MW01247265

Sound-Blind

Sound-Blind

American Literature and the Politics of Transcription

ALEX BENSON

The University of North Carolina Press Chapel Hill

This book was published with the assistance of the Authors Fund of the University of North Carolina Press and Bard College.

© 2023 Alex Benson
All rights reserved
Set in Charis by Westchester Publishing Services
Manufactured in the United States of America

Library of Congress Cataloging-in-Publication Data
Names: Benson, Alex, author.
Title: Sound-blind : American literature and the politics of
    transcription / Alex Benson.
Description: Chapel Hill : The University of North Carolina Press, [2023] |
    Includes bibliographical references and index.
Identifiers: LCCN 2023020749 | ISBN 9781469674629 (cloth ; alk. paper) |
    ISBN 9781469674636 (paperback ; alk. paper) | ISBN 9781469674643 (ebook)
Subjects: LCSH: Boas, Franz, 1858–1942—Criticism and interpretation—
    History. | American literature—History and criticism. | American literature—
    Themes, motives. | Writing—Social aspects. | Writing—Political aspects. |
    Discourse analysis. | Paralinguistics. | Settler colonialism—United States. |
    People with disabilities in literature. | Race relations in literature. | BISAC:
    LITERARY CRITICISM / General | LANGUAGE ARTS & DISCIPLINES /
    Translating & Interpreting
Classification: LCC PS88 .B46 2023 | DDC 810.9—dc23/eng/20230602
LC record available at https://lccn.loc.gov/2023020749

Cover illustrations: Six gestural drawings from David Efron, *Gesture and Environment* (1941), 26–31.

Contents

Figures

Sound-Blind

Introduction

·······································

Transcription is political. That's less a claim of this book than its premise. At one scale of analysis, transcription is political because the small, situated practices of making something into a text—whether those practices are manual or mechanical, and whether that something is the content of an utterance, the sound of a cry, the logic of a gesture, or simply the script of a different document—are always socially embedded.[1] The choice of which features of some discursive source material to represent (or not), the anticipation of a reader to whom one hopes to make something legible (or not): these variables hinge on negotiations of public life that are no less urgent for their localization. At another scale, transcription is political because the very idea of textuality has featured so centrally in the imagination of colonial modernity as a conversion from orality to literacy—and, too, in practices of resistance to the violent implementations of that imagination.[2] *Sound-Blind* reads American literary history across these scales.

But first: "sound-blind"? My choice of this archaic medical term as a title has to do, in part, with its peculiar coordination of the aural and the visual, of medium and ability. Although the chapters that follow this introduction will rarely make direct reference to sound-blindness, these relations will recur throughout. My choice of title has just as much to do, though, with the particular spaces that this term has drawn together in the history of its circulation. So I'll begin with two stories about its career in print.

1. On January 10, 1888, the U T K Clothing House ran one of its regular newspaper advertisements in the *Minneapolis Journal*. The Nicollet Avenue store had a well-established rhetorical niche: the header and first several sentences of any given ad would often pull copy directly from a recent news item, something slightly off the beaten path. Then through some abrupt mischief of wordplay, each ad would pivot toward its point. Low prices. Quality control. New hats. This time the point was a clearance sale, and the source material for the ad copy was an item about a curious medical hypothesis in a recent edition of the paper. This item itself was taken from the newswire, with dozens of newspapers throughout the United States publishing a version of the story in late 1887 and early 1888. The piece was offering

an explanation of variations in young students' facility in learning to spell. It had been observed among schoolchildren in England that some students, when writing dictation, consistently confused certain letter pairings, switching *v* and *p*, for instance, or hearing *e* as *o*. These confusions were not, per the report, easily explained by a difference in educational preparation. Under the header "Sound Blindness," the U T K ad, like its source material, described this "inability to distinguish particular shades of sound"—*shades* registering an analogy with color-blindness—"arising from some organic defect in the ear, which is distinct from deafness as that term is commonly understood." Then the commercial pivot: "Dig the wax out of your ears and listen to the U T K. This is the season of 'Blowouts.'"[3]

2. A year later, in the January 1889 issue of *American Anthropologist*, Franz Boas—the German American anthropologist, still in the early years of what would be a field-changing six-decade career—cited the idea of sound-blindness in an article titled "On Alternating Sounds." The piece as a whole is concerned with the problem of linguistic transcription. A number of ethnographers, Boas noted, had recently observed that their notations of non-Western speech often included inconsistent spellings. These observers attributed the anomalies to the irrationality of the languages being spoken. Boas spied a fallacy. Rather than an objective record of inconsistent speech sounds, these wayward notations were, he argued, the artifacts of the observers' own auditory predispositions. The problem had to do with listening and writing across entirely different systems of phonemic habit and expectation—differences that make it difficult, when listening to an unfamiliar language, to register a meaningful versus an insignificant variation in two very similar-sounding utterances. Explaining this difficulty in reference to the science of psychophysical measurement, the field in which he had written a dissertation about perceptions of seawater color, Boas argued that what others called "alternating sounds" were in fact merely the effects of "alternating apperception," a kind of low-grade perceptual category confusion.[4] To frame this point, Boas offers sound-blindness as an analogy, citing an 1888 study of the phenomenon by the Boston educator Sara E. Wiltse, rather than the earlier London report that was the basis of the piece in the *Minneapolis Journal*. In Boas's analogy, the condition is not imagined as congenital. Instead, it figures the bias introduced by the simple fact of being more at home in one language than another.

The second story is better known than the first. To clarify why I place it alongside that newspaper advertisement—and how their juxtaposition leads into the method of reading that this book develops—I need to follow the afterlives of Boas's piece a little further. In many tellings over the past several decades, this citation of sound-blindness has been positioned as a kind of origin point for the discourse of multiculturalism. "On Alternating Sounds" is most commonly referred to as a crucial early articulation of the critical upheaval that aimed to displace the racist hierarchies of nineteenth-century social evolutionism and to advance a newly pluralistic concept of culture. That displacement involved new diction: "cultures" becomes say-able with an *s* for the first time in English usage, as a new way to describe the sources of human custom in all its variation (even as "culture" in the singular continued, and continues now, to be used to refer to a kind of pro-gressive *exception* from everyday custom: the culture you get when you break your routine to linger in front of a painting).[5] The plural form appears in anthropological writing at the end of the nineteenth century. The new usage is tied to the nascent discipline's embrace of empirical fieldwork and, in the interpretive summation of the resultant data, its emphasis on histori-cal particularism. By a few decades into the twentieth century, "cultures" becomes widely common. In a certain progressivist version of this narra-tive, the lingering determinisms of racialist thinking constitute a vestige of the colonialist imaginary that hadn't yet caught up with this turn in Amer-ican English and perhaps, too, in American "culture"—except that this ver-sion of the narrative, as I've just rehearsed it, assumes a correspondence between linguistic and cultural particularity that, while it has come to seem like common sense, was precisely the thing at issue.

"On Alternating Sounds" never uses any form of the word "culture." Still, for historians of American anthropology, in this essay about linguistic ex-perience Boas "applied his cultural relativism to his own culture as well as to those he studied 'in the field,'" and the essay's "anti-evolutionary stance in interpreting variation of categories across phonological systems was, in fact, the paradigm for his entire anthropological oeuvre."[6] For scholars in literary history and American studies, a consensus about the essay's status as "a foundational text in the formulation of the culture concept" has meant that "alluding to alternating sounds has become a way to shorthand the emergence of pluralist thought."[7] The essay's importance to the priorities and methods of salvage anthropology (the project of creating durable records of folk customs and speechways imagined to be in danger of disap-pearance) "cannot easily be overstated."[8] Its importance to "the history of anthropological thought," more generally, "is impossible to exaggerate."[9] If, this historiography supposes, Boas gave us a way to talk about cultures, sound-blindness gave him a way to think about them.

Without rejecting this supposition on its own terms—some of the works just quoted, in my aggregate construction of this motif, have made possible the idea of this book—we might ask what happens to our conception of sound-blindness when we bracket what has in retrospect become its predominant association. Even within the narrow orbit of American anthropology, after all, the idea of "On Alternating Sounds" as a paradigm-shocking thunderbolt would have been a perplexing take for the first seven decades of the essay's existence in print. Over that span, the essay receives only an occasional passing reference: in, for instance, a 1900 article on ethnomusicology, whose author mentions having perused "an old number of the *American Anthropologist*" and, as if dusting off some forgotten print ephemera, "chanced on an article by Dr Boas"; in a 1930 exploration of the possibilities of objective observation afforded by the "strobophotographic" analysis of soundwaves; and in a wide-ranging 1944 summation of Boas's many contributions to linguistics.[10] Meanwhile, major studies of his career by his own students during the same period do not cite the essay at all.[11]

Of course, any historical revision must say something about the past that the past didn't say about itself. Still, if we follow the path of this belated canonization, it becomes clear that there are some important spaces it never crosses. Two texts are key to the formation of that path. In a 1965 essay, George W. Stocking Jr.—whose work greatly broadened the scope of our understanding of early American anthropology—argues that "On Alternating Sounds" "foreshadows" the concerns not only of Boas's own later work but also of twentieth-century cultural theory.[12] Then, in *To Wake the Nations* (1993), a book that pressed scholars of American literature to reckon more consistently with the dialectics of race, Eric J. Sundquist cites Stocking's account in order to position "Boas's argument as a general paradigm" for the relationship of "two conflicting yet coalescing cultural traditions— 'American' and 'African,' to use for the moment an inadequate shorthand." Remarking that he almost titled the book after a phrase drawn from Boas's essay, Sundquist takes the alternating-sounds argument as a hermeneutic: "Just as anthropologists are likely to misperceive the 'sounds' of another culture they attempt to record or analyze, so readers and literary critics . . . are likely to misperceive and misunderstand the signs generated by another cultural tradition."[13] For Stocking, the intellectual historian, the idea of sound-blindness anticipates an account of culture. For Sundquist, the literary critic, it tropes it. Notice that in Sundquist's account, both the markers of tradition ("'American,'" "'African'") are in scare quotes, and "'sounds,'" too, while "signs" are left in the unmarked position of the real.[14] That shift from sound to semiotics has allowed "On Alternating Sounds" to speak outside itself in powerful ways. It has allowed it to speak, for instance, to the ethnocentric biases that may condition any act of representation. Yet the way this application has settled into place has also risked obscuring the essay's own mediation of particular spaces of colonial aurality and textuality.

To ask, then, what else sound-blindness means and does—less what it foreshadows than what it sideshadows—would be to build on work that has productively fractured our sense of the theories of human variation that were operant around the turn of the twentieth century; it would be to observe, with Brad Evans, that what the retrospection of literary history often reads as "cultural" representation was often conceived otherwise.[15] It would be to question the relationship between such theories and the period's political realities, recognizing, with Audra Simpson, that the scientific priorities of Boas and his influential students, however progressive their political beliefs, assumed the coming disappearance of Indigenous peoples in ways that were commensurate with social evolutionism and convenient for settler colonialism.[16] And it would be to ask, with David Mitchell and Sharon Snyder, about the materialities of metaphoric applications of disability, about the ways in which representations of disabled experience have served as prostheses for narratives of American literacy and for theories of human variation along many axes.[17] More than the legal or social production of medicalized disability, it is this kind of discursive prosthesis that the chapters here will critically attend to. It's with some reservation, I should also note, that I use the terms "disability" and "disabled." They are imperfect frames of analysis in their generality and in the negative logic of their prefix. At the same time, this book is, in large part, *about* those frames: about the slippages of thought by which alternatives of linguistic modality are made to serve as the grounds and expressions of political exclusion. *Sound-Blind* understands transcriptions as processes in which those slippages are generated, refused, and redirected. This understanding will take the pages that follow in a number of directions—to phonetics and fiction in Indian Territory, to experimental notations of diasporic gesture, to the entanglement of anti-Blackness, ableism, and allyship in the editorial history of a poem that never got written. And to other sideshadows.

For now, it can take us back to the first story I sketched, that of the Minneapolis clothing store advertisement. The first thing to say is that it shares a basic logic with the second story. They both begin with a representation of disability that turns out to trope something else. In the U T K ad, a hypothesis about congenital hearing impairment serves as the background for an exhortation that the reader figuratively clean out their ears so as to better receive the news of some serious sale prices. In this, it is only a more abrupt, sardonically humorous expression of the widespread prejudice of "audism" (the term proposed by Tom Humphries and then influentially applied by Harlan Lane and many others in Deaf studies and activism): that is, the association of hearing with cognitive privilege, an association grounded in a narrow sense of language as a thing of vocal utterance and auditory perception.[18] As it happens, two days after the ad about sound-blindness, the U T K extends this very theme in another ad placed in the *Minneapolis Tribune*. Here, the ad copy comes from another recent item in the papers about "whether the blind or deaf suffer the worst affliction." The former are, it's claimed, better off because "the deprivation of spoken language is in our civilization the most serious deficiency" (though all will be well served, the ad assures, when shopping at the U T K).[19] This commonplace assessment—the idea that hearing is more essential than sight to vocal communication and therefore to public life—clarifies the political stakes already implicit in "sound-blindness," even in its early medical usage, where the phrase bridged forms of sensory impairment that carried very different connotations within normative audist models of linguistic community.

This confusion of the eye and the ear gave the phrase a frisson of curiosity. If this may help explain why "sound-blindness" briefly caught widespread public attention, including the attention of at least one advertiser, it may also be part of the reason that it didn't last very long in scientific usage. Nobody loved the label. A "very awkward designation," the *Wisconsin Journal of Education* called it.[20] "The name I do not at all like," complained the mathematician Joseph LeConte.[21] Boas himself pointed out that the implicit parallel with color-blindness was misleading, in that a more precise analogy would involve "a case of lacking faculty to distinguish the key of sounds," rather than phonetic differences.[22] And Sara Wiltse, in a revised version of her research published in a 1902 collection of essays, used it as "as a title, not because of its fitness, but because it is one in most common use and is made to cover as many shades of physical disorders as used to be classed under heresy in the region of morals."[23] Of dubious "fitness," the term itself, like the conditions it so loosely names, is taken to stand in want of correction.

The referential blur of the term makes it a good fit, though, for the critical modality of this book.[24] To think by way of sound-blindness, to sit in the grammar of its hyphen (or, in some iterations of the phrase, in the space where the hyphen would go), is to reckon with the converse whose possibility it implies in negation: seeing sound. The early usage of the phrase may position "-blindness" as an awkward figure for category confusion, but this also has the effect of orienting us toward the forms of visual experience and exclusion associated with notation on paper. Which was, of course, the site where sound-blindness became thinkable. The data were always to be found on the page, in the orthographic choices of a bad transcription, whether that of a young student just learning to spell or of a philologist limited by their own ear. To read these records as evidence less of what's said than of what's heard is to displace the logic of the sonic waveform (techniques for the production of which were being fine-tuned during the same period, and by some of the same people who concerned themselves with sound-blindness): if the dream of phonographic inscription is to represent sonic material so faithfully that it could be played back from the page—even "heard" in the mind's ear, as in a more perfect form of musical sight-reading—a sound-blind transcription records sound as phenomena rather than as material.[25] The transcript's visible errancy (not its perfection) is what implies some prehistory of aural experience.[26]

"Why can't sounds be visible?" asked the experimental composer Pauline Oliveros in 1968. "Would the feedback from eye to ear cause fatal oscillation?"[27] Let's hope not. That feedback is something like the key in which the readings here are scored. Those readings are often very granularly developed, practicing a decelerated attention—close reading by way of deep listening—that is imagined not in distinction from historical contextualization but as a way into the question of how and when history comes, or doesn't, to appear on the page. This kind of attention needn't assume the static autonomy of texts; it can open up relations across and outside them, their makers, and the worlds of their making.[28] This principle sometimes keeps *Sound-Blind* close to details of "transcription" as the alphabetic representation of vocal exchange (the primary meaning of the term in early discussions of sound-blindness, both medical and anthropological). Yet the larger questions of historical representation at issue here also unfold toward a set of adjacent linguistic, graphic, and literary practices: translation, transliteration, transmediation, revision, redaction, reproduction. There are versions of a study of the politics of transcription that would focus on the social histories of stenography and shorthand, the ideological histories of phonetics or grammatology, the technological histories of audio recording, the scientific histories of fieldwork, or the generic histories of dialect literature. This book contains aspects of each but has in mind another project: it is an experiment with literary history as textual history as sonic history.[29]

This involves thinking about sound while writing about the graphic record, and vice versa. It means taking the format of the page and understanding its effects as constituted only in relation to other media of inscription and expression. It means reading and listening across those media in a way that is informed by analyses of the soundwork of print in Black studies, by turns to the detail and the partial explanation in feminist criticism, and by debates about the critical affordances of weak and nontotalizing theory in queer and modernist studies.[30]

Invoked in the same breath, the terms "transcription" and "weakness" may, for some readers, call up a widely influential distinction in late twentieth-century political theory: James C. Scott's sense of the "public transcript" versus the "hidden transcript." Neither is necessarily a materially *textual* transcript, for Scott. Instead, a public transcript involves the kinds of utterance acceptable to the powerful, while a hidden transcript names forms of quiet (anonymous, grumbling, gossiping, subversive, tactical, life-supporting) discourse in which the weak express critical alternatives. Scott draws a first example of "the possibly dramatic disparity" of these modes from the memoirs of the abolitionist and suffragist Mary A. Livermore, first published in 1888.[31] Much of her writing focuses on her work as a nurse during the Civil War, but prior to that, she had been employed as a governess by a slaveholding family whose housekeeper, a person they claimed to own, was known as Aunt Aggy. According to Livermore, in a conversation between herself and Aggy one day before the war—and shortly after Aggy's daughter had been attacked by the slaveholders—the housekeeper privately expressed a prophetic sense of the apocalyptic justice that would eventually be visited on white people. For Scott, this interaction reveals the existence of a subversive millenarian discourse contrastable with the more accommodationist registers in which Aggy most likely, out of necessity, spoke with the slaveholders, and "our glimpse of Aggy's hidden transcript, if pursued further, would lead us directly to the offstage culture of the slave quarters and slave religion."[32]

Although *Sound-Blind* is likewise invested in the "infrapolitics" of discursive spaces conceived as minor or everyday, the same example can help illustrate a difference in approach. There are prior questions I'd want to ask about the local mediating practices that allow and restrict the "glimpse" opened in Aggy's voice. Her reported utterance comes to Scott's book indirectly, through an earlier study by Albert J. Raboteau, morphing in small, normal ways through the typographic telephone game of each of these quotations. But there's a basic structural change to the situation of the utterance that needs articulating. Livermore's own account had framed the prewar conversation not only in autobiographical retrospect, as she looks back across the decades, but also through a specific intermediate event: a chance reunion at a postwar prayer meeting, where the two women talk *about* that prior talk. Given on the page as a conversation-within-a-conversation, Aggy's prophecy is enmeshed with a complex set of other discursive conditions, including—and these are only some obvious and immediate elements of the scene as Livermore presents it—an analogy between memory and photography, the identifying patterns of gestural habit, the group dynamics of the prayer meeting, and the conventions of racialized dialect writing.[33] These frames disappear when the utterance is given as an unmediated, first-order example of political practice. Of course, they are barely present on this page either, in the abstracted list of my summary. But marking them makes a difference. It bears pragmatically on the kind of thing that one asks next. In this case, that might not be (as Scott suggests) a question about the discourse of the slave quarters. It might instead be a question about the work of memory *after* the formalized end of slavery. The status of that "end" is, of course, in the deepest way, another question entirely. The point is that this, too, might be better considered through the details. What becomes legible in Livermore's memory of Aggy's voice includes the intersections between a post-Reconstruction surge of white-supremacist violence and the bigoted linguistic premises of certain forms of dialect writing that were, in the late nineteenth and early twentieth centuries, at the height of their popularity.[34]

The textual histories traced here unfold around the same moment, from the 1880s to the Second World War, with a few tendrils looping out to points of attachment further back and forward. Aside from the shifts in anthropological thought playing out across these decades, this is also a period in the United States of proliferating linguistic intersections and transformations due to urbanization and massive immigration flows (and also of nativist legislative restrictions on the latter); of new audio technologies from the laboratory to the cinema hall; of expanded programs of linguistic assimilation in the form of boarding schools, part of the state's intensified genocide of Native peoples; of strenuous debate about sign language and vocal training in the field of deaf education; and of legal expansions and retractions of political franchise, often spoken of in terms of the possession or dispossession of "voice."

Each of these developments comes into play here. I resist coordinating them as a grand narrative. The mode of attention practiced here takes historical time as an effect of localized relations, relations produced as people work to articulate and revise the extralocal transformations in which they are caught up.[35] Sustaining this kind of attention also means that, after this introduction, my engagements with recent secondary sources will play out almost entirely in the notes. This approach should not be taken to minimize my own situatedness in the form of my debts to prior scholarship (which are considerable, as I hope the notes properly credit), nor to reinforce a hierarchy where specialized knowledge murmurs archly to itself behind the velvet rope of the citational apparatus. The idea, instead, is to trust the theoretical depth of a wide range of discursive materials, animating their urgencies by way of textual-historical narratives plotted through relations of proximity and recursion. So even as the writers considered here make a heterogeneous group (poets, public intellectuals, college students, organizers, linguists, newspaper editors, novelists, critics, scientists, teachers, politicians, folklorists), I identify, where possible, the common spaces of their transit, the reviews they wrote of each other's work, the mutual friends, kin, antagonists. Some of those spaces look familiar to me, while— as a settler scholar, nondisabled as of now, who has written much of this book on unceded Muhheaconneok (Stockbridge-Munsee Community) land in New York State—I'm an outsider to others. Such geographies subtend this book's interest in a model of literary meaning, and of what the musicologist Dylan Robinson calls "hungry listening," that foregrounds the social trajectories indexed in situated practices of writing.[36] When I position literary production both through and *as* transcription, part of what I mean to do is to underscore similar forms of indexicality.

I use that term here, "indexicality," to signal this book's investment in conditions of material connection in representation. A figure who himself crossed paths with some of the writers considered in this book, the philosopher C. S. Peirce defined "the action of indices" as dependent not on the resemblance between two associated objects (he called such resemblance "iconicity") but rather "upon association by contiguity." Common examples would be the association of footprint with foot and smoke with fire; more germane here would be that of manuscript with hand and of echo with sound. Such contiguities, Peirce writes, tend to "direct attention to their objects by blind compulsion."[37] (Note the use of "blind" to connote involuntariness. In one of Peirce's examples of indexical compulsion, when someone points at something, creating an associative contiguity between finger and object, the effect is to make you look.[38] The irony of the sight-based example of "blindness" goes unacknowledged.) Just as relevant here, though, is the uptake of Peirce's concept in linguistic anthropology, where indexical relations describe the way that speech acts register the social structures that allow their efficacy, as well as the way that those structures are, in turn, pragmatically reconfigured by such speech acts.[39] To read for these forms of indexicality in all their messy material embeddedness is, epistemologically, to privilege a semiotic space outside what is normatively given as the proper, exceptional sphere of human language—that is, symbolic abstraction.[40] And it is, methodologically, to test, proliferate, and reorder claims of causation, while shuttling between questions of rhetorical form and of material circulation. The kind of chronology one gets from this approach is less nonlinear than multilinear: crisscross.[41] If the historical location of this book is the late nineteenth and early twentieth centuries, this is a period drawn not in outline but as the shade of a crosshatch.

On that note, having followed "On Alternating Sounds" forward through its reception, we might also follow it back a few years the other way. Often the piece is framed as a response to one or another of Boas's scientific contemporaries. Horatio Hale and J. W. Powell are prominent names in this conversation; each is, no doubt, relevant, as is Daniel G. Brinton, whose claim in an 1888 lecture that many Native American languages feature "alternating" consonants and "permutable" vowels seems a likely object of Boas's critique.[42] But different angles open along the citational chain of Boas's references to sound-blindness. Published in January 1889, "On Alternating Sounds" was dated, on its final page, as composed in November 1888. This was the same month that an item was published on sound-blindness, without byline, in the journal *Science*, where Boas worked as an assistant editor.[43] Both of these texts—Boas's *American Anthropologist* article and the anonymous *Science* story—cite the study of sound-blindness published by Sara E. Wiltse in the August 1888 issue of the *American Journal of Psychology*. As Wiltse writes there, the psychologist G. Stanley Hall had, in March 1888, asked her to research sound-blindness in Boston schools, sending her the clipping of a *previous* piece on the same topic from *Science*.[44] That earlier *Science* piece had been published (like the later one, anonymously) in November 1887 with the header "Sound-Blindness." It became the basis for a newswire story that resulted in articles about the phenomenon appearing in dozens of newspapers nationwide from late November 1887 through the middle of the next year. These included the *Minneapolis Journal*, which led to that U T K ad. The two stories I started with are the same story.

Because Boas's 1889 essay ties the term "sound-blind" to Wiltse's 1888 piece in a scholarly journal, it has been accepted that this is where he learned

Introduction   11

of the term.[45] But given his job at *Science*, he almost certainly knew of it from the brief summary published in 1887. At the very least, he would have read that piece. Depending on whether he had any responsibilities related to the short "digest" section in which it appeared—combing scientific periodicals, drafting summaries: these would be likely tasks for an assistant editor—he may have even helped write it or prepare it for publication. He may, in other words, have been partially responsible for getting the term into wide circulation in the United States in the first place. I make this point not just to set the record straight on a footnote of intellectual biography (the arc of Boas's career matters to this book without being its central concern) but to cue a more general orientation to the continuity of fields often treated separately as "intellectual history" and "print culture." Backdating Boas's introduction to the idea of sound-blindness matters, in other words, because it allows us to understand the way that "On Alternating Sounds" erases its own ties to popular print—a move of scientific purification, whether deliberate or kneejerk, that reinforces certain discursive hierarchies even as the essay so famously flattens others.[46]

The 1887 *Science* piece that was, I'm proposing, Boas's probable introduction to the term "sound-blindness" was itself a summary of an article in London's *Journal of Education* by J. C. Tarver, an educator and literary critic who would later write books about Flaubert and about secondary education. It was a transcription of poetry, Tarver writes, that first drew his attention to the possibility of sound-blindness. A nine-year-old student, writing down a line of verse memorized by ear, "had spelled the word *very*, *voght*. I found that he could hear no difference between *very*, *perry*, and *polly*." Suggesting that the difficulty of distinguishing phonemes may be not simply a cognitive but also a sensory condition, Tarver muses on consequences for pedagogical practice: "how should a man learn to spell even phonetically to whom not only the printed sign, but also the distinction of sounds is arbitrary and conventional? and how should he not learn whose ear is a torturing conscience?"[47] He does not cite previous references to sound-blindness. He wasn't the first to use the term, though. "Sound-blind" had recently appeared in the 1869 memoirs of a soprano, quoting a doctor's piteous description of "children who have no ear"; in an 1876 lecture on the sounds of grasshoppers, with vibrations so high in pitch that musicians can't identify their key and some people can't hear them at all; and in an 1882 complaint about the philistine, who is, in response to poetry, "as one who is colour-blind; he is sense-blind or sound-blind."[48]

But one text in particular—A. H. Sayce's *Introduction to the Science of Language* (1880)—seems a more likely influence on Tarver than any of these, given not only the time and place of publication but also some close parallels of content and phrasing. Where Tarver refers to children's "inability to distinguish particular shades of sound," Sayce had described a "childlike inability to distinguish between sounds" in certain dialects.[49] The problem may arise, Sayce writes, either from within the system of speech ("the sound being formed at the neutral point, as it were, intermediate between two distinct sounds") or in the moment of hearing. The former is a matter of phonetics and "takes us back to the time when man was gradually fashioning the elements of articulate speech," while the latter "is analogous to colour-blindness, and has most to do with the imperfections of childish utterance or the substitution of *r* for *l* so often heard."[50] Sayce makes this distinction in an argument about the evolution and geographical spread of the "Aryan" language family; his general position on the matter was that this language family originated in Scandinavia rather than in South Asia (an argument that echoes in the Nordicist theme of twentieth-century white supremacism in the United States, as I'll discuss in chapter 3). He speculates that the speakers of "Parent-Aryan" had, in their linguistic evolution, already left behind the stage of phonetic confusion, meaning that any inconsistent pronunciations would have been attributable not to "imperfection of utterance" but "rather to sound-blindness."[51]

The break in the citation chain between Tarver and Sayce, if a "break" is what it is—to call it that presumes the continuity in question—has consequences for how we think about the reference to sound-blindness in "On Alternating Sounds."[52] To read that reference without Sayce in the background is to understand that Boas uses sound-blindness as the metaphorical vehicle for a point about perceptual relativism imagined to escape old geographies of human difference. To read that reference *with* Sayce in the background is to take this metaphor as emergent *in* those geographies. In the former mode of reading, the politics of transcription become legible where disability tropes culture. In the latter, they become legible where disability intersects with concepts often construed as culture's opposite— race, land, nature.

Each chapter of this book tracks the interplay of these modes.

Chapter 1, "Harjo's Brand: Alphabetics and Allotment," starts from the seed of a small graphic element embedded in a line of text. In 1907, John M. Oskison published a short story that includes the image of a cattle brand.

A mark of property that also generates a "fantastic" moment of aesthetic irreducibility, the brand simultaneously registers histories of Indigenous media and, in a visual reflection of sound-blindness, makes a kind of "mute appeal" (to reapply a phrase of Oskison's) that frustrates protocols of phonetic transparency associated with the expansionist state. Introducing Oskison's ironic sensibility at the hinge between studies of territorial politics and of linguistic media, the chapter navigates the conventions of local-color fiction; the historiography of the syllabary circulated by Sequoyah in the 1820s, which Oskison, a Cherokee Nation citizen, addresses in his historical novel *The Singing Bird*; and the representation of the land-allotment process in Indian Territory periodicals at the turn of the century. Through these contexts' overlap at the site of the Harjo brand, the chapter unfolds the political bivalence of the idea of a rationalized writing system—an idea mobilized in narratives both of US expansionism and of Cherokee sovereignty.[53]

The idea of mute refusal that is key to Oskison's engagement with those narratives derives its rhetorical traction from the representations of linguistic impairment and assimilatory education that circulate in the period. Here Helen Keller's name is ubiquitous, both as a discursive reference and as a print object. Her signature has been a popular illustrative inset since the beginnings of her celebrity in the late 1880s. What does the image do for the editors who print it and the readers who encounter it? The answer offered in chapter 2, "Helen Keller's Handwriting: Audism and Autography," involves the submerged connections between alphabetic literacy (including both the Latin and the manual alphabet, or fingerspelling) and Oralist vocal training. Tracing both the norms of vocality and the taxonomic imaginaries that surround the autograph, I argue that its circulation refracts ideas of disability as an object of spectacle and therefore as proximate to the visibility of the racially marked body. First inferring this dynamic from representations of Keller's literacies across media, from 1880s magazine pieces to films made later in her life, the chapter then turns to a text about Keller by W. E. B. Du Bois for an anthology published in 1931 (though the content of the text sketches a history of acquaintance that begins four decades earlier). Others have found in the same document evidence of allyship or philosophical continuity between Keller and Du Bois; I find in the text's production history a more fractured scene—one that helps explain the cryptic connection that Du Bois draws between Keller's ability to "understand without sound" and her "blind[ness] to color differences."[54]

From the first two chapters' accounts of the political contestations that have, in the United States, surrounded writing systems other than the Latin alphabet (the Cherokee syllabary, the manual alphabet), *Sound-Blind* turns next to what can be read and written in the paralinguistic movements of the body. How does one transcribe a gesture? What can a tic transcribe? And what kind of noise is produced in the channel between motor habit and text? Chapter 3, "Gatsby's Tattoo: Music and Motor Habit," considers these questions by bringing F. Scott Fitzgerald's fiction into conversation with ethnographies of gesture (particularly David Efron's study of Jewish and Italian American communities in 1930s New York); with contemporaneous discourse about the temporalities (and, for reactionary critics, the pathologies) of jazz improvisation; and with the materials of Fitzgerald's own revision practice. The focal point for this discussion is the passage of *The Great Gatsby* (1925) in which one character drums a foot on the floor and another turns toward him suspiciously. Some "blind compulsion," Peirce might say, makes the latter look. But when that compulsion is elaborated more fully, it turns out to index an anxiety about able self-control that is inseparable from the visualities of race and the racialization of sonic aesthetics.[55]

Boas makes appearances in the first three chapters. He speaks at Oskison's college, he most likely comes into contact with Keller at the Chicago world's fair, and he supervises Efron's research. Chapter 4 returns to his writing more directly. The central text in chapter 4, "No-Tongue's Song: Fieldnotes and Fiction," is a 1922 volume of short stories by anthropologists, *American Indian Life*, edited by Elsie Clews Parsons. I focus on two entries: one coauthored by Parsons and Thomas B. Reed, a Hampton Institute student from a Deg Hit'an community in Alaska, and the other a text by Boas (his only published work of fiction) that repurposes Inuit song-texts transcribed during an 1883–84 expedition to Baffin Island. Boas reprinted the same texts, in multiple translations, several times over the decades, but it's only in fiction that he attributes the compositions to a character named "No-tongue." Does the "tongue" here negated refer to a language, the organ used to express it, or the quality of that expression? It's left unspecified. Chapter 4 proposes that the figure connects the problems of aural experience that Boas once described as sound-blindness with the colonialist geography that is the condition of anthropological writing; and it asks how the song-texts themselves might sound space otherwise.[56]

The archival spaces through which these chapters move and the archival gaps across which they sometimes speculate are far from exclusively "literary" in a conventional sense. But one of the brighter threads woven through these textual histories is the question of that category, the literary, as a continually, variously, locally emergent effect. What are often taken as fundamental structures of fictional and poetic expression—perspective, character, plot, poetic lineation, implied authorship—take shape in the histories offered here in relation to particular sites of sensory politics.[57] Of course, this approach, situating literary effects at pragmatic scales other (smaller, larger) than the national, also throws into doubt the idea of an "American" literature referred to in this book's subtitle.[58] I refer to this term precisely because the same doubt is alive throughout the material I treat. Fraught with the ideologies of hemispheric hegemony and imperial exceptionalism, Americanness, as it operates in and around the texts I'll discuss, coordinates and haunts the spaces of contested sovereignty, assimilatory coercion, ableist linguistics, and the aesthetics of daily life. Like the singular form of "literature"—dubious given not only what has come to be called "cultural" diversity but also the simple fact of the plurality of writing systems—this imprecise national designation serves, in the chapters that follow, as a problem, not a premise. Here, that is, "American literature" is more than a distinctive space for second-order reflection on, among many other things (love, death, dirt, theft), the forms of textual production and reproduction that emerge in and against the settler nation. It is also, and first, a name for those forms.

1 Harjo's Brand

Alphabetics and Allotment

. . . .

H-I. Three lines of equal height stand like fence posts, bisected by a horizontal rail. Or rails, maybe, since, just to the right of the middle post, the slightest of gaps divides the horizontal element of the structure into two colinear segments. The total figure looks roughly like an uppercase letter *H* in the Latin alphabet, reflected across the axis of its right-hand post (or "stem," to move from the language of enclosure to that of typography) and then, in that microscopic gap in the rail (or "crossbar"), cut. Almost but not quite duplicated, the letter becomes something stretched and staggered. It also becomes something impossible to pronounce, at least—and this particularity matters—for a speaker of English. Starting with "aitch" seems like a good way in, but then what?

The problem of this utterance sits at the intersection of alphabetic print culture and colonized territory. The source of the figure is "The Problem of Old Harjo," a 1907 short story by John M. Oskison. The titular character, a rancher, lives in an unspecified part of Indian Territory—perhaps Muscogee Nation, given that Harjo is identified as Creek. The plot is driven by the efforts of a young missionary to convert him, efforts that are complicated by the fact that Harjo has two wives. When the missionary visits the ranch in hopes of sorting this out, Oskison embeds an image right in the middle of a sentence: "Three cows, three young heifers, two colts, and two patient, capable mares bore the Harjo brand, a fantastic '**H-I**' that the old man had designed." This brand has no self-evident bearing on the course of events, which arrives at an inconclusive end in the missionary's inability to conceive of a response to the "mute appeal" expressed in Harjo's eyes.[1]

Born in 1874, Oskison grew up in Indian Territory, got an undergraduate law degree at Stanford followed by a year of graduate study at Harvard, and spent the rest of his life largely in New York but somewhat peripatetic, taking up residence elsewhere on the East Coast as well as in Northern California, the Southwest, and Europe, with many returns to home in what had, by his middle adulthood, become Oklahoma. Prior to his service in the Great War, he published numerous short stories and essays. From the 1920s until his death in 1947, he turned to book-length works of fiction, biography, and history. He was a Cherokee Nation citizen through his mother's side of the family, with his enrollment confirmed in 1903.

Recent scholarship has paid increasing attention to the unique ways in which Oskison's body of work mediates histories of land, law, gender, and species. This chapter brings these concerns into conversation with questions of linguistic mediation. In itself, this isn't a novel gesture within the study of American regionalist literature of the late nineteenth and early twentieth centuries. The genre's representations of dialectal English have been discussed from many an angle. But while Oskison's work does, occasionally, include such representations (as often in the pronunciation of ethnically marked white characters as in the grammar of Indigenous speakers), the space of Indian Territory also asks us to redraw the political, linguistic, and chronological boundaries of the genre. As influential studies have argued, readers' fascination with local color mediated both the energies of North-South sectionalism (in the wake of civil war) and of newly conspicuous forms of overseas imperialism (with the occupation of the Philippines, in particular).[2] But in Oskison's work, the regional, the local, takes shape in the transit between the US interior and the multiple national externalities, often marked as linguistic alterities, that this "interior" encompasses—and that it doesn't, the state's sovereignty being, not unlike the enclosure of a broken fence (or one never finished), less than total.

"Old Harjo" remains the best known and most anthologized of Oskison's texts. Critical and editorial commentaries on the story, often underlining the ethical dilemma produced by incommensurable cultural norms, have been silent on its one curious illustration. I don't point this out in the spirit of correcting an outrageous oversight. The brand asks to be ignored. Interrupting the plot without advancing the story, it reads as the kind of insignificant notation said to facilitate the reality effect of fictional representation, "scandalous" in its superfluity.[3] Plus, in this case, there's a practical dissuasion from critical remark: the image in Oskison's text presents a minor headache for quotation, not only aloud but also in print.

Oskison made a similar move at least one other time. *The Brothers Three* (1935), a semiautobiographical novel based loosely on his own family and their ranch during the decades of transition from Indian Territory to Oklahoma, also includes an image of a brand in the middle of a line of text: "Ꝋ (circle-I)."[4] But there the image—an oval from approximately the center of which rises a vertical line segment, which is capped by a shorter horizontal line—seems more justified. The figure illustrates a metonym of

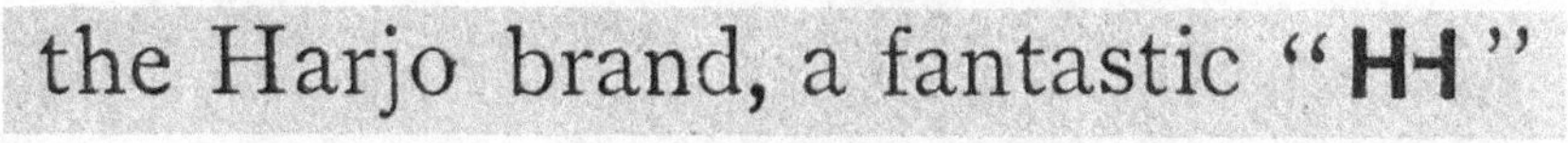

the Harjo brand, a fantastic "H-I"

FIGURE 1.1 The Harjo brand as printed in a copy of the April 1907 *Southern Workman* issued to the subscriber "Mrs Wm B Rogers"—probably Emma Savage Rogers—of Boston.

the ranch itself, whose prosperity and decline constitute the central drama of the plot. Confusingly, "ठ" seems to present a circle-*T*, not a "circle-I." There's a crossbar at the top of the stem but not at the bottom. This could have been a typesetting error. We may never know. As with Queequeg's mark (described in the narration of *Moby-Dick* as a "queer round figure" but represented on the page as a cross), we lack a manuscript in the author's hand to compare with the figure set in type.[5] Whether wrong on the cattle or in the text, though, this incongruous figure is drowned out not only by its immediate parenthetical translation into verbal form, "(circle-I)," but then also, across hundreds of pages, by dozens of repetitions of this phrase in both dialogue and narration.

In contrast, neither the Harjo brand nor the bodies into which it is burned are ever mentioned outside of the sentence in which they first, and last, appear. The brand's excessiveness is further underscored by the fact that it must have demanded an extra moment of improvisation from the typesetters of the Hampton Institute's *Southern Workman* (where the story was first published), given that the typeface of the *H*-like figure does not match that of the rest of the text.[6] The terminal points of the first letter in the name "Harjo"—the initial that the brand might represent—have serif flares that the brand does not (fig. 1.1). Here, too, we lack an extant manuscript through which to assess the origins of the brand's form. Features such as font styling and that small central gap may be authorial choices or artifacts of typographic bricolage, one of the Hampton students who set the magazine having perhaps created the figure by altering pieces from some other font set that had been moldering in a corner of the shop (fig. 1.2). Still, whatever exactly it looked like in Oskison's hand, we might ask, Why did he bother with this ink out of place in the first place?

It's tempting to settle immediately on one or another iconographic reading of the figure—for instance, to assert that the brand, referencing its designer's name, also depicts in its shape the structure of his predicament. Its doubled, divided form seems to visualize the double consciousness that Du Bois, a decade earlier, linked to the feeling of embodying a social "problem," here the so-called Indian Problem.[7] This is, no doubt, one meaning

FIGURE 1.2 Frances Benjamin Johnston, *Compositors Working in Printing Shop, Hampton Institute*, photograph, Hampton, Virginia, 1899 (or 1900). Frances Benjamin Johnston Photograph Collection, Library of Congress, Prints & Photographs Division, LC-USZ62-110215 (b&w film copy neg.), loc.gov/item/94502417/.

that the brand might generate. But to commit to it requires taking a rough graphic resemblance for a smooth semiotic commensurability. (Even the "rag of scarlet cloth" once famously discovered in a custom-house storeroom "assumed the shape of a letter" only after "careful examination"—as Nathaniel Hawthorne writes in a novel that, as I'll develop, has an afterlife in Oskison's writing.)[8] So instead I hope to work up an account of this figure's significance and of its insignificance that is at once more cautious and more expansive, traversing the social and textual spaces opened in the simple fact of its status as a mark of agricultural property and in the self-evident problem of its graphic/alphabetic shape.

The brand's function is one starting point. Cattle branding is a crucial sign system in Indian Territory at the turn of the twentieth century, ranching having been a dominant aspect of the regional economy for decades.

One 1859 estimate put the number of Cherokee-owned cattle at a quarter million.[9] Over the two decades prior to Oklahoman statehood in late 1907, land allotment legislation—the Dawes and Curtis Acts—led to the parceling of lands that had been held communally according to Indigenous land tenure conventions. (Often, those lands had also been leased to individual ranchers, as was the case with Oskison's father.) This legislation led to large-scale dispossession, facilitating white settlers' expropriation of parcels. It also set the conditions for the transition to statehood. The transformations under way during Oskison's youth can be narrated, in part, through the material of fences and brands, complementary techniques of enclosure and inscription.[10]

The brand's form, indistinctly tied to the Latin alphabet, registers another Cherokee history: that of the syllabary introduced in 1821 by Sequoyah, also known as 4·Vᵒⵞ, George Guess, and by orthographic variations thereof. A writing system based on syllabic units rather than on the roughly phonemic model of many alphabetic scripts, the Cherokee syllabary adopts a sizable minority of its glyphs (eighty-six in total, later standardized to eighty-five) from the shapes of the Latin alphabet, divorced from the sounds those marks may indicate in English. Sequoyah and the syllabary drew Oskison's attention at multiple points in his life. The incomplete manuscript of his autobiography, for instance, refers to his exposure, as a child, to the *Cherokee Advocate*, a newspaper printed in both the Latin alphabet and the Cherokee syllabary; he discusses Sequoyah more than once in essays in the 1910s; and in the novel he left unpublished at his death, a work of historical fiction titled *The Singing Bird: A Cherokee Novel*, Sequoyah is a significant character. In the novel, Sequoyah's daughter describes having collaborated with him on the syllabary: "We both listened carefully to the people's talk, and put down a sign for each syllable."[11] In considering this scene's relevance to "Old Harjo," a couple of qualifiers are needed. The titular character of "Old Harjo" is not Cherokee but Creek in nationality; and a specifically Creek context is germane here, as I'll later discuss, through his potential association with Chitto Harjo, a prominent opponent of allotment.[12] It is also important to note that the Harjo brand does not precisely match any particular grapheme in Sequoyah's syllabary or in the Creek alphabet. But the specification that Harjo himself designed his brand invokes, in the context of Oskison's work, the story of Sequoyah and his daughter listening carefully—the story of the syllabary is commonly told as a parable about aural precision and the perfectibility of transcription—and then "put[ting] down a sign." This parable's circulation during Oskison's lifetime is inseparable, as I'll discuss, from a political history, at once intra- and transnational, that enfolds multiple Indian Territory constituencies.

There's more to say about the iconographic details of Harjo's brand. The end of this chapter will consider them again. But its indexical relations to such histories of graphic representation, aural imagination, and territorial dispossession are why *I* bother with this ink out of place. My account of those relations leans frequently on material published in small-circulation periodicals, both to give a granular sense of the spaces in which Oskison moved and on the premise that this approach can attune us to the method of an author whose fiction came increasingly to draw on similar archives. The primary question that I follow across this material has to do with how ideas of phonetic transmission—and of the interruption of such transmission by a refusal of speech marked as muteness—get threaded into histories of social reproduction, including, especially, those that play out in the contested historiography of Sequoyah's invention and in the imagined dilemma of Harjo's conversion.

Two suggestive facts of linguistic history may encourage us to follow these threads. First, if the design of the aleph derives from the horns of an ox, that of the letter *H* descends, through the line of Phoenician alphabetics invented, according to myth, by Cadmus, from a grapheme based on the image of a fence.[13] Second, as a 1904 article about the Cherokee syllabary noted, when it was first circulated—and this was according to one Reverend Rope Camell of Cooweescoowee District, Cherokee Nation, who, at 112 years old, claimed to have personally known the inventor in his youth—"Sequoyah's method was at once associated with the idea of branding cattle."[14]

Soil Stories

When, late in Oskison's half-century writing career, he recalled how it all started, he pictured talking protozoa. I'd like to start with this recollection as a way into one of the quieter through lines of that career: the writer's concern with the politics of attributing discursive intent to ostensibly nonlinguistic life. The question of this concern is caught up with ideas of "Nature" that Oskison directly engaged, with theories of "culture" that he conspicuously dismissed, and with the conventions of local color writing that his work—particularly the college publications and early magazine pieces on which this section focuses—both adopted and transformed.

Oskison offers the anecdote of his first publication twice, with minor variations in emphasis: once in *The Brothers Three* and once in his autobiography, left in manuscript form at his death. In *The Brothers Three*, the character of Henry Odell serves as the author's proxy. Like Oskison, he grows up on a ranch a few miles outside of Vinita, a Cherokee Nation ranching town with a population of about 2,000 at the turn of the twentieth century (in what was then Indian Territory and is now Oklahoma). Also like Oskison, he leaves to study at Stanford and then to build a writing career in New York, returning to his hometown regularly throughout his life. Late in the novel, his sister-in-law asks, "When did you first actually write things?" He was bored in a college biology class, Odell explains. Observing "a smear of one-cell microbes," he began "imagining them as human" and wondering what these microbes might have to say about those who were trying to study them. Absorbed in his scribbling, he fails to notice the approach of one Professor Jenkins. Jenkins picks up the pages and reads. To Odell's surprise, rather than scold him for his distraction, Jenkins encourages him to submit the piece to the *Sequoia*, Stanford's literary magazine.[15] Oskison's autobiography corroborates this account of how he wrote a "dialogue between two . . . microscopic playboys" in the lab, adding that it was his friend Dane Coolidge, an English major and one of the *Sequoia* editors, who then helped him to get his "Two on a Slide" into print and soon thereafter to join the magazine's staff. Before long, Oskison starts publishing the kind of "vignettes of range and farm life" that will become his mainstay.[16]

Oskison positions the amoeba sketch as his entry both to publishing his own fiction and to the editorial work that would sustain him for decades. But the anecdote is misleading on multiple counts. What he later called "Two on a Slide" fills two pages of the magazine's February 5, 1897, issue under another title: "A Laboratory Fancy." The discrepancy of the title reflects another. The sketch does not, in fact, depict two protozoa, as Oskison later wrote. Instead, a single such "animalcule" addresses the student-narrator.[17] The dialogue comes to a foreseeable conclusion: it was all a dream, the student having drifted off at the microscope. The fact that the story's dialogue occurs across species lines is key to its rhetorical energies. Through the distinction between the Paramœcium (loosely coded as Indigenous) and the narrator (addressed by the Paramœcium as white), Oskison satirically explores the analogies and entanglements between ecocide and genocide and between zoological and anthropological taxonomies. He does so, too, while satirizing the position of the narrating settler-scholar who has "unpacked his kit" on Indigenous land, insisting on the practice of a science that he also mocks.[18]

The title that Oskison forgot captures some of these complexities, even in its generic simplicity. "A Laboratory Fancy" surely refers to the dream of the writer, to the poetic fancy *in* the laboratory. But it may also suggest the necrotic fancy *of* the laboratory, echoing the Paramœcium's critique of taxonomic violence. The cynical tautologies of the student's rejoinders make good fodder for this critique. "Of what import is your life when I must put a drop of Methyl Green on you pretty soon," he asks rhetorically, "and try to discover from your dead body just where the living center of your highly magnified corpse is located."[19] Here the designation of bare life involves logic that could only work in a dream. The reveal of that dream in the story's ending may feel predictable as an ending, and we could write this off as a hallmark of juvenilia. But the story is also *about* the trouble with prediction—about the violence that so often attends claims to know how something is going to end. When the predictable reveal of the dream does arrive, and the student awakens in the lab, the other foregone conclusion that the dialogue had centered on—the death of the amoeba—is never explicitly realized, neither within the dream-space nor in the waking world of the frame narrative. The death drive gets diverted into a principle of plot.[20] The amoeba's life is not explicitly ended; instead the voice with which it would query that ending's necessity is silenced by the machinery of a narrative cop-out.

The questions that attach here to "fancy"—With whose perspective is it associated? And with what aesthetic, ethical, and ecological implications?—are explored by Oskison in another early *Sequoia* piece. Titled "Heard at Random," the sketch presents a dorm-room debate centering on the pathetic fallacy. This premise suggests that, a decade before Oskison drafted Harjo's "fantastic" design, he was aware of "fancy" as a significant term in aesthetic criticism (in debates among figures such as Samuel Taylor Coleridge, Matthew Arnold, and John Ruskin), a term connected not just with caprice and ornament but also with arguments about epistemology and anthropomorphism. In the sketch, "sentimental Tommy" argues for Nature's intrinsic sublimity; meanwhile, the skeptical Crawford—for whom "Nature . . . is only a heterogeneous mass of things more or less useful to us"—sees literary history as a misguided series of faddish paradigms: Romanticism in the early nineteenth century, the "sectional eccentricities" of local color in the late, and perhaps (as Crawford scornfully forecasts) theosophy in the early twentieth?[21]

The phrase that Oskison uses for the title, "Heard at Random," is a typical column header in newspapers of the period. Usually, it introduces several very short items. They might be anecdotal, sensationalistic, humorous, or even aphoristic in nature. In some small-circulation papers, these items might take the form of a list of brief personal updates from various locals, written in the first person.[22] The *Sequoia* had no such feature; placing this phrase as the title of a long academic dialogue, Oskison playfully repurposes it. In the context of a novice writer's effort to find a place in the medium, navigating among genre conventions, the title seems to announce a commitment to an unadorned realism. A mere report. But any implication that the sketch is simply a neutral transcription is undone by its conclusion. When the interlocutors finally disperse for the night, the narrator is left "to write an essay for the next day on Nature."[23] The suggestion is that the text that one has just read is the same that the narrator would submit to an instructor. It's revealed to have been an instrumentalized fabrication all along, the heterogeneities of random overheard speech converted to "more or less useful" material for academic credit.

These two *Sequoia* pieces imagine a turn to the aural as the condition of representing Nature. This turn is obvious in the framing of "Heard at Random," whose narrator is hardly dramatized except as a student whose writing is parasitic on others' speech, but is also crucial to the structure of "A Laboratory Fancy," dismissing visual technology except as it happens to occasion dialogue. The odd phrasing of the story's conclusion is telling. After the instructor interrupts the dream, the narrator notes, "I was on the point of relating my dream, when I heard that I'd have to stay and make up the time I put in sleeping"—not "I was told" or "Professor Jenkins said to me" but, awkwardly, "when I heard." It's as if this news were a rumor drifting by happenstance into the narrator's sphere of attention. Obscuring the source of the sound, this moment offers an apt conclusion to the text's representation of sensory experience, which locates the occasion of writing—and in the author's retrospect, the birth of the writer—in a turn away from the visual observation assigned to the student at the microscope and toward a dream (for the narrator, a sleeping dream; for the author, a daydream) in which he hears an impossible voice. That voice fades back and forth across thresholds of audibility. The student notes that he misses the first part of the speech, and then, as the Paramœcium begins to dry on the slide, its voice weakens. At that point, the narrator eagerly revives it: he administers water, almost as if caring for a machine but also comparing the action to the way that "a fresh quid of tobacco, administered to an old mountaineer at the right time, will open the pores of his memory, and he will tell marvelous tales of other days."[24] If the image is peculiar—having absorbed the nicotine through the pores in his gums, the mountaineer then emits stories through the pores of some other membrane, as if sweating them out—it is also fitting for a comparison with a voice that emanates unexpectedly from the cell membrane of the eukaryotic body.

The image of a flat, round source of sound, its most functional features visible only through a microscope, was specifically evocative of novel audio technology in the 1890s, the same decade that wax cylinders begin to give way to flat-disk phonographic records. The Paramœcium's speech is first introduced in the terms of this very technology: it "answered in a voice which resembled the squeak of a phonograph."[25] Given the premise of the Paramœcium's imminent death, this reference, in which the microscope's visual magnification is supplanted by the fantastic vocal possibilities of audio recording, carries an additional resonance.[26] As cultural historians and historians of technology have noted, the phonograph was often marketed in the period as a device by which to hear the voices of the dead; this was also the decade that saw anthropologists such as Jesse Walter Fewkes first taking the phonograph into the field.[27] The technology carries particular meanings in light of the amoeba's association with Indigenous life, imagined in a necropolitical colonial fantasy and by salvage anthropologists as imminently vanishing. The phonographic "squeak" in Oskison's laboratory story invokes a chorus of voices recorded not "at random" but because of their predicted disappearance. None other than Boas spoke on the same theme at Stanford during Oskison's first year there, giving a talk, according to a report in the *Sequoia*, about "the almost extinct tribes of the Pacific Coast."[28]

Oskison's own memory of his first publication turns out to have been a porous record in still another way: chronology. "Heard at Random" appeared in November 1896, a few months before "A Laboratory Fancy." The story he called his first wasn't.[29] So why was it the amoeba sketch, rather than the earlier "Heard at Random," that he would later come back to and claim as an origin? Maybe he simply forgot, of course. But this just shifts the terms of the question: Why did "A Laboratory Fancy" stick better in the memory? Perhaps an amoeba bursting into expression offered an irresistible trope for a writer's small beginnings. Another factor may have been that this was his first publication dealing explicitly with issues of Indigenous politics—while also, in a heightened form of the rhetorical obscurity that has occupied scholars of his mature work, focalizing these themes through an erratic settler consciousness.

The anecdote's fictional retelling in *The Brothers Three*, four decades after the fact, opens another line of possible explanation. One 1935 reviewer of the novel noted that "Mr. Oskison joins that group of writers who are realizing that the 'soil' story is one of our country's blessings"; another reviewer—Oskison's second wife, Hildegarde Hawthorne, throwing any conflict-of-interest qualms to the wind—wrote that "from the first page . . . you are drawn into the life of the Odell family so vigorously and honestly portrayed that it is difficult to believe, when you have read the final page, that these men and women, these growing youngsters, are of imagination all compact, that as you close the book they cease to be."[30] Protesting a bit much against the hypothetical reader who might detect echoes of Oskison's own family, Hawthorne's denial of the autobiographical aspects of the novel might have read with a wink to people in the know. In the phrase "imagination all compact," she links Oskison's fancies with those of *A Midsummer Night's Dream*.[31] But at bottom, this Oklahoma soil story is a novel of economy. Its representations of land and of nonhuman lives revolve around their commoditization. The dollar values attached to livestock, land, and extracted mineral resources feature with staggering frequency.[32] Here the muddy voice of a life on the line between flora and fauna, instrumentalized by a form of knowledge production tied to territorial incursion but still bearing witness, might have provided a telling counterpoint.

Oskison is now remembered as the first Native American graduate of Stanford University.[33] The institutional claim was not always so straightforward. When a *Washington Post* article noted Oskison's success as a short story writer in 1899, just a year after his graduation, the campus newspaper, the *Daily Palo Alto*, proudly printed a notice of the piece but also went out of its way to correct the *Post*'s "supposition that Oskison is a full-blooded Indian, whereas he is, more properly speaking, a white with some Indian blood in his veins."[34] Oskison did not himself tend to frame the question of his blood quantum in the same way. But in his half-remembered "Laboratory Fancy," another fraught "first," he seems to have anticipated these ethnological tensions in the reception of his work and of his person, placing his own participation in the academic institution under scrutiny. (Two were on the slide, after all.) If his early narrative of a protozoon and its observer complexly allegorizes the taxonomic imagination that conscripts racialized and deracinated subjects into the colonial project, the story also nests such an allegory of personhood in particular histories of land use. In it, he begins to experiment with the capacities of fictional fancy—of the counter-fantasies of identification afforded by narrative—both to ventriloquize and to critique the logic of settler expansionism.[35] He concretizes this ambivalence not only in dialogue but in a narrative voice that both originates in and alienates his experience—a vocal irony born not of distance but of sharply felt contradiction.

Over the several years after Oskison graduated, he became more self-reflective about the models he wished to follow as a writer. He read Henry James (at least *What Maisie Knew* and *The Turn of the Screw*) while spending a year studying at Harvard and balked at the "obscurity of language" favored by both James brothers; William gave a guest lecture in his psychology class and Oskison found it agonizing.[36] He read J. M. Barrie and found him too sentimental; the assessment was reached through sniffles, Oskison self-mockingly admits. He read William Dean Howells, who represented "another kind of realism" that Oskison admired, but he felt he could not himself rise to the heights of the *Atlantic Monthly*. (This is despite the fact that he had begun to publish in East Coast magazines with a highly visible entry in the *Century*, where he had won a prize in 1899 for the best short story by a recent college graduate.) But while Howells signified a distant elevation, Oskison did feel that "it might be possible to become a more or less worthy disciple of Hamlin Garland," the author of the 1891 story collection *Main-Traveled Roads* (with an introduction by Howells) and of the influential set of essays in *Crumbling Idols* (1894).[37] Such touchstones help us coordinate the author's later understanding of his work's place in literary history, but we can turn to his magazine fiction itself for a more textured sense of the relevant print-cultural geography—and for a sense of how Oskison extended his earlier explorations at the intersection of the biological and the political in a fictional practice that was self-reflexive about its relationship to land.

Take Oskison's second piece for *The Century*, "'The Quality of Mercy': A Story of the Indian Territory," published in a 1904 issue that also featured work by Garland. In its opening, a character raises the same question that the illustration in "Old Harjo" does: Why put a cattle brand into print? Venita Churchfield has just returned from college in St. Louis to her hometown, Black Oak—presumably the Black Oak in what is currently Arkansas, given the subtitle. Churchfield finds the local newspaper, the *Sachem*, exasperatingly provincial. If she had her way, the paper's editor, Mr. Efferts, would do away with one of its regular features: the cattle brand page. It "occupied a considerable share of the four pages devoted to keeping the little prairie town of Black Oak informed of the world's doings." Efferts, though, insists that "spreading the knowledge of a brand throughout the country" and also printing the "ugly, raw news" of regional outlaws like Missouri Bob the cattle thief should take priority over, say, "editorials about Ruskin." "Cattle made Black Oak," he says to Churchfield, "and they made the 'Sachem,' too." Churchfield's desire for more cosmopolitan material, meanwhile, has motives outside of her own readerly experience: she hopes to have Efferts as an "ally in the work of introducing culture—an exceedingly vague something, meant, for one thing, to suppress the unseemly shooting at sign-boards when, on occasion, cow-boys, full-bloods, half-breeds, and whites came in at night to 'paint the town.'"[38]

The dismissals and qualifications in this statement about "culture" signify complexly. Although the line represents Churchfield's viewpoint, it also clearly integrates the earthy skepticism of the fictional editor—and perhaps the implied author. Through this blur of narrative voicing, Oskison efficiently sends up the obscurity of E. B. Tylor's catch-all description of culture as "that complex whole which includes knowledge, belief, art, morals, law, custom, and any other capabilities and habits acquired by man as a member of society."[39] But that isn't the only definition of culture that the line plays with. Churchfield's preferences seem to lean toward an Arnoldian sense of "culture" as distributing, across class differences, "the best which has been thought and said in the world"—and what that distribution can do, it's hinted, is to moderate the potential for social conflict.[40]

Oskison's writing never sustained a direct engagement with the question of the culture concept. Yet both his writing and his advocacy do suggest his awareness of contemporaneous debates. Setting aside glancing encounters such as he could have had with Boas at Stanford in 1895, Oskison's most direct connection with professional anthropology derived from his later involvement in the Society of American Indians, the pan-Indian advocacy organization in which he was a leading member and a close colleague of the anthropologist Arthur C. Parker. The two of them, with the artist Angel De Cora Deitz, formed a subcommittee tasked with selecting the society's logo design; they were also members of a larger committee tasked with drafting its constitution.[41] Parker, an anthropologist strongly influenced by Lewis Henry Morgan (who had worked closely with his uncle, Ely S. Parker), is a likely source for the reference to social evolutionism in the 1912 mission statement, committing the society to "the advancement of the Indian in enlightenment which makes him free, as a man, to develop according to the natural laws of social evolution."[42] The comparative hierarchies of social evolutionary thinking would seem a fitting ideology for an organization that has sometimes been presented as assimilationist. However, as more than one recent account has remarked, talk of social evolutionism in such organizational language probably did not represent a committed theory of human variation.[43] Rather, such references were of a piece with the heterogeneity of anthropological theory in the period, characterized by Alfred

Kroeber in 1917 as "this current confusion between the organic and the superorganic," a confusion attributed by Kroeber to a persistent application of social-evolutionary alongside historical particularism, of racialist thinking alongside cultural pluralism.[44]

A version of such confusion is visible in the list of rowdies—"cow-boys, full-bloods, half-breeds, and whites"—that draw Venita Churchfield's disapproval in "The Quality of Mercy." She smiles wryly at Efferts's embrace of these locals' "incongruousness," referring to their inappropriate modes of occupying public space. A more evident incongruousness, though, is produced by the list itself. When "cow-boys" is followed immediately by "full-bloods" and then "half-breeds," the effect is to imply that these terms name distinct categories. This implication trades on *Century* subscribers' likely assumptions about the whiteness of cowboys. But the conclusion of the same list with "whites" then triggers a weird redundancy, a quiet cousin to the comic paradox that the humorist Will Rogers, Oskison's childhood friend, generated in publicizing himself as "the Indian cowboy."[45] As the connection with Rogers might suggest, part of the difficulty of attributing to Oskison an adherence to any given theory of cultural variation—a difficulty reflected in scholarly disagreements about his politics—stems from his investment in the aesthetic and comic effects enabled by the *production* of confusion.[46] "Irony is meat and drink to us," says Henry, the writer, in *The Brothers Three*, explaining the sensibility of the Odell family (and, if we accept the novel's autobiographical implications, of the Oskison family as well).[47]

A travel piece that Oskison wrote in 1914, titled "The Road to Betatakin," shows what happens when this sensibility comes into direct contact with ethnographic writing. Published in two installments in *Outing* magazine, the piece makes a running joke out of the navigational guidance offered by the Smithsonian anthropologist Jesse Walter Fewkes's *Preliminary Report on a Visit to the Navaho National Monument, Arizona*, which Oskison carried with him on the backcountry excursion. It was published in 1911 by the Bureau of American Ethnology (of which Fewkes would become president in 1918). One can certainly detect in the book the confusion of theories that Kroeber will identify in the discipline later in the decade. Yet where Fewkes applies the term "culture" in the book, he consistently assumes the diffusionist methods of early Boasian anthropology. Rather than taking cultural variations and syncretisms as the expressions of particular societies' essential qualities or their social-evolutionary positions, he speculates about the dissemination of ideas and objects across geographical spaces. Fewkes infers from techniques of kiva construction, for instance, that "the prehistoric migration of culture was down rather than up the [San Juan] river."[48]

The only time Oskison uses "culture" in "Road to Betatakin," though, it is to imply that he is drawn to Fewkes's volume *despite* the latter's interest in such theories: he finds in it an enchanting description of a romantic terrain "hidden in a page of talk about the peculiar culture of the Hopi clans."[49] The implication is not that Oskison dismisses this "talk" as theoretically flimsier than, for instance, Parker's social evolutionism. It's that "culture" presents an exceedingly vague something that can be done without.[50] The questions it carries distract Fewkes from the more picturesque experiences of the field. The more practical, too. Attempting to follow the itinerary that Fewkes lays out in the volume, Oskison and his companion get badly lost, and he comically rues having "rel[ied] upon the printed words of the Government man."[51] Associating the inflated authority of this "Government man" with "printed words"—a paper trail, the piece suggests, laughably removed from the rough trails of the West; a map that cannot be trusted as true to the territory—Oskison links ethnography with state power and frames epistemic authority (and its lack) as a question of medium. And he plays on the fact that his own report from the trail will, likewise, circulate as talk printed on the page.

In "The Quality of Mercy," too, "culture" is nested within conflicts of social distinction (low, high), of geographic affiliation (local, cosmopolitan), and of modes of occupying public space (rowdy, bookish). These oppositions define the representational spectrum of local color writing, a narrative mode often understood, in the period, as mingling folkloric report and fictional fabrication. In the influential essay "Local Color in Art" (published in *Crumbling Idols*), Hamlin Garland—of whom, again, Oskison considered himself a "disciple"—calls for writing that merges what is "indigenous" to the space of the writer with what qualifies as "beautiful" across broader spatial and temporal contexts. This synthesis is troped as a union across caste positions: "Beauty is the world-old aristocrat who has taken for mate this mighty young plebeian Significance," Garland writes, defining "Significance" not as global truth but as localized meaning—the "native element, the differentiating element" that keeps literary history safe from dry rot, reflecting its own emergence from a rooted position in time and place in "a statement of life as indigenous as the plant-growth."[52]

For Oskison, in stories like "The Quality of Mercy," the making of such meaning tends to be conspicuously concretized in vernacular graphic systems: cattle brands, newspaper advertisements, editorial columns, bullet-ridden sign boards, and telegraph messages. (In the conclusion of the story, the Shakespearian phrase of the title is used as a code, sent by wire.) All of this collides in the figure of speech that Churchfield uses to describe the rowdies' behavior: painting the town. This phrase names activity that is, on the one hand, and despite being "ugly" and "raw," an integral part of the complex, immanent whole of the particular culture of this town—culture in what Tylor calls its "wide ethnographic sense."[53] On the other hand, this behavior is directly opposed to culture in the sense of an elevated, pacifying force, exemplified in the fine arts. "To 'paint the town'" resolves this opposition in an aesthetic figure, superimposing the object and the medium of local color.

Although Oskison sets "A Quality of Mercy" elsewhere, he hints that he is painting his own hometown as well. Let me follow a few paths in this direction, less to develop a biographical interpretation than to trace a bibliographical arc: as Oskison's writing begins to appear in magazines on both coasts, his work also insistently registers print-cultural contexts specific to Indian Territory. In Venita Churchfield's first name, to begin with, Oskison barely changes the spelling of Vinita, and then he signs off from "Vinita, I.T." at the end of the text as well, despite the fact that he was primarily living in New York at the time, working for the *New York Evening Post*. In the name he gives to Black Oak's fictional newspaper, meanwhile, the *Sachem*, he takes the title of Vinita's major periodical, the *Chieftain*, and translates it into the anglicized version of an Eastern Algonquian term for "leader."

After Oskison began publishing in the *Sequoia* in 1896, his college sketches were often reprinted in the *Chieftain*. His name was becoming increasingly familiar in its pages. When he graduated from Stanford in 1898, the paper printed a proud notice.[54] The same edition, on the following page, also included space for cattle brand advertisements, as the *Chieftain* almost always did (fig. 1.3). In the *Chieftain*, though, as opposed to the fictional *Sachem*, the brands usually occupied just a single column of a back page—often just part of that column, rather than the three front-page columns that annoy Churchfield.[55] And the Vinita paper did, in fact, sometimes print "editorials about Ruskin" or at any rate referring to him. In 1897, for instance, the *Chieftain* quoted Ruskin's assertion that "crime cannot be hindered by punishment" in the context of a brief editorial note on the importance of education as an instrument of social harmony.[56] (Churchfield would approve.) In early 1904, just a few months before "The Quality of Mercy" was published in *The Century*, the *Chieftain* printed a notice of upcoming

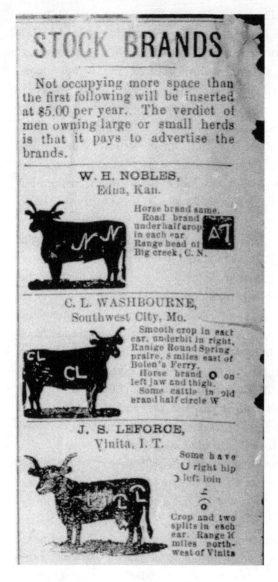

FIGURE 1.3 Cattle brand ads in the *Weekly Chieftain* (Vinita, Indian Territory), June 9, 1898. The Gateway to Oklahoma History, Oklahoma Historical Society, http://gateway.okhistory.org /ark:/67531/metadc71545 /m1/4/.

meetings of a new Vinita women's literary club whose schedule included a session on Ruskin.[57] Formed in 1903, the group called itself the Sequoyah Club.

While Sequoyah had long been a luminary in histories of Cherokee nationhood, his name was being uttered and printed even more than usual at the moment. As plans for Oklahoman statehood crystallized during the allotment period, some Indian Territory groups attempted to preemptively avert the consolidation of Indian and Oklahoma Territories under white set-tler control by creating a separate state, named Sequoyah, out of Indian Territory. The movement ultimately failed—pursuant to the Oklahoma En-abling Act of 1906, Oklahoma's statehood was ratified in 1907—but it leant the name a special valence in the first several years of the twentieth century.

This valence applied even when statehood was not directly at issue. On January 17, 1905, for instance, the *Daily Chieftain* printed a piece about Se-quoyah titled "The First Indian Writer." It opens by briefly describing the work of John Eliot, the Massachusetts Bay Colony missionary who in the seventeenth century "published the first Indian Bible" in a transliterated version of the Wôpanâak (Wampanoag) language. Leaping from Eliot to Sequoyah without offering any explicit connection between them, the arti-cle implies that the former's linguistic legacy is extended, elevated, by the latter's invention. Sequoyah is cast as the heir to a Puritan national prehis-tory.[58] The piece ends by noting that "Sequoia, the botanical name of the big trees of California, is the only memorial the white man has given to Sequoyah, this truly American genius"—as if to imply that the state name could be a gesture of recompense.[59] If Oskison read the story, its closing refer-ence to California flora would have echoed his own associations between the originator of the Cherokee writing system and the origin story of his own career in a magazine named after the same big trees; and those associations themselves fit a pattern in his writing in which the markers of the organic and the superorganic (nature and culture, tree and paper) move in sustained mutual collapse, a movement well figured as an irony you can eat.[60]

That the name of Sequoyah would bridge such different contexts for Os-kison was not improbable. Sequoyah was of exceptional importance in the imagination not only of Cherokee Nation but also of nineteenth-century print culture. Before moving to Vinita, Oskison's family had lived for a time outside of Tahlequah—where, he later writes, "they published *The Chero-kee Advocate*, a weekly newspaper printed half in English and half in the Cherokee characters devised more than forty years before by Sequoyah."[61] Elsewhere, he referred to the *Chieftain* as "one of the earliest successors of the Cherokee Advocate, the official paper of the nation."[62] The *Advocate* itself was the inheritor of an important legacy, carrying on the bilingual formatting of the *Phoenix*, which had begun to print Sequoyah's syllabary in the late 1820s. Production of the *Advocate* as a national Cherokee publi-cation was halted in March 1906, though, due to the transition to Oklaho-man statehood. (Subsequently, the *Phoenix* resumed publication and remains in business today.) Most issues of the *Advocate* published while Oskison lived in Indian Territory featured about a page of print in the syllabary, with the rest of the four-page paper printed in the Latin alphabet. These proportions were not usually the even split, half and half, that Oskison suggests. But they're near the proportion of brands to writing in the fictional *Sachem*.

If it sounds like I'm heading toward a claim that the brands referred to in "The Quality of Mercy"—those that Venita Churchfield wants replaced with more cultivated matter—are metaphorical substitutes for the printed characters of the syllabary, that is not quite my destination. It's close, though. What I want to emphasize, more precisely, are the metonymies generated by Oskison's sense of social conflict as practically mediated not only in but as the proximity and contestation of graphic systems, such as that between the branding of cattle and the printing of Sequoyah's syllabary. So just after the federal government steps in to stop the presses on the principal distributor of the syllabary (the *Advocate*), Oskison goes out of his way, in 1907, to get the mark of the Harjo brand onto the page of a magazine. This unsayable quasi-alphabetic mark, burned onto the fleshy sides of fictional animals (a technique, like the microscopic slide, for making a speechless organism knowable in two dimensions) is a minor response, if not to the closure of the *Advocate* in itself, then to the massive program of linguistic hegemony and resource extraction of which that closure was a part. Because the syllabary has often occupied, for Oskison and others, a major place in the history of such responses, I'd like to turn in the following pages— before returning to "Old Harjo"—to representations of Sequoyah's invention and to the metanarratives of orality, literacy, and nationhood that its characters come to carry.

The _____ Cadmus

Unfolding in Indian Territory across several decades in the mid-nineteenth century, during and after Removal, Oskison's late novel manuscript, *The Singing Bird*, places Cherokee figures from that period, John Ross and Sequoyah among them, alongside a group of fictional white missionaries.[63] The historical narrative—involving Cherokee factions, negotiations with the federal government, the creation of schools, and the distribution and typesetting of the syllabary—intertwines with a series of romantic triangulations. Driving much of that drama is the magnetic and cynical Ellen, who is married to, and eventually cheats on, the pious missionary Dan. Late in the novel, Ellen reflects on her indiscretions: "I've been naughty, and must be stood in a corner—not with a dunce's cap on my head, but—Paul, do you happen to have an iron for branding on my forehead the letter 'A'?" In drawing a comparison between her own iniquity and Hester Prynne's, Ellen would have been alluding, in the timeline of the novel, to a brand-new book (one that happens to have been written by the author's grandfather-in-law, through his spouse, Hildegarde). Ellen's friend Paul, the novel's narrator, gets the reference: "The Scarlet Letter? No; we don't even brand our cattle. . . . The Cherokees seem to have convinced the cattle thieves that it would be bad luck to steal from us" (165). If Paul proves himself here a true expert in changing the subject, the conversation also aptly reflects how often, in *The Scarlet Letter*, Hester Prynne's letter—and the forms of discipline given expression through it—is compared to the kind of mark burned in flesh.

Nathaniel Hawthorne had a long-standing interest in the history of languages and, particularly, of graphic systems. We know, for instance, that he read both Charles Davy's and Charles Kraitsir's tomes on the alphabet.[64] In *Grandfather's Chair: A History for Youth* (1842), Hawthorne includes a brief account of John Eliot's linguistic work (Eliot also features in *The Scarlet Letter*; Arthur Dimmesdale is returning from a visit to him when he has a pivotal meeting with Hester in the woods).[65] In *Tanglewood Tales: A Wonder-Book for Boys and Girls* (1853), Hawthorne tells the myth of Cadmus, the Phoenician prince who slayed a dragon, who grew an army by planting that dragon's teeth in the ground until they sprouted into soldiers, and who also, the story goes, invented the alphabet (or at least introduced it to Greece). Hawthorne concludes his own account of Cadmus's adventures by noting that he "used to find time from his kingly duties to teach [his children] their A B C—which he invented for their benefit, and for which many little people, I am afraid, are not half so grateful to him as they ought to be."[66] A few chapters into *The Scarlet Letter*, the impertinent child Pearl, strongly associated with Hester's letter itself, is implicitly compared to the founder of Thebes. Pearl plays poorly with other children, but she is able to fantasize and give voice to a whole host of made-up playmates, "her one baby-voice" representing "a multitude of imaginary personages." These personages are not friends. Instead she "seemed always to be sowing . . . the dragon's teeth, whence sprung a harvest of armed enemies."[67] Linguistic ingenuity, soldiers spawned of dragon teeth: here we have an American Cadmus.

That nickname is already taken, though. It is Sequoyah's. An article on him appeared in the *American Magazine of Useful and Entertaining Knowledge* in the same month, January 1836, that Hawthorne accepted a job as the magazine's editor. The piece describes Sequoyah's persistence in his efforts to create the writing system, despite skeptics who discouraged him from trying to "emulate a *Cadmus*."[68] Given the timing and Hawthorne's personal fascinations, the piece must have come to his attention (even if, as he had written a few months earlier, he did "abhor an Indian story"); and six months later, he published a piece on John Eliot's translations in the same magazine himself, just as he resigned as its editor.[69] In accounts of Sequoyah from the late 1820s through the twenty-first century, the comparison with Eliot largely falls away, with exceptions such as the 1905 piece in the *Chieftain* that I discussed earlier. But the Cadmus analogy appears with remarkable frequency across works of journalism, historiography, oratory, and poetry.

The earliest instance of the mythical comparison in print may have been in an 1829 account by Samuel Knapp, titled "See-quah-yah: The Indian Philosopher." Knapp explains that although news of Sequoyah's invention is already widespread, he had the advantage of having met him in DC when a Cherokee delegation traveled to the capital for one of the Removal negotiations and so can report firsthand that "the manners of the American Cadmus are most easy."[70] The piece was excerpted in the July 29, 1829, issue of the *Cherokee Phoenix*—whose title may have made a reference to the Phoenician prince seem especially fitting—before appearing in Knapp's *Lectures on American Literature*. In the fuller context of the book, the enthusiastic account of Sequoyah's syllabary sits ill at ease with Knapp's celebration of the expansion of English. "Our mother tongue," he writes, "is becoming the triumphant language of mankind."[71] It also contradicts his description of Indigenous American peoples as "a thinly scattered race of rude men" obstructing "the founding of an empire larger than the world had ever seen."[72] In Knapp's account, the same thing that prevents Sequoyah from participating in that obstruction also allows him to create the syllabary: his disability. When a diseased knee "confined him to his cabin" only to turn into a permanent condition limiting Sequoyah's mobility, he was able to turn in earnest to his contemplations of graphic technology: "Deprived of the excitements of war, and the pleasures of the chase . . . his mind was again directed to the mystery of the power of *speaking by letters*."[73]

If the contradictions in Knapp's account of Sequoyah, both racist and celebratory, are compressed in the story of Sequoyah's immobility, they also reflect a larger linguistic quandary. The continuity of Anglo-American language and ethnicity was a major warrant for the claims of higher

civilization that underwrote expansionism; at the same time, this continuity undermined assertions for a distinct new national voice. At stake for
Knapp is nothing less than national evolution: "The literature of a nation,"
begins the section on Anglo-American literature that immediately follows
his account of Sequoyah, "affords the best criterion, by which may be
judged the principles and powers of a people, as well as their rank in the
scale of civilization."[74] Knapp's positioning of Sequoyah at multiple stations along that social-evolutionary scale (as a traditionalist adherent to
the customs of a "rude race" and at the same time as a rare genius of "easy
manners") produces a protean figure that can imaginatively resolve the impossible antinomy of an American literature. Indigenous and, at the same
time, fancied in some sense as English, this figure's voice comes through
with the strangest of clarities: Knapp claim to share what he has learned
"from the lips of the inventor himself," as if he and Sequoyah spoke to each
other in the same language, despite the fact that Sequoyah, who did not
speak English, spoke to him through interpreters.[75]

That slippage fits a broader pattern: as the Sequoyah story begins to be
more widely circulated, the figure of the inventor becomes available for rhetorical conscription in non-Cherokee linguistic and national narratives.
This was already evident in small ways when Knapp's 1829 account was
excerpted three years later in the *American Annals of Education*.[76] The excerpt is immediately preceded by a piece about English orthography, which
makes a case about the irrationality of the language—or rather, due to the
irregularity and nonsystematic nature of spelling in English, of the two languages, written and oral.[77] This complaint about the usage of the Latin alphabet is often, in decades to come, in the background of stories about the
syllabary's status as an extraordinarily transparent medium of both aural
and oral transmission, accurately reflecting the sounds of the spoken language and smoothly transferring into correct utterance.[78] While Knapp's reference to the "American Cadmus" appears in the excerpt, an editorial
reference to the article in another piece ("Self-Taught Men," appearing immediately before the piece on orthography) refers to the "Cherokee Cadmus"
instead.[79] In the long history of the comparison to Cadmus, the qualifier is
never fixed. Oskison himself uses different versions across his career. In
1914, he writes of the *Phoenix* that "by 1828 the Cherokees had a weekly
newspaper—half of it printed in English and half in the characters which
this Indian Cadmus had made familiar to his people"; in *The Singing Bird*,
though, Paul refers to Sequoyah as "the Cherokee Cadmus" (and the novel
also plays on the reference in other ways; the missionary Dan alludes to the

myth but implicitly associates Cadmus with US power, which "has sown the dragon's teeth and must needs harvest the terrible crop").[80] Both within and outside Oskison's imagination, the Cadmus comparison displays remarkable plasticity in its national affiliations.

Traveller Bird, in *Tell Them They Lie* (1971), underscores this plasticity more forcefully. In this account, Sequoyah—that is, the image of Sequoyah that commonly appears in the academic and governmental historiography—is a false substitute, "the bastard Cadmus of a white man."[81] Claiming privileged knowledge of the real Sequoyah through oral tradition and documents passed down by kin, Traveller Bird argues that the generally accepted biography has twisted the facts of Cherokee history in ways that serve the projects of nineteenth-century missionaries and expansionists. Sequoyah did not, Traveller Bird writes, participate in Removal negotiations as part of the Cherokee delegation to the US government, as in Knapp's report of meeting him in DC. He was, instead, "a fighting warrior-scribe" who resisted this process so fiercely that a kangaroo court convened by Major Ridge and other elements of the pro-Removal party punished him by disfiguring his fingers and ears and branding him on both the back and the forehead.[82] According to Traveller Bird, Sequoyah did indeed help teach and circulate a Cherokee writing system, but this happened in the 1790s rather than the 1820s; the system of symbols had long been in existence. This offers an alternative explanation of why full Cherokee literacy could be realized so "quickly" when the printing presses of missionaries and of the *Phoenix* were put into use three decades later: the signs were already familiar.[83]

Unsurprisingly, Traveller Bird's version of events has produced recurring historiographical disputes over the five decades since its publication. Yet it also problematizes in advance the terms of such dispute. Professing indifference as to whether the story corresponds with the reader's sense of truth, the book presents "the truth as it exists in the hearts and minds of some 13,000 fullblood kinsmen . . . who still speak, read and write our native language."[84] I have no standing to speak in the space of this claim. The limited observation I would offer has to do with how, in the reference to a "bastard Cadmus," one truth interprets another: the phrase repurposes the classical comparison as evidence of a false Sequoyah's status as a colonial construction. While "bastard" may serve the general function of a negative epithet, it also pointedly invokes an illegitimate claim to inheritance—preserving a space for the legitimacy of another Sequoyah as a proper steward, rather than the lone inventor, of the revolutionary weapon of Cherokee writing.[85] The cultural dimensions of the critique slide into the sphere of property relations. In this way, Traveller Bird's counternarrative, while contested by other histories of Sequoyah (both Cherokee and non-Native), tunes our ears to how the idea of the syllabary has sometimes been mobilized within the nationalist discourse of the expansionist state—and how, also, it can be retold and mobilized otherwise, since the stories of listening and literacy that circulate around Sequoyah have served to dramatize the scripts both of settler-colonialist modernity and of Indigenous futurity.[86]

Both scripts become audible, if the latter at a lower frequency, in an event that took place on June 6, 1917: the unveiling of a statue of Sequoyah in the National Hall of Statuary, commemorating Oklahoma's transition to statehood ten years earlier. (Two decades after this ceremony, Oskison's friend Will Rogers would be added next to Sequoyah.) The sculpture was designed by Lavinia "Vinnie" Ream Hoxie—the namesake, as it happens, of Oskison's hometown of Vinita, founded in 1871—but she died before completing the piece; it was finished by George Julian Zolnay, the Romanian American artist best known for his sculptures of Confederate officers (many of which, today, have recently been deinstalled).[87] Several elected officials spoke at the unveiling. Their remarks—what's said, what goes unsaid—merit a few moments' attention, as they are revealing both of the long-standing commonplaces that circulate around the syllabary and of the more localized texture of their articulation during Oskison's career.

A contrast between Cherokee and English spelling—the former perfectly reflecting the sounds of speech, the latter a broken mirror—was reiterated numerous times at the unveiling. Introduced as "the most lovable man in the United States," the Speaker of the House, Champ Clark, kept his remarks brief, but they included a searching question about the syllabary (which he called an alphabet): "What is the philosophy of this alphabet? It has one letter for each and every sound the human throat can make. That is precisely what it is." It is not. Rather than encompassing the entire range of human vocalization, the syllabary mediates the syllabic units specific to Cherokee speech. But the false premise allows Clark to make a stronger contrast between the syllabary and the Latin alphabet and thereby to highlight the dire necessity of spelling reform for the purposes of education in the English language. "My father believed in phonetics and I believe in phonetics," Clark attests; "we spend one-fifth of our lives learning how to spell, and we don't know yet." Here, the *Congressional Record* indicates "[laughter and applause]."[88]

The thrust of Clark's comments was consistent with other remarks at the unveiling. In sharp contrast with earlier philological rejections of syllabaries as inferior to alphabets due to the greater number of graphic characters required, the speakers celebrated the efficiency of Sequoyah's system.[89] Charles Carter (Chickasaw and Cherokee), representative of Oklahoma's Third Congressional District, complained that "the European alphabet goes too far in providing analysis of sound and permits such large variations in spelling that it is a task of years to learn how to spell correctly in any of the European languages," whereas the syllabary enabled a Cherokee student to "learn to spell in one day."[90] Robert L. Owen, senator of Oklahoma and Cherokee Nation citizen—and an early editor of the Vinita *Chieftain*—argued that this "phonetic alphabet, with a character representing every sound in the tongue of his tribe," had rapidly elevated Cherokees from a "benighted" state to literacy.[91]

At this ceremony, the syllabary is not just part of a "civilizing" program that includes literary education, the fine arts, or, say, Ruskin. It is a technology that brings the noise and wilderness of the frontier within the compass of representation, that takes the irreducible surround and makes its materials fungible. (Crawford, the cynical anthropocentrist of Oskison's "Heard at Random," would approve.) For the purposes of this narrative, congressmember Tom D. McKeown finds in Midas an even better figure than Cadmus, musing that Sequoyah's "footsteps turned the hills into rich lead and zinc, the highlands into coal, oil, and gas, and the prairies into fields of fleecy cotton and golden grain."[92] Troping the invention as an instrument of agriculture and resource extraction, McKeown links Sequoyah's work with the subsequent transformations of land that, in their connection with the transfer of territorial sovereignty, were a precondition of the statue's installation at the Capitol.

The two themes that thus dominate the event—the syllabary's qualities of auditory precision and its relationship to land—dovetail in the remarks of Thomas A. Chandler (an enrolled member of Cherokee Nation, from Vinita as well, representing Oklahoma's First Congressional District):

> The only voice of advice or learning that came to Sequoyah was the sound of nature. As the phonograph records the songs of the impressario and the tenor, Sequoyah recorded the songs of the birds, the clap of thunder, the roar of the beasts of the forests, the music of the zephyrs, combining these with the myths, he recorded them into an alphabet, as communicative to his primitive people as the phonograph of to-day.

From flittering noises in the dark, reaching him from the mystic unknown, he created a medium of understanding transmission from the ear to the eye.[93]

If the audience may have puzzled at "the songs of the impressario"—impresarios are, no doubt, linked with the performing arts but not usually as singers themselves—this is not the only strange representation of voice in Chandler's analogy. The phonograph and the writing system are intuitively compared with each other as mediators of sound, but the expression of this comparison seems to mismatch each technology to its function: here, the linguistic medium of the syllabary records all kinds of nonhuman noise *other* than speech (birds, beasts, weather), while the phonograph, which one might think to be better suited to transmitting such noises, is associated *only* with the singing voice. Beneath this apparent confusion, though, is a unifying idea of the syllabary as a technology of order alongside the plough, plantation, mine, and fence. The relevant distinction here, then, is the one between a mythic, aural wilderness ("the sounds of nature"; "noises in the dark") and a sense of reasoned communication tied to the faculty of sight and so associated less with the phonograph than with, say, the microscope.

In this paradigm, the syllabary becomes, as Chandler puts it, "a medium of understanding transmission from the ear to the eye." This formulation ignores the capacity for transmission in the other direction as well, as in the demonstrations of reading aloud that Sequoyah and his daughter are said to have performed for skeptical Cherokee Nation leadership. In *The Singing Bird*, Oskison has Sequoyah recall the well-known story: "I sent my daughter clear away, wrote down words that were said, and went away myself before my daughter came back and read on the paper what they had said" (77). While obviously the dictated text is central to the scene, it is the moment of vocal performance, the act of reading it back, that secures approval for the syllabary's distribution. Chandler's remarks in Statuary Hall, though, are all about the eye. This orientation conforms with what has been called the "audiovisual litany," a Western metaphysics of the vision/hearing distinction in which vision both "takes us out of the world" and "bathes us in the clear light of reason"—as opposed to the impressionistic, passive immersion imagined to characterize hearing.[94] If the privileging of the eye here serves a narrative of Enlightenment—allowing even those who do not read the syllabary to look at it as a treatment for their sound-blindness—it's also a fitting idea on the occasion of an unveiling: the visual reveal of the sculpture dramatizes the imagined transition from noise to reason, from oral to literate culture, that the technology of the syllabary is taken both to reflect and to produce.

Reading aloud, eye to ear, did have a place at the ceremony, though. Two poems were included in the proceedings: J. S. Holden's "The Cherokee Cadmus" and Alex Posey's "Ode to Sequoyah," which also deploys the Cadmus analogy: "The mysteries enshrouding Cadmus' name / Cannot obscure thy claim to fame."[95] Both poems also seem to set the syllabary's durability, the permanence of the textual record, against a narrative of Cherokee disappearance. "In ages yet to come / When his nation has no place," writes Holden, "His memory shall live in history's page," while Posey writes of the "inevitable doom" that will sweep away "the last fragments / Of tribes," except for the enduring letters Sequoyah made.[96] The understanding of those letters as having been selected almost at random, the grapheme-phoneme relation unburdened of such histories as trouble English spelling, frames the syllabary as a clean break from the "fragments" of the past. Even as it undermines the hegemony of English, this motif of rationalization happens to suit a state narrative of the path forward to clear, total sovereignty, by way of a return to a Cadmean origin.

Yet other details of these recitations sit less easily within the state narrative that the ceremony advances. Posey's "Ode to Sequoyah" was read first. The author, a Creek Nation citizen and well-known poet who served in 1906 as secretary to the Sequoyah State Constitutional Convention, had died in 1908. The reader was introduced simply as "a young Cherokee lady, Miss Anne Ross."[97] Anna Ross (later Anna Ross Piburn) was from the Tahlequah area, born there a couple of decades after Oskison, but was in DC in 1916 as Zolnay was completing the sculpture.[98] Because all the extant images of Sequoyah were based on copies of a single, destroyed painting by Charles Bird King, Zolnay wanted to work from life in creating a new likeness. When he met Ross, it occurred to him that because she was, like Sequoyah, "of mixed Cherokee and white blood," her face would make for a fitting model.[99] But Ross's own claims of descent also tell another story, separate from Zolnay's sense of ethnological aesthetics. She was the great-granddaughter of Sequoyah's contemporary John Ross. Principal chief of Cherokee Nation for four decades beginning in 1828, he was a promoter of the syllabary's use and strongly associated with the history of resistance to Removal—with, that is, the claim that the sweeping away of the nation is not an "inevitable doom" at all. Posey's ode does not mention John Ross but does acknowledge his political rivals (signers to the Treaty of New

Echota agreeing to Removal): "Waitie and Boudinot / The valiant warrior and gifted sage." Anne Ross had herself been talking about her great-grandfather a lot, though. The reason she was in DC, according to an April 1916 interview, was to seek government audiences for a frank discussion of the Cherokee territory that had been claimed by the state in contravention of treaties promising it in perpetuity (promises broken after discoveries of oil in the region, as she notes).[100] Asserting Cherokee exceptionalism, she claims that Cherokee Nation is "the only Indian nation that has its own written language—not a sign language, but one with an alphabet—and a literature of its own," and decries the fact that the United States prohibits education in the Cherokee language and has "stopped even the production of our newspaper, The Cherokee Advocate."[101] Describing the syllabary without mentioning Sequoyah, she downplays the lore of the lone genius in favor of an ancestry narrative that foregrounds the ongoing work of the syllabary's circulation as part of the project of sovereignty.

After Ross read Posey's poem, Charles Carter, who had recently been appointed chairman of the Committee on Indian Affairs, read "A Cherokee Cadmus." He noted that he had "been requested to read the following poem, by J. S. Holden."[102] What "by" attributes to Holden is probably the poem's authorship, but it could also be the act of the request, since Holden was in attendance. A well-known newspaper editor in northeastern Oklahoma, he had been a leading advocate in the State of Sequoyah Movement.[103] Given that this movement was conceived as an alternative to Oklahoma statehood, the subsequent choice of the figure of Sequoyah for the statue commemorating the new state can read as either irony or consolation.[104] Holden's poem, originally published in Indian Territory periodicals before the statehood question was settled, reflects this history most explicitly in its exhortation that "the future State should bear Sequoyah's name." The *Congressional Record* gives the full text of the poem as follows:

> The Cadmus of his race,
>   A man without a peer,
> He stood alone, his genius shown
>   Throughout a hemisphere.
> Untutored, yet so great,
>   Grand and alone his fame—
> Yes, grand, great, the future State
>   Should bear Sequoyah's name.

In ages yet to come,
　　When his nation has no place,
His memory shall live in history's page,
　　The grandest of his race![105]

When Carter reads that seventh line, where the repeated adjectives "grand" and "great" slide from Sequoyah's person to "the future State," the Hall of Statuary resounds for a moment with a possible history that had been foreclosed by the very events commemorated by the ceremony. Curiously, though, this tension seems already to have been predicted in the tenth line of Holden's poem, which suggests that Sequoyah's memory will live on even "when his nation has no place." This line seems incongruous—and not only because, if it were to conform with the pattern of the first two quatrains of this metrically conservative poem, it would be in iambic trimeter. Isn't the point of the "future state," according to its proponents, precisely that it offers a strategy, however compromised, for preserving the nation's place? If the poem serves as a rallying cry, why does this line prophesy doom?

Part of the answer: Holden changed the line. The poem exists in at least three versions that differ in small, significant ways. It was first printed in Holden's paper, the *Fort Gibson Post*, in 1899, before the Sequoyah movement became a going concern. Here lines 9–11 read, "In ages yet to come / When time shall all efface / His memory shall live in history's page."[106] Then, when Holden reprinted the poem in 1904, as the movement gathered steam (if briefly), he revised line 10, replacing its acceptance of oblivion ("time shall all efface") with an affirmation: "When his Nation has a place."[107] Here the anapest sneaks in. More pertinently, this was the version of the poem that circulated in many Indian Territory articles and pamphlets about statehood in 1904 and 1905. Days before Carter recited it at the 1917 ceremony at the Capitol, an article about the unveiling in the Muskogee press reprints the same 1904 version, noting that it had been "widely quoted" during the statehood movement and "afterwards included in the school readers of Oklahoma."[108] This seems to be true, according to an earlier piece in the *Fort Gibson New Era* (which Holden edited after the *Post* and whose masthead boasted that it was printed with the same typeset and press as the *Cherokee Advocate*). At some point in the decade between statehood and unveiling, though, Holden had also introduced a third version. Going back again to the same line, he changed "a place" into "no place."[109] This re-revision circles back to the line's original theme of erasure: "time will all efface." But now it's history, not time, that does the effacing.

If these revisions, taken in sequence, reflect the chronological rise and fall of the State of Sequoyah movement, their staggered reprinting, distribution, and recitation also limn a more conflicted sense of counterfactual simultaneity. At the moment of the 1917 ceremony, multiple versions of the poem were still in circulation. The poet was in the room, and the most recent revision was the one read aloud. When Carter recited the text into the *Congressional Record*, the dissonance of its paradoxical tenth line might have rung in the ears of some attendees—such as Robert Owen, who had advocated the State of Sequoyah—as an acerbic comment. For others, that line's reiteration of a commonplace narrative of disappearance would have sounded all too right. It offered an unsurprising reference to the premise of vanishing nations against which, in some tellings, the fuzzy outlines of Sequoyah's invention acquire their romantic definition.

Placed against the same backdrop, the little brand printed in Oskison's 1907 short story, written on the threshold of the closing of Indian Territory, becomes both more legible and less so. The end of this chapter will take this detail as a reflection on the politics of transmission and territory that also register in the name of "Sequoyah," curving back toward Oskison through another name that also circulated widely during the allotment era: "Harjo."

A Mute Appeal

Not everyone thought that the inventor of the syllabary would be the best namesake for an Indian state in 1905. "Why not name it 'Crazy Snake,'" asked the *Daily Oklahoman* in September of that year, "in honor of an illustrious Indian and also typifying the movement?"[110] The reference was to Chitto Harjo, also known as Wilson Jones and as Crazy Snake.[111] A prefatory "old" was often attached to any of these names. The idea that the state might be named after him was offered by the *Oklahoman* in a contrarian spirit, but it did not come out of nowhere: as the leader of the 1901 Crazy Snake Uprising against allotment, Chitto Harjo was at this point the figure most strongly associated with Indian Territory opposition to increased federal control of the region.

Not every member of Oskison's immediate audience for "The Problem of Old Harjo," the readers of the *Southern Workman*, would have heard of Chitto Harjo. Some might have recognized "Harjo" as a common Creek name. It was the family name, for instance, of Alex Posey's mother. But if they knew that much, or if they had been paying any attention to the politics of Indian land, they probably also knew the specific name of Chitto

Harjo, because he was an outsized figure in both news and local-color anecdote at the moment. Oskison could reasonably have expected that, for such a reader, the choice of "old Harjo" as the name of a "full-blood" Creek elder who makes trouble for a white bureaucracy—a bureaucracy in which allotment, language bans, heteronormative intermarriage, and the measures of blood quantum all served as technologies of assimilation to the category of able whiteness—would call Crazy Snake to mind.[112]

A report of a 1905 conversation between Crazy Snake and Posey gives a sense of the persona. The poet was working as a field interpreter for the Dawes Commission at the time. Most enrollment interviews happened centrally at the commission office. Indeed, in Oskison's "Old Harjo," the Creek man "went to Muscogee to enroll himself and his family in one of the many 'final' records ordered to be made by the Government preparatory to dividing the Creek lands among the individual citizens" (237). But as Oskison hints by putting scare quotes around "final," some cases, particularly those in which enrollees were not so forthcoming, had to be completed through information-gathering in the field. The *Muskogee Times-Democrat* noted that the job of Posey's field team was "really the winding up of the odds and ends" of allotment files.[113] As Posey himself wrote, though, their remit also included "conciliat[ing] the Snakes."[114] Within a few months of taking the job, Posey and the stenographer Drennen C. Skaggs were already known for coming back from these excursions with "their usual quota of stories."[115] Usually the stories that made it to print were quick vignettes (the kind that could be placed in a "Heard at Random" column), but the description of their meeting with the Snakes' leader got two columns in the *Times-Democrat* under the headline "Old Crazy Snake Is Full of Talk." This lengthy piece was the likely catalyst for a satirical dig printed in the *South McAlester News* a couple of weeks later: "We shudder to think what would become of Alex. Posey if Crazy Snake should cease, either from death or paralysis of the vocal cords, to furnish material for copy."[116]

As a commission employee, Posey found himself in de facto opposition to Crazy Snake, and some of Posey's earlier editorial work implied a view of civilizational progress in which traditionalist Creeks had little place.[117] He also romanticized the elder, though, having once referred to him in verse as "the one true Creek."[118] The monologue that Posey ascribes to Harjo in 1905, in a translation that probably takes substantial liberties, illustrates this ambivalence. "I am at my own home here on my own ground," Crazy Snake is reported to have said to the poet; "I do not try to make others listen to my views and no one has any right to tell me at my own house, in my own yard, what I should do." Repeating the word "own" four times in one breath and connecting this ownership to a sense of ethical autonomy, Crazy Snake claims his place. At this implicit rebuke of the very conditions of the conversation, the visitors' nonverbal responses reveal their unease: "Posey emitted a great 'Ugh!' while Skaggs measured the distance to the buggy standing in the roadway."[119] They are stunned into inarticulacy. The effect of verbal paralysis, in contrast with Harjo's eloquence, is particularly comical given their professional roles as interpreter and stenographer. The former can grunt out no more or less than the monosyllabic exhalation of "Ugh!"[120] The stenographer, meanwhile—that avatar of accurate, efficient mediation from ear to page—eyeballs the measure of the land not for the parcel records of the allotment commission but as preparatory to saving his own hide.

Unlike old Chitto Harjo, the old Harjo in Oskison's story poses no apparent threat.[121] The problems he generates for the settlers with whom he engages derive from a partial conformity. He voluntarily enrolls at the Dawes Commission office, and he actively wants to convert. But here, too, muteness and mortality are entwined in ways that become apparent on the occasion of a house call—an encounter that reveals the settler-colonial logic in which, even under their own roof, the Native lives in trespass.[122]

When the young missionary in the story, Miss Evans, takes on the project of converting Harjo, she is optimistic, since he has recently arrived at an enthusiastic belief in Christ. But a dilemma emerges. On the one hand, as church authorities remind the junior missionary, the old rancher's salvation is precluded by the fact that he is married to two women, 'Liza and Jennie. Evans's superiors in the church administration note that she will need to convince him to part ways with one wife (unless one of them is going to die soon; they're younger than he is, so probably not). The polygamous marriage must be actively dissolved for Harjo to become a member of the church. "Just out from New York," Evans decides it will be best to go to "the Creek's own home where the evidences of his sin should confront him as she explained" (235, 236). During that visit, when she makes her explanation, at first Harjo thinks she must be speaking sarcastically. Surely she's only parroting her superiors' self-evidently silly rules. 'Liza, Jennie, and Harjo joke with each other in Creek about running a race to decide who will stay and who will go. When Evans confirms, to Harjo's shock, her seriousness—"the church cannot be defiled by receiving a bigamist into its membership"—he moves to expel the presumptuous visitor on the grounds that "it is not good to talk like that if it is not in fun" (238). At this point, though, Evans, second-guessing herself, asks Harjo to describe how the family came into this arrangement. Harjo explains that he and 'Liza had been unable to have children, and when Jennie found herself without any local relatives, they took her into the family both out of hospitality and in the hopes (unfulfilled) that she might bear a child. Finding herself sympathetic, Evans realizes that to disband the family would be "cruel and useless" (240).

From here, the narrative proliferates, without resolving, a set of double commitments and double binds that entail different levels of conflict, from the harmonious to the irreconcilable: each spouse tied to two partners, the convert committed to two normative systems of uncertain commensurability, the missionary divided between humanist sympathy and the imperative of salvation. After Evans visits Harjo—at his "*double* log cabin," for what it's worth—the story plays out its central tension for a while. He comes to church. She agonizes. But then it just ends, not with the synthesis of two social groups giving "each to each other those characteristics which both so sadly lack" but rather in a problem so particular that its resolution can't be imagined.[123]

> Month after month, as old Harjo continued to occupy his seat in the mission meetings, with that mute appeal in his eyes and a persistent light of hope on his face, Miss Evans repeated the question, "What can be done?" . . . Harjo was her creation, her impossible convert, and throughout the years, until death—the great solvent which is not always a solvent—came to one of them, would continue to haunt her.
>   And meanwhile, what? (240-41)

Here "haunting" occurs not after but until death. In this context, it's a familiar temporality. "The only way to make me raise my right hand is to kill me," Crazy Snake is reported to have said to Posey and Skaggs, "and raise it when I am dead."[124] It's a statement of resistance that also recognizes empire's view of those who contest its territory as spectral, as living in the future-perfect tense—an idea that Oskison had been exploring since "A Laboratory Fancy." The fictional old Harjo's conversion, which the missionary tries to carry out on the grounds of his own home, reads in this light as a metonym for the assimilatory branch of a genocidal project of territorial dispossession.

These forces meet in the word "solvent." The reference to death as "the great solvent" here, in the penultimate paragraph of the story, presents a chemical figure for the dissolution of the "Indian Problem." It also echoes the line that immediately follows the presentation of the Harjo brand:

"Materially, Harjo was solvent; and if the Government had ever come to his aid he could not recall the date" (237). Harjo's avoidance of the debt mechanism central to settler-colonial land management makes the fact of his family's childlessness—which is, as he explains to Evans, one of the motivating conditions of their polygamy—all the more important: allotted land with a clean, no-lien title but also without a clear line of succession might look, to the state, like *terra nullius* in the making. Harjo's material solvency may be the problem most in need of solving.

This doesn't yet explain why, in that penultimate paragraph, death is "*not* always a solvent," nor what it means for Evans to reflect on her *own* mortality as a possible escape: "until death . . . came to *one* of them." Of course, the latter clearly suggests the character's desperation, yet both of these details also have to do with how the story imagines conversion, catching its characters in contradictions that will not be dissolved no matter how their immediate circumstances might change. If conversions are, among other things, narratives, the narrative of Harjo's conversion lacks an ending.[125] But the radical change narrated here is not primarily in the life of the new Christian, who comes to his belief in the first sentences of the story, but in the ethical outlook of the proselytizer. That secular conversion is left unresolved precisely because it is disallowed by a religious imperative that has not been abandoned. In fact, its urgency has been reinforced by a new believer's enthusiasm. And that enthusiasm seems genuine. This is perhaps most emphatically evidenced in its nonvoicing, in Harjo's patient silence in the pews. Muteness recurs across Oskison's fiction: in *Brothers Three*, one sibling becomes mute after a traumatic accident; in "The Biologist's Quest," a naturalist loses his voice to dehydration, like the amoeba in "A Laboratory Fancy"; in *The Singing Bird*, Ellen, grazed by a bullet, suffers "a partial paralysis that will prevent speech" for a period that seems to coincide with her moral redemption.[126] But Harjo's "mute appeal" is particular in two ways. First, it performs a silence that would invoke, in late nineteenth-century American Protestantism, an appropriate mode of faithful supplication. "A mute appeal" to "the divine man . . . moves his benevolent heart," said J. P. Greene in an 1888 sermon transcribed in the *St. Louis Globe-Democrat*, in which newspaper Oskison recalled reading sermons in his youth.[127] Second, rather than serve—as the figure of the vocally "dumb" subject often does—as a kind of passage through disability that is finally redeemed in a purer speech, Harjo's appeal is still, at the end of the story, speechless.[128]

"And meanwhile, what?" The final question, a gnomic ending to the story, is legible in part because it reiterates two prior lines in the preceding paragraphs. First Evans cries out to herself, "What, what can be done!"; then we learn that "month after month . . . Miss Evans repeated the question, 'What can be done?'" (240). The final line of the story repeats the same question, but now with a key phrase—"can be done"—elided. The quotation marks have also disappeared. The voices of narrator and character blur, reproducing the irresolution of the plot as an indeterminacy of voice (of the kind that narrative theorists call free indirect discourse). The reader is asked to simultaneously inhabit the character's quandary (What should I do?) and the implied author's (What should I write?). Given that the conditions of this crisis involve the missionary's own self-image as a kind of author—"Harjo was her creation," she laments—it's apt that this problem marks a limit of narrative horizon as well.

This possessive attachment, culminating in a final paralysis of the narrative vocal cords, implies other affective energies as well. The final question goes unanswered but is not necessarily unanswerable. There are other solutions. Evans could join the family. Her ecclesiastical superiors would find this reading a provocative stretch, but the text has also prepared us for it. We are never given any reason for Harjo's sudden desire to convert except that, as the story's opening lines inform us, he has been inspired by "the fire in the new missionary's eyes and her gracious appeal" (235). And when she goes to his cabin, even before she learns of his sense of humor and his practical virtue, she takes in the appeal of his person as well: his "broadening smile of welcome," "his abundant grey hair," and "his eyes, clear and large and black," which gave off "the clear light of hospitality." "Thus Abraham might have looked and lived," she muses (237). If the Old Testament comparison raises doctrinal doubts about the prohibition on polygamy, the fact that the similarity comes to mind at this moment also raises the question of how Evans sees herself in relation to this scene. As, possibly, a surrogate mother like the biblical Hagar?[129] It's a possibility that the missionary would not allow herself to voice.

It's also just the sort of thing that Sequoyah, as Oskison characterizes him in his last novel manuscript, would come right out and say. Midway through *The Singing Bird*, Sequoyah causes a stir by pointing out, "half seriously" but accurately, the romantic triangulations that have been simmering among the missionaries. Noticing that Miss Eula assists Dan, Ellen's husband, with special devotion, Sequoyah says, "In the old days, when it was permitted to take more than one wife, I would have asked my uncle to go to your mother and arrange for you to keep my second fire—as you are doing for the head man here." After ensuring that Sequoyah understands that she has no sexual relationship with Dan, Eula is flattered by the recognition of her service; but Ellen spies hypocrisy in her pious husband and his colleagues: "in all of your kind, the passion for serving God is stimulated by the desires of the flesh" (81). However jealous and vain, Ellen is also cast as perceptive and even—in direct contrast to the naïve narrator, Paul—writerly in her linguistic invention. "She had been playing on my imagination with words," Paul agonizes (93). His resentment of her "scornful irony" signals (in an irony that Paul himself can't understand) Ellen's affinities both with the novel's author and with the ur-author figure of Sequoyah, seemingly the only other character in the book who knows how to wink (161).

Without an ironic Cadmus to step in and tell it like it is, "The Problem of Old Harjo" provides shakier ground for the potential resolution I suggest. Evans's own polygamous conversion is here in the mode of the possible, present in its absence if that, and as such it sits alongside other possibilities— the white fantasy of Native adoption, for instance.[130] We can't tell because Evans can't say: her potential union with the family, in any role, is bounded by social stigmas that the narrative does not name, much less transcend. The story closes by asking us to inhabit her experience of dilemma. Any social "problem" becomes immanent to the missionary's individuation as an ethical subject. Viewed from this angle, the presence of 'Liza and Jennie plays a crucial role in the scene at the Harjo home—or rather, the role they *don't* play is crucial.[131] 'Liza and Jennie aren't exactly silent subalterns: they joke and laugh about Evans's requests, and in so doing, they seem to take up the perspective closest, of all the characters here, to the satirical angle we might attribute to the author. But what they say is given in the text only through Harjo's relay, interpreting in English. Oskison did elsewhere represent non-English speech directly *as* English speech. *The Singing Bird*, for example, has Sequoyah speaking in Cherokee at the level of the story but given in English at the level of the text. So the approach to the Creek women's speech in "Old Harjo" does not derive from some principled avoidance of representing one language in another. It has to do with a localized choice to inscribe the linguistic world of this story primarily within the experience of the missionary and, in so doing, to make the limitations of that experience visible—and to make them *visual*, too, in that the social pragmatics of an imagined oral scene are concretized in choices not only of verbal but also of typographic representation, choices about whose speech ends up inside quotation marks.

Which brings us back to the typography of the Harjo brand. Unlike the circle-I brand in *Brothers Three*, this "**H⊢**" is surrounded by the same kind of inky tadpoles that often indicate dialogue. Syntax makes it obvious that this isn't their function here.[132] Still, in combination with the fact of the brand's unsayability, the typography suggests, in uncanny negation, the direct discourse of a voice transcribed. In this light, it's fitting that, to whatever extent Harjo's design resembles a character in the Latin alphabet—insofar as it is made of marks that are traceable, if also finally irreducible, to that system—it's the same character that spelling reformers have more than once tried to eliminate. The primary association of *H* with aspiration, the argument often goes, makes it a mark more diacritic than vowel or consonant, more spirit than letter.[133] Sometimes Sequoya's name is spelled without it.

So if the quotation marks around the brand imply the capacity of text to record speech, the thing that they enclose resists playback. It is antiphonographic. A grapheme unmoored, the figure disrupts the "understanding transmission" tied to alphabetic technology in general and the syllabary specifically. For Oskison, the meaning of such disruption is both more extended and more localized than the conception of "culture" that he held at a satirical distance and through which the dilemma of his best-known story has often been framed: more extended in echoing centuries of discourse about the "civilizing" channels of translation and textual communication; more localized in the dynamics of Indian Territory's transition to statehood at the turn of the century. The linguistic refusal of the Harjo brand sits in uneasy relation, not simple opposition, to the logic of individual recognition that is central to state subject-formation processes like allotment.[134] In something like the way that Crazy Snake's resistance to the state can be invoked in demands for recognition by the state, so do the refusals of Harjo's brand to legibility involve a demand for the consideration of his property rights whose logic is not incommensurable with the political philosophies of expansionism.

It matters that the Harjo brand is designated as his own design. In its adjacency and irreducibility to the Latin alphabet, the brand invokes histories of Indigenous writing most famously epitomized by Sequoyah's system. It's no surprise, then, that, when the missionary sees the mark, it is described as "fantastic": wonderful, that is, but also, like Evans's "impossible" creation himself (and like the "fancy" Oskison dreamed up for the *Sequoia*), a thing that strains belief. If this fence-like image evokes the (incomplete) process of territorial enclosure, it also suggests and refuses another pertinent wooden object: it includes multiple bisections but, thanks to the slight central gap, not a single cross. Those quotation marks come into play here too.

As with the scare quotes around the "final" administration of enrollment, this is a figure that registers as dubious. There is a long history in that dubiousness of refusals of Indigenous artistry, a history that Traveller Bird traces in settlers' responses to the syllabary: "the idea of a Cherokee native method of writing and reading was rejected and fought by the missionaries living in the nation, who felt that anything of Indian origin was repugnant and savage."[135] Oskison did not tell the same story in *The Singing Bird*; his fictional missionaries generally embrace the syllabary as an instrument for distributing the gospel. But there's a hint of the same recoil in that "fantastic." The sign of Harjo's property and artistry leaves Evans—and the narration that is, at this moment, focalized through her perception—with nothing to say, leaving her to look, without reading, at a mark that cuts the tie (a tie sometimes termed "literacy") of the visual to the aural. So we get an "Ⱶ" to go along with Posey's "Ugh!"

Because this is Oskison's most widely distributed text, its little graphic anomaly has come to the attention, if not of critics, then of numerous editors and typesetters. Whatever Oskison wrote or drew in his manuscript at this point, the students in the Hampton print shop took it and, by making their own design of Oskison's design of Harjo's design, set something else in motion. If Oskison's manuscript ever resurfaces, what it shows will expand but not contradict the multiple interpretive lines that the graphic choices of those students have, in this chapter and in many readers' experiences, made possible. Among those choices, the brand's difference in form from the surrounding typeface has a peculiar effect. In the context of the brand's quotation or republication, this difference seems to call for visual reproduction. There's thus one more thing we might see in the near-duplicate shape of the brand: a copy sliding out from an original. In fact, the brand's nearly symmetrical shape teases a specific element of print technology in the period: the reverse form of wood and metal type. This image looks *almost* the same in both a typesetting case and in the printed text, but if one cares about the location of the gap (left or right), the brand must be constructed in advance as its mirror image.

That mechanical consideration disappears with the digital typesetting that dominates by the time the story begins to be anthologized in the late twentieth century. Other complications emerge. Some republications, such as that in the *Heath Anthology*, where I first read it and realized I couldn't read it (certainly not aloud, possibly not otherwise), aim to match the brand's shape, as first printed, as closely as possible; others ignore the distinction between the brand and whatever serifed print surrounds it, alphabetizing the figure as "HH," "H-I," and "-H-"; still another ("**H—I**") maintains the typeface distinction in the shape of the posts while extending the crossbar, the rail, into an enormous em dash, discontinuous not only with the central post but also with the one on the right.[136] The fence expands. The breaks multiply.

Such alterations of the text, and sometimes conversions of the figure *to* text, may not seem ideally faithful to what appeared in the *Southern Workman*. But the idea of graphic fidelity isn't exactly neutral here either. Ink distribution not being absolutely uniform in the printing process, the brand looks different even in different copies of the 1907 publication. The idea of fidelity always requires a little leap of faith.[137] In the abstract, this problem may sound like a question of mechanical reproduction no different from other examples of illustrations set into the lines of narrative prose (a coffin, an eyeball, a muted trumpet, a cut in stone). And the process of formal iteration was also, of course, already there at the imagined scene of the ranch itself; surely the brand looked a little different on each animal body it marked, too. Yet that scene also stages what's distinct about this case: the political particularities of its emergence in the flow of aural and graphic histories that are inseparable from transformations of land use and sovereignty in the long nineteenth century. As these processes extend into our present, the Harjo brand's mute appeal—a claim to property but also a refusal to make that claim readily legible to a form of perception exemplified as a missionary's desiring vision—reiterates itself whenever readers and editors puzzle over the sound and shape of its design, reproducing its fancies as real.

2 Helen Keller's Handwriting

Audism and Autography

• •

The frontispiece of Helen Keller's *My Religion* (1927) features two images, one above the other. One is a portrait. The subject sits in ninety-degree profile, looking to the left of the frame. The obscure foliage of the background, the dark flower tucked into her clothing, and the wicker construction of the chair all suggest a garden setting. Her left hand, the one visible to the camera, rests on the arm of the chair. Its fingertips and the heel of its palm make contact with the braided rattan. The palm itself is cupped, lifting an inch away from the surface. The knuckles are slightly bent. Keller's hand—the organ that is to her, she elsewhere writes, "what your hearing and sight together are to you"—seems ready to read, spell, write, gesture.[1] The second image, smaller, occupies the lower fourth of the page. It reproduces a sentence in Keller's own handwriting: "If you can enjoy the sun and flowers and music where there is nothing except darkness and silence you have proved the mystic sense."[2] Following the sentence is a long underscore and then, in the same lettering—"a cross between printing and penmanship," as one Waco, Texas, journalist described it in 1915—Keller's name.[3]

A portrait of the author, a maxim bearing her signature: these are not surprising elements for the front matter of the book. They interact, though, in surprising ways. At first blush, the sentence below seems to caption the portrait above. Even as Keller addresses a second-person "you," she seems to characterize the experience that she herself, as pictured above, is having in that garden. She may sit in "darkness and silence," common terms in the representation of Keller's sensory disabilities, but the capacities of her interior experience afford an "inner" or "mystic sense" (conceptualized here through the thought of Emanuel Swedenborg) that is independent, the sentence implies, of external conditions. As one reads down from portrait to passage and back up, the static object of the page becomes host to a shifting play of medial effects. If the upper image first seemed, in C. S. Peirce's terms, an iconic and indexical representation of real space—the photograph linked to the garden scene both by visual resemblance and by the physical relays of optical reflection—after reading the passage below, it might read also as a symbolic representation of virtual experience.[4] What's illustrated by Keller's serene profile, in the rhetoric of this page, becomes less the enjoyment of the actual garden than an inner state ideally indifferent to "sun and flowers and music."

The object of Keller's handwriting, meanwhile, introduces an anomaly of format—the rest of *My Religion* is, as one would expect, set in type—that asks one not only to read but to look. In this regard, it resembles the illustration at the center of my argument in chapter 1. Of course, Keller's handwriting does not present exactly the same troubles of pronunciation that Harjo's brand does; but its circulation does, I'll argue, have much to do with the question (a question of significant public fascination) of Keller's own capacities for speech. Like chapter 1, then, the argument here will revolve around a kind of graphic object that, though not itself a self-evident *example* of oral transcription, is conditioned in its effects and its circulation by the political meanings of the interface between orality and the page. At the same time, the print-cultural status of the Harjo brand and Keller's handwriting could hardly be more different. Whereas the image in Oskison's story has mostly presented a necessary inconvenience in republications of that text, the Keller autograph is something that, since the beginnings of her celebrity in the late 1880s, countless editors have gone out of their way to place as a prominent inset in texts ranging from popular magazine pieces to scientific journal articles to her own memoirs.

The motives for these reproductions, the mute appeal that Keller's autograph is taken to make, the problem that its publication is imagined to solve—these things are hardly ever articulated. Inferring them will be among this chapter's aims. I should note at the outset that by the word "autograph," I mostly intend the now rare sense of a manuscript or piece of writing in the author's own hand. Yet the more common contemporary usage, referring to the fetishized object of a celebrity's name in signature, is relevant here too. The history of reproducing Keller's handwriting is inseparable from the ways that her famed persona has been instrumentalized in multiple narratives of human difference and of US polity. Autographic reproduction materializes the oscillation of this persona between writing subject and inscribed object.[5]

A scene that can begin to illustrate that oscillation plays out during Keller's 1893 trip to the Columbian Exposition in Chicago. This was, not surprisingly, a site at which a number of the figures discussed in this book crossed paths (including Oskison and Will Rogers). Keller was accompanied by Annie Sullivan, who had been her teacher and closest daily companion since 1887 and who famously succeeded in teaching Keller to communicate verbally by means of the manual alphabet. Keller's account of their trip to the exposition was published in *St. Nicholas*, an illustrated magazine for children. (Hildegarde Hawthorne, a year younger than Keller, would start publishing there a few years later.) As Keller recalls, she and Sullivan visited the Anthropological Building—toward the south end of the fairgrounds, not far from the livestock and agricultural equipment—with the anthropologist Frederic Ward Putnam and Alexander Graham Bell, who helped to sponsor Keller's education and long remained close with her.[6] Keller doesn't mention Putnam's chief assistant, Franz Boas, nor does she mention that she herself served as a featured performer of sorts in one of the eight "laboratories" that Boas coordinated at one end of the Anthropology Building.[7]

The psychologist Joseph Jastrow ran the laboratory focused on measuring sensory experience and mental acuity. Jastrow had studied with Peirce, in 1884 coauthoring a paper with him on psychophysical measurement and the question of a "least perceptible difference" in experiences of similar sensations.[8] Psychophysics was one field of interest that Jastrow also shared with Boas, as illustrated by the latter's discussion of procedures for measuring the "differential threshold of two sensations" (particularly phonemic sensations) in "On Alternating Sounds."[9] At the world's fair, Jastrow used the occasion of Keller's tour to draw attention to his exhibition of perceptual measurement devices, having her undergo a wide array of tests and staging a comparison of her levels of sensitivity to other fairgoers in attendance. In "mental anthropometry" as in physical measurement, as Jastrow writes in an essay summarizing the results of Keller's testing, "the first object is to ascertain the normal distribution of the quality measured."[10] Keller was already, even in preadolescence, a long-standing subject of scientific assessment. Public discussion of her capacities of information retention had intensified in the previous year in the context of a plagiarism scandal, the crux of which was the question of how well, and with what degree of intention, Keller might have been able to reproduce the text of a short story that was once read to her. At the fair, taking Jastrow's tests, she could have anticipated that, whether within "normal distribution" or not, her sensitivities would be interpreted as exceptional: higher than normal, lower than normal, or surprisingly normal.[11]

Perhaps Keller's resistance to this inevitable framing explains why Jastrow's measurements don't come up in her own account of the visit for *St. Nicholas* magazine. Perhaps it's also relevant to that omission that one of the tests measured sensitivity to pain.[12] What Keller emphasizes instead is her own interest in the ethnographic collections. She recalls observing with fascination "the curious and interesting things in the Anthropological department," especially the Incan relics, given to her to touch as Putnam and Bell explained to Keller, with Sullivan interpreting in the manual alphabet.[13]

The trick with presenting this aspect of the event (Keller observing rather than observed) as if it stands in opposition to Jastrow's research is that Keller's powers of "observation" are just what he was out to measure. This is not a trick that Jastrow missed. His article about the event concludes by commenting on "the remarkable alertness and receptivity of mind displayed by her in visiting the exhibits at the World's Fair": "it certainly was most interesting to observe the rapidly-varying expressions of her animated features, and listen to her comments, as one specimen after another from the ethnological collections was placed in her hands."[14] Keller simultaneously occupies the positions of anthropological observer and anthropometric patient. Her relation to the measure of the normal, a concept used to police the boundaries of both ability and ethnicity, ramifies across all angles of this complex position.

Keller's name isn't the only one on the frontispiece of *My Religion*. Between the two images I described earlier, there is another small strip of text (typeset, not handwritten): an image credit at the bottom right corner of the portrait: "Photo by Edward S. Curtis"—Curtis being the photographer best known, both in the 1920s and now, as the creator of *The North American Indian*, a multivolume project of photographic salvage anthropology. The attribution of the photograph performs a legal function and also a generic one. Together with the choice of the right-angle side profile, a favored framing in the visual language of ethnology, it cues a reader that the attention they are meant to pay here involves the position of this subject in a human taxonomy. If the sentence in Keller's handwriting retrains the sighted reader in how to look at the photograph above—offering the scene as a metaphorical disclosure of interior experience—the image and its attribution also remind them of the registers of racial difference in which the settler nation audits its own image. And the name of the writer in the writer's own hand is asked to perform a particular function in that audit. Consider the conclusion of Theodora Kroeber's *Ishi in Two Worlds* (1961), which quotes the habitual "phrase of farewell" of the so-called last wild Indian— "YOU STAY, I GO"—and then, without comment, reproduces an image of his signature.[15] Ishi's farewell, Kroeber implies, makes space for the continued presence of his interlocutors. These include not only the museum staff and anthropologists with whom he interacted on a daily basis—particularly, Kroeber's late spouse, A. L. Kroeber, one of Boas's most prominent students—but also, implicitly, the readers of Kroeber's biography. The signature authorizes its own substitution for the person.

This chapter argues that the deaf-blind celebrity's autograph participates in—but also serves as a site for unsettling—an ableist phenomenology of literacy in which sight and hearing are inseparably but differently construed as channels of linguistic assimilation. Because of Keller's ambivalence toward this phenomenology, an ambivalence that sometimes seems like an acquiescence to audism, I will for the most part avoid the capitalized Deaf-Blind (a signifier of cultural autonomy) in characterizing her position.[16] The larger question here has to do with how disability mediates narratives of national belonging and difference—a question approached here through the circulation of biographical narratives rather than, for instance, through the legal histories of citizenship. The chapter moves from autographic reproductions in print to depictions of Keller's education in other media, especially film, and concludes with the textual history of a print object (a text by W. E. B. Du Bois) that doesn't involve Keller's handwriting directly but that does help to show its relation to the politics of voice and visibility within the horizon of Jim Crow.

If it is conspicuous to my reader by this point that this chapter hasn't included a visual reproduction of Keller's handwriting, whether from the 1927 frontispiece or elsewhere, this choice has to do with the argument that I'll make about its functions within the discursive spaces of able-bodied normativity and of racialization. But the idea is not so much to avoid as to pause in the trouble of this low-key spectacle's ongoing reproduction.[17] I avoid "avoid" because it's not clear that my argument doesn't, in the final telling, participate in the reproduction of Keller's autograph. This chapter has, after all, already referred to qualities of that object, and it will soon include images of her writing transcribed into other media forms. While these representations haven't and won't involve straightforward facsimile, to imagine that they don't visually reproduce Keller's autograph would be to reinforce ontologies of image and text—and, it turns out, of voice—that her work asks us to think across.

Blindness and Inset

In Keller's last year of college at Radcliffe, she made national news for receiving a package: a four-volume Wordsworth collection in Braille, sent from

London. According to a news story widely republished in January and February 1904, the Boston Custom House required her signature to confirm that this package contained nothing "dangerous, dark, or dutiable."[18] (Did it contain "danger, difficulty, or death"? A different question.)[19] The clerk who brought it to Keller's door expected to get her signature on the form in ink. As a member of the house staff explained, Keller always used pencil when writing by hand, "for when she writes she follows the point across the paper with the forefinger of her left hand, and it is evident that anything but a fairly hard pencil would blot."[20] When the customs clerk insists, an alternate solution presents itself. Another agent of the state is called in. The following day, Keller—presumably with Sullivan or someone else literate in the manual alphabet present to aid as a mediator in communication—swears to her own signature in the presence of a notary public.[21]

Anybody who has ever scrawled a random mark in receipt of a package might wonder why blotting seemed such a problem. Keller, though, knew that her signature would serve as what another customs officer once called a "queer vehicle of fame," even in contexts where it was only intended for distribution as a legal instrument.[22] The following year, for instance, in January 1905, a piece in the Birmingham, Alabama, press reported that a local resident had come into possession of a property deed bearing Keller's signature, "remarkable for the fact that every letter was exactly on the line left blank for Miss Keller to sign" and written in a "bold, vertical hand."[23] A smeared signature on a customs form might have received a similar, but less favorable, report.

Reproductions of Keller's handwriting circulate as early as 1888, when *Science* reprints a letter from her to Bell across two pages.[24] A high-profile instance appears in April 1902, with the first excerpt of *The Story of My Life* published in the *Ladies' Home Journal*. A line in Keller's hand features prominently in the heading. It seems to serve primarily as evidence of the author's literacy, given that it is placed just below a title that is anxiously redundant about its attributions—"Helen Keller's Own Story of Her Life: Written Entirely by the Wonderful Girl Herself"—and just above an editorial preface at pains to clarify for skeptical readers just how the "almost incredible" fact of her writing was achieved (namely, through a process of drafting and revising that made use of Braille, typewriting, and the manual alphabet).[25] But the text of Keller's handwriting is itself worth note. "I have tried to show that afflictions may be looked at in such a way that they become privileges," she writes.[26] Here the visual figures both rhetorical demonstration ("to show that") and perspective ("may be looked at"). Taken one way, the line is an expression of DeafBlind gain. Taken another way, it articulates an ableist logic in which looking at a sign of Keller's affliction (the lettering telegraphing in its form the probability that its making relied on some technological prosthesis beyond the stylus) turns into a reflection of the sighted reader's own privilege.[27] The autograph becomes a looking glass for sightedness.

In some contexts, this mirroring effect verged on scientific formalization. A letter that Keller received late in life provides a good example. Despite the loss of much of her personal correspondence in a 1946 house fire, Keller's papers in the archive of the American Foundation for the Blind still include innumerable requests from admirers for her autograph. In 1952, Dorothy McRonald of Reading, Massachusetts, wrote a letter to Keller requesting "a few lines" of her handwriting. McRonald explained that she had recently seen a mention of Keller's handwriting in *Readers' Digest* and would like to analyze it through the methods of grapho-analytical psychology—"character-reading through the strokes in writing."[28] A distinct method of the science of personality interpretation through handwriting (often termed "graphology"), "grapho-analysis" was popularized in the early twentieth century by Milton N. Bunker. When McRonald writes to Keller that, over the past five years, she has "analyzed hundreds of writings, including . . . writing done by holding the pencil in teeth, by hospital patients," she probably refers to a case study included in Bunker's *What Handwriting Tells You about Yourself, Your Friends, and Famous People* (first copyrighted in 1939 and republished in 1951). Reproducing a sample of Helene Wilmone Wilhemi's writing, Bunker instructs the reader to "study this next specimen," which is not "handwriting" even though it looks just like it and "even though it was written with a pen." The explanation of this paradox: Wilhemi "was born without the use of either arms or legs, and this letter was written with the penstock held between her teeth. . . . She guided the pen with the movement of her head but her writing still told the truth"— the truth, that is, of her "persistence and determination, both of which show plainly in her writing." The (non)handwriting also contains a counterfactual truth: "It reveals what might have been. If Helene Wilhemi had possessed an ordinary body she would have made a remarkable dancer."[29] Keller's handwriting would have served, for a grapho-analytical character reader, as evidence for a parallel line of inquiry—*What if Keller could see and hear?*

The opportunity to investigate that question is not given to McRonald. Keller is out of town when her letter arrives, and Keller's secretary, Evelyn

Davidson, responds on her behalf, explaining that she is sorry not to "have a specimen [sic] of Miss Keller's writing since she uses the typewriter most of the time. I do have her autograph which I am enclosing herewith."[30] Here the autograph as the celebrity's name in signature, not more generally as a specimen of handwriting (that meaning having started to fade from usage by midcentury), is identified in alternative to, not in satisfaction of, the desire to witness the spectacle of the disabled author writing.[31]

That desire had precedents, even in Keller's childhood. In fact, in Keller's telling, a similar autographic spectacle is already present at the very scene where it was first imagined that her education might be possible. In *The Story of My Life*, Keller notes that it was what Charles Dickens wrote about his encounter with Laura Bridgman, the deaf-blind student of Samuel Gridley Howe, that first inspired Keller's mother to contact the Perkins School. In *American Notes for General Circulation* (1842), Dickens quotes at length from Howe's summary of Bridgman's education. Then in his own voice, he describes his experience of reading Bridgman's diary, which the school gives him to peruse. Its contents, Dickens writes, are "written in a fair legible square hand, and expressed in terms which were quite intelligible without any explanation." Mark-making and meaning-making dovetail in the "legib[ility]" of Bridgman's writing. Just as her diary entries are "intelligible without any explanation," so too, as the passage turns to a description of how Bridgman writes physically, her process seems self-sufficient, in need of no prosthesis. When Dickens asks "to see her write again," Bridgman's teacher "bade her, in their language"—that is, the manual alphabet— "sign her name upon a slip of paper, twice or thrice." Dickens "observed that she kept her left hand always touching, and following up, her right, in which, of course, she held the pen. No line was indicated by any contrivance, but she wrote straight and freely."[32] "Twice or thrice" is revealing: when it came to writing her name, Bridgman had practice. The autograph was sold to visitors to the school on cards attached to Bridgman's craftwork (crocheting "and other fancy articles"), a kind of gift-shop souvenir.[33] This generated income for her. But with Howe also sometimes requesting additional copies for other professional purposes, the repetitive task became, according to Bridgman's teacher Mary Swift Lamson, "often very irksome."[34]

In a text published in 1892, Keller herself described the process of her handwriting with the same grooved boards and the same "square-hand" technique that were in use at the Perkins School when Bridgman was there—and that Bridgman herself generally used, if not, in Dickens's report, for her autograph.[35] Keller's account of this technique appears in *St. Nicholas*, in the context of an illustrated article in the magazine about a visit she had paid the previous year to the Abbot Academy in Andover.[36] The article is written by the Abbot student Adeline G. Perry, but the editors also include an inset letter in Keller's own hand. The first half of the letter's opening sentence—"It gives me very great pleasure to send you my autograph"— implies either that the editors had requested her to supply it for the story or that, even absent such a request, Keller knew that the demand was there. The commodity form in which her autograph circulated wasn't the same as in Bridgman's case, but the existence of a market of fascination is continuous across the two careers. Keller's letter, offered as both text and illustration, caters to that fascination.

Yet even by the end of its first sentence, Keller has begun to control the meaning of her handwriting's circulation. She is pleased to send the autograph, she writes, "because I want the boys and girls who read *St. Nicholas* to know how blind children write." She does not just mean *how* as in a visual or verbal style but as in a practical method:

> I suppose some of them wonder how we keep the lines so straight so I will try to tell them how it is done. We have a grooved board which we put between the pages when we wish to write. The parallel grooves correspond to lines and when we have pressed the paper into them by means of the blunt end of the pencil it is very easy to keep the words even. The small letters are all made in the grooves, while the long ones extend above and below them. We guide the pencil with the right hand, and feel carefully with the forefinger of the left hand to see that we shape and space the letters correctly. It is very difficult at first to form them plainly, but if we keep on trying it gradually becomes easier, and after a great deal of practice we can write legible letters to our friends. Then we are very, very happy. Sometime they may visit a school for the blind. If they do, I am sure they will wish to see the pupils write.[37]

All but naming the implicit logic in which the object of the autograph is taken to verify the literacy of the disabled author, Keller gives the sighted reader their visual artifact and even attests to its provenance. But this explanation interrupts the autograph's usual mirroring effect: when the sighted read what she writes here, they are not given back the privilege of their sight. They are instead told about a scene—the grooved boards, the manipulation of the paper, the left finger moving along each line without ever leaving a trace, the incessant practice—that they can only "wish" to see.

Meanwhile, this scene involves its own kind of sight, neither literal eyesight nor a metaphor of special insight but a transsensory scriptorial practice: "we . . . *feel* carefully . . . to *see* that we shape and space the letters correctly." The discontinuous print of the letters produced by the square-hand technique may index the writer's difficulty with producing cursive script, but the spaces between the letters also register a kinetic space of text-making that remains invisible to the reader (in ways more commonly associated with typewriting).[38]

The question of "how blind children write" was not one that the Abbot students expressed any interest in, as far as Perry's *St. Nicholas* piece reveals. The question does, however, closely parallel one that Keller herself posed to the students on the day of the visit: "How does Dickens write?" The story of this question is unfolded in the main text of Perry's piece, just to the right of the inset letter. (The autograph takes up a full page vertically, but because it's slightly narrower in layout than the magazine page, there's room for a slim column of typeset print alongside it.) Keller and Sullivan were with students and staff in the school library, and somebody mentioned Dickens. Keller jumped at the opportunity to interject with her question, as the setup to a joke. After a beat, nobody answering, "her face aglow with fun," Keller gives the answer: "All of er Twist!"[39]

The homophonic play on the Dickens title is, in itself, strong. Put it on a popsicle stick. The joke doesn't quite land in the way that this genre usually works, though. Its semantic sense ought to be relatively self-evident, whereas "All of er Twist" gives a slightly perplexing answer to the question "How does Dickens write?" While the joke is not original to Keller, she does compress it in ways that contribute to this confusion. According to an anecdote reprinted in the humor section of more than one nineteenth-century periodical, Dickens was posing for what would become a famous photograph of the author at his desk. When the photographer asked him to hold his pen more "naturally, like you do when you're writing one of your novels," Dickens replied, "I see—all of 'er twist."[40] Even here, the exact physical reference is less than self-evident. The apostrophe in "'er" implies a (Cockney) abbreviation of "her" rather than, say, a dialectal pronunciation of "a" (as in the idiom that predates the naming of Oliver Twist: "I'm all of a twist"). But just what "her" is getting twisted? The pen held in the curl of the hand? The body torqued over the desk? Whatever the precise referent, the context of Dickens's response, in the prior iterations of the joke, is clearly the embodied practice of writing. When Keller changes the setup to "How does Dickens write?" she improves things by virtue of compression, but she further confuses the question of what is being twisted. We could now be talking about penmanship or posture, but we could also be talking about writing as the process of verbal artistry, at the level of either prose style (syntactic contortions) or narrative structure (plot twists; narrative lines twisted around each other as the strands of a rope). Keller's compression dispenses with the cues that would allow her audience to differentiate between writing as penmanship and writing as expression.

The joke's ultimate payoff, then, is in the inset autograph that appears with the published article. The content of the letter's text transforms the visual aspect of Keller's lettering, evenly spaced along parallel lines, from a static object of graphic wonder to the traces of a deliberate expressive manipulation—from handwriting to handwritten, from fetish to medium. Linguistic acts located far apart in time and space, with the letter composed well after the school visit, joke and autograph twist toward each other on the page. The point here isn't that Keller, however precocious, anticipated the effects of this juxtaposition. (After all, we don't know whether the *St. Nicholas* article represents what she said at the school accurately; Perry could have been the one to compress the joke in transcription.) It's instead that this juxtaposition becomes probable within a particular rhetoric of reading in which literacy is associated with sightedness.

Attending to this rhetoric, and to how Keller inverts it, also allows a fuller understanding of the aural confusion produced by the compression of the Dickens joke. This confusion is not just an incidental effect of a joke told too hastily. It derives from the way that the joke makes voice—a voice marked as nonnormative, in the Cockney *h*-dropping of "er"—split from meaning. While the Abbot students may not have expressed any interest in the process of how blind students write (if they did, Perry's story doesn't report it), they cared a great deal about how a deaf student spoke. Several paragraphs of the *St. Nicholas* article are devoted to the marvelous success of Keller's study of vocalization and her demonstrations of speech during the visit. "Her voice is necessarily peculiar," writes Perry, "and listening to its monotonous tones, one can better appreciate how important hearing is to modulation and expression."[41] But while the person who hears may get the pun of Keller's joke, they are less likely to understand—because they haven't been given sufficient information about—the imagined exchange between photographer and Dickens that is its occasion. If the autograph's content blinds the sighted reader, the bad pun deafens the audience of the joke. It turns their hearing into the very thing (a modality of experience without access to linguistic meaning) that an audist theory of communication, taking speech sounds as metonyms for language in general, associates with *non*hearing.[42] The discontinuity of Keller's lettering is important here, as the formal opposite of the kind of graphic line produced by technologies like the phonautograph—technologies imagined, by a figure like Bell, to carry the potential to so perfectly and legibly render speech sounds on paper, in a continuously flowing line of sonic script, that the deaf child, once literate in the waveform, would be able to read it and speak.[43]

When Perry, at the end of the article, describes Keller rising to address the children at the conclusion of the visit, it's almost as though the lesson of the joke—the reminder about the limits of aural ability—has been taken to heart: although she gives Keller's oration word for word, she also hedges her bets about the fidelity of her own transcription. "She was led to the desk," Perry writes, "and spoke with self-possession something like this:"— with the text of Keller's address, as Perry recalls it, then given as direct discourse inside quotation marks.[44] *Something like*: instead of again describing how Helen Keller speaks—Perry's earlier description of her "monotonous tones" having emphasized the value of the ear to proper enunciation—*likeness* here reflects the imprecision of an aural transcription that is nevertheless put on paper as if it were a verbatim record. The next section will stay with the interactions of voice and letter that are materialized in representations of Keller's own linguistic education. Beginning with a discussion of the speech instruction that she started to take not long before the visit with the Abbot students, I'll then move toward a particularly well-known scene of pedagogical "miracle," as its narrative details vary across texts and performances and as those variations register the priorities and exclusions of an assimilatory American promise.

W~A~

"Am I socially related," asks the French sociologist Gabriel Tarde in *The Laws of Imitation* (1890), "to an educated deaf mute who may closely resemble me in face and figure?" Without hesitation: "No, I am not."[45] This, anyway, is how Elsie Clews Parsons renders Tarde's rhetorical question in the 1903 English translation of his text.[46] Tarde had here written, "Suis-je en rapport social avec un sourd-muet *non instruit* qui me ressemble beaucoup de corps et de visage? Non."[47] Parsons adds emphasis, doubling down on the rejection of the "deaf-mute" person by rendering "non" as "no, *I am not*." And her translation of "corps" as "figure" rather than as, for instance, "body" softens the literalism but preserves the premise of the qualifier at the end of Tarde's sentence: even corporeal—by implication, racial—similarity cannot transcend so radical a difference of ability.

But there is also a more direct transformation of the wording here. The person whom Tarde imagines encountering is, in fact, *un*educated: "*non* instruit." In the original version of the line, the experience of sociality across abilities hinges on education. In the translation, education isn't enough. Perhaps Parsons's reference to "an educated" person was a slip of the pen, a typesetting error, or an artifact of dictation (the doubled sounds of "*an un*educated" potentially sounding like an accident of voicing rather than a choice of wording)—but in any case, the incorrect wording might have escaped attention because of its powerful normativity: to be educated but nonvocal is, from an audist perspective, to stay in a state of exception.

Oralist methods of deaf education had been developed for several decades before Keller's exposure to them. It was during her childhood that they began to be institutionally integrated in widespread ways. In the same year that Keller was born, 1880, at the Second International Congress on the Education of the Deaf convened in Milan, Bell infamously coordinated a ban on the teaching of sign language in schools. The convention supported instead "the 'intuitive' method" in the instruction of "the speaking deaf": "setting forth first by speech, and then by writing, the objects and the facts which are placed before the eyes of the pupils."[48] Some schools in the United States, such as Gallaudet College (now University), did maintain sign-language instruction. One of those that embraced the Oralist program was the Horace Mann School for the Deaf in Boston. When, in 1888, Sara Wiltse, at the suggestion of G. Stanley Hall, carried out her research on sound-blindness, she found that one student's ostensible "feeble-minded[ness]" was actually, after an examination by the aurist Clarence Blake, found to be attributable to "early trouble with the inner ear." This child was then sent to Horace Mann to be trained in "the use of his vocal organs"—as a fortuitous alternative, Wiltse writes, to "the School for Feeble-minded Children."[49] The program at Horace Mann was well established by the time Keller moved, with Sullivan, to Boston in 1888 to have access to the Perkins School for the Blind.[50] In the spring of 1890, with the instruction of the Horace Mann principal Sarah Fuller, Keller began to learn to vocalize (to relearn, more accurately, since she had also done so in infancy). In early lessons, she could only produce "broken and stammering syllables," she writes in her first memoir, "but they were human speech. My soul, conscious of new strength, came out of bondage, and was reaching through those broken symbols of speech to all knowledge and all faith."[51]

"Brain Bursts Its Bonds," ran a *Boston Globe* headline about Keller's lessons with Fuller, marveling at the pedagogical achievement.[52] The article opens with an allusion to scripture. "The multitude wondered when they heard the dumb speak." Because it bears on a larger question about how Oralism was imagined, we might take a moment to notice that this is an unusual construction from Matthew 15:31. The King James version, for instance, reads, "The multitude wondered, when they *saw* the dumb to speak" (my emphasis). The alternate version in the *Globe* may possibly have been the ready-at-hand translation for this journalist; it's an extremely rare but not absolutely unique formulation.[53] More likely, it may have seemed an intuitive phrasing ("intuitive" in precisely the audist sense of the Milan convention) of a half-recalled line, presenting the speech of the dumb as a miracle heard, not seen—and avoiding the risk of muddying a specific contrast of linguistic modality. The idea of talk as visible sounds less like oral articulation than like sign language, after all.[54] The fact that Bell's father, Alexander Melville Bell, muddied that contrast in marketing his phonetic system, a set of graphemes modeled on the physiology of articulation, as "Visible Speech" may take the opposite approach rhetorically (steering into the confusion of modalities, rather than sidestepping it). But that approach works toward the same polemical end as this article in the *Globe* and many other celebrations of Keller's Oralist lessons: the point is to supplant the visible speech that is signing in favor of a graphic apparatus designed with the idea of reproducing, pedagogically, an orality that is ostensibly universalized in human physiology (even if that physiological norm is in fact an accidental tendency of biological history).[55]

A displaced contrast in linguistic modality mediates this bias, insofar as the politics of sign language inform the discourse around Keller's education despite her not using ASL. The contrastive effects that I'll follow in the rest of this section take shape primarily within the triadic relationship of vocalization, the Latin alphabet, and fingerspelling in the manual alphabet, and they focus on a familiar moment in the popular imagination of Keller's life, a moment of ostensible liberation by means of the "broken symbols of speech." If Sequoyah's syllabary was the most celebrated linguistic invention of the nineteenth century (in part because it seemed to promise to repair those broken symbols), this moment of Keller's education may be the most famous linguistic epiphany of the twentieth century (in part because it seemed to promise to repair speech itself).

Filling a pitcher at the well pump in the fading Alabama daylight, with her teacher Anne Sullivan at her side, the child feels the water run over onto her hand, drops the vessel roughly to the ground, and struggles into speech: "Wah. Wah. (*And again, with great effort.*) Wah. Wah."[56] Most accounts of the event—including those offered when a representation of Keller at the well pump was installed in 2009 as one of Alabama's two statues at the US Capitol—refer to Keller as seven years old, but, having been born in June 1880, she was a couple of months shy of her seventh birthday; we know from a letter that Sullivan wrote about it at the time that the incident occurred on April 5, 1887.[57] Although it's thus squarely in the nineteenth century, my reference to it just a moment ago as a scene of the twentieth century was intentional. This is not just because it wasn't until 1903 that the story became widely known through the publication of Keller's first memoir, which includes a transcript of Sullivan's letter in its appendices. It is also because key elements of this version of the story only develop much later, in William Gibson's *The Miracle Worker*, a teleplay in 1957, then a stage play in 1959, and then a 1962 film. It was Gibson's drama, with Keller's cry as its catharsis, that made a household phrase of "wah, wah," thanks partly to Patty Duke's Oscar-winning turn in the Keller role and also to numberless actors in regional theater and school productions. Together these performances have cemented the well-pump scene as the crucial tableau in a parable of progressive education.[58]

The same tableau, iterated across time and media—I'll address a limited set of these iterations—encapsulates much of what has made Keller a fraught figure for several decades, most pointedly in the sphere of Deaf cultural critique. Keller herself, in a letter of gratitude to Fuller in the fall of 1890, wrote, "God . . . wanted you to teach me to speak because he knew how much I wished to speak like other people. He did not want his child to be dumb, and when I go to him He will let his angels teach me to sing."[59] The young Keller casts the incapacity or choice not to speak as unpleasing to God, with vocalization as a kind of redemption that can be worked toward in life but fully realized only with one's death.

She did, in fact, sing in public during her lifetime, even before she and Sullivan took to the vaudeville circuit, and she did so in the specific role of Oralist advocate.[60] At a 1912 convention of otologists, she first delivered an address in English, German, and French. Then, accompanied by a pianist from the New England Conservatory of Music, she sang, "giving the ear specialists the benefits of some lessons in vocal culture which she has recently undertaken." This performance of melody and multilingual articulation was not only a spectacle of impairment overcome, though. Keller's address to these "leading aural experts of the world" also uses the occasion to critique their general neglect of the social dimensions of disability.[61] Her insistence that they pay more attention to Oralist education involves an exhortation to move beyond their "study of the organ of hearing and to the treatment of its diseases" and to attend to "the deaf pupil and the deaf citizen as well as the diseased ear."[62] Similarly, essays like "What the Blind Can Do" (1906)—subsequently reprinted in *Out of the Dark* (1913), the collection of essays in which Keller most explicitly develops her position as a socialist—subordinate the tragedy of impairment to the injustice of built environments: "the school, the workshop, the factory are all constructed and regulated on the supposition that every one can see," with the consequence that "the blind as a rule are poor."[63] Especially in the first two decades of the twentieth century, Keller increasingly espoused this kind of economic critique of the material conditions that produce disabled subjects as a dependent class.

Still, her cry at the well pump remains the central scene in the hagiography of an individual "supercrip" for whom disability is to be mastered through a heroic force of individual spirit.[64] This tension is to some degree reflective of an irresolution within Keller's own politics. Yet the anecdote's far-reaching reverberations make it all the more important to note that the cry is William Gibson's invention and interpolation. It does not come from Keller's own report of the breakthrough. Nor does Sullivan's 1887 letter mention any vocalization at this moment. The six-year-old Keller had already become fairly proficient in fingerspelling transcription, without yet fully comprehending its utility for identifying objects. Sullivan reports, on the day in question, that she "spelled 'w-a-t-e-r' in Helen's free hand. The word coming so close upon the sensation of cold water rushing over her hand seemed to startle her. She dropped the mug and stood as one transfixed. A new light came into her face. She spelled 'water' several times."[65] In *The Story of My Life* Keller emphasizes that, in this moment, her "whole attention [was] fixed upon the motions of her fingers," and through these motions, "the mystery of language"—exemplified in the fact "that 'w-a-t-e-r' meant the wonderful cool something that was flowing over my hand"—"was revealed" to her.[66] Nowhere in Sullivan's or Keller's representations does the child speak. In fact, in two separate passages of her memoir, Keller writes that as she became proficient in the manual alphabet and learned to spell "water," she gradually *stopped* making the sound that she had been making ever since she was a baby (spelled once with and once without the aitch): "wah-wah" or "wa-wa."[67] Within this arc, the incident at the pump implicitly confirms the child's growing sense that vocalizing is less useful than transcribing. Sullivan's letter italicizes the same point: "She has learned that *everything has a name, and that the manual alphabet is the key to everything she wants to know.*"[68] Keller will elsewhere represent the manual alphabet as constraining, but here it is something that opens: a "key." She may have become an Oralist, but she wasn't one yet.

The Miracle Worker's climactic resolution at the pump conflates episodes of Keller's biography that express contradictory linguistic attitudes, eliding a moment that had, in the source material, assumed the robust capacities of the manual alphabet. To be clear, Gibson's Keller does fingerspell both before and after the cry, exuberantly so, but this modality is dramatically subordinated to the catharsis of vocal expression. *"And now the miracle happens,"* per Gibson's stage directions: *"at last it finds its way out, painfully, a baby sound buried under the debris of years of dumbness."*[69] There's a thin line between linguistic politics and dramaturgy here: for the playwright, the character's mental transformation may have seemed to demand a conspicuous performative break—a new kind of action for a new kind of thought. The articulations of fingerspelling may have involved movements too fine to be legible even to an audience literate in the system (particularly when partly obscured from view by the tactile way in which Keller and Sullivan used the alphabet with each other, pressing the manual shapes into one other's hand).[70] So instead, as a convenient metonym for linguistic discovery, Gibson adds—by temporally displacing—a sudden vocalization, despite the fact that, in Keller's view, at least for a few years of her childhood, the voice was precisely what this same moment of discovery had rendered irrelevant.

The effects of the utterance of "water" are sharpened by an incidental phonemic feature: its first syllable, the one Keller repeats, is also the common vocable for that "cry of deprecation" which "wells out of itself from the human vocal organs under certain sudden emotional excitements" (differing from, say, "ugh" in its more specific association with affliction).[71] This is the characterization offered by Grant Allen (novelist, critic, and science writer), not in direct reference to Keller but in an 1894 essay titled "The Beginning of Speech." Inquiries into the origins of language may have been stigmatized as unscientific by some professional linguists in the period (discussions of the topic having famously been banned at an 1866 convention in Paris) but were sustained in the discourse of social evolutionism. For Allen, the etymological descent from "wah" (as a universal form of involuntary outburst) to "woe" (as a lexical abstraction) is also a parable of the primitive origins of language in indexical immediacy: whereas "early people and simple minds" occupy themselves with "the Here and Now," the development of linguistic complexity brings with it a capacity for "abstract subjects" and "absent interests."[72] This capacity is, of course, just what Keller and Sullivan identify as the pedagogical outcome of the well-pump scene. That outcome is not, though, a sudden burst into language from nonlanguage. Rather, it involves a movement away from the indexical and iconic proximities of gestural communication—Keller had, prior to Sullivan's instruction, developed an idiosyncratic repertoire of several dozen meaningful signs—to the symbolic abstractions associated with alphabetic representation.[73]

The fact that Keller's cry does not seem to have caused much audience confusion across the decades, its ironies seeming appropriate, probably owes something to a further alteration that the play text makes to its source material. Gibson changes how teacher and student get to the well in the first place. In *The Story of My Life*, the scene occurs during a calm, typical instructional session. In *The Miracle Worker*, it arises as the result and redemption of the child's own violence. Keller has been uncontrollable at the dinner table. Lashing out at her parents and teacher, she upends a water pitcher. When Arthur Penn directed Patty McCormack in the Keller role for the 1957 CBS teleplay, he instructed her to "forget her table manners . . . and act like a dirty little animal."[74] Sullivan, furious, drags her outdoors, wild-haired and thrashing, to refill the pitcher. In her letters, the historical Sullivan does describe Keller often breaking things in this period of her life—"if she finds anything in her way, she flings it on the floor, no matter what it is: a glass, a pitcher"—but she does not refer to such behavior in relation to the well pump.[75] It's been argued that *The Miracle Worker*'s emphasis on Keller's wildness challenges sentimentalist framings of disability.[76] But this behavior's incorporation in this scene, disrupting a dinner-table debate over whether there is any hope for her education, also relies on and redeploys a long narrative tradition in which the exile or incarceration of the disabled subject is deemed necessary due to the danger of their wanton behavior.[77] (Consider the way that Billy Budd's stammer, in Melville's novella, is taken to divert the energy of linguistic expression into a lethal extrajudicial force that must be contained—an example that was playing out on American movie-theater screens at the same time as *The Miracle Worker*, via Peter Ustinov's 1962 adaptation.) With Keller's wild physicality raising the risk of her permanent exclusion from the common life of the species, her final pained cry—accompanied by another drop of the pitcher, this time not wanton but ecstatic—can read both as feral and as linguistically original. It's the last gasp of a gestural infancy that alphabetization has begun to displace.[78]

During the middle years of Keller's adulthood, the relationship between the kinetic and the alphabetic was reshaped in the gestural intensities and textual devices of silent film.[79] *The Miracle Worker* was not the first on-screen depiction of the well-pump scene, and I'd like to turn now to an important earlier iteration. The biographical film *Deliverance* (1919) was written by Francis Trevelyan Miller; George Foster Platt produced and directed; and Keller and Sullivan provided consultation and were closely involved throughout the process. Keller appears on-screen, playing herself, late in the film. As one article about the production indicated in the summer before its release, she "was a most apt screen actress." *Apt*: Keller as student, always. She took "many of her directions by means of sound vibration and without the ordinary method of communication, such as the code employed by her and her teacher."[80] According to other reports, though, while Platt did direct Keller by stamping his foot when she was on camera, sending vibrations through the floor to where she stood, she did in fact communicate with Sullivan through the "code" of the manual alphabet, as Sullivan relayed what was happening to Keller "by pressing in the palm of her hand." Working with Sullivan in this way, Keller often "stopped the rehearsals to correct the director or to explain to little Etna just what it was she did and how she felt when that particular incident really happened."[81] Keller as teacher, too.

"Little Etna" refers to Etna Ross, the child actor who played young Keller in the first part of the film, including the well-pump scene. In *Deliverance*, this scene makes for a significant but not climactic moment in the early section of the biography—and perhaps this is part of the reason that, while scholars have attended to Keller's own participation as an actor in later sections of the film, this sequence has received little attention. Neither of Gibson's most conspicuous alterations of the scene for *The Miracle Worker* feature here. In *Deliverance* as in *The Story of My Life*, the scene remains centered on fingerspelling (without any cry), and no tantrum precedes the incident. The 1919 film presents a relatively close adaptation of the story as Sullivan and Keller first told it in the memoir and then, perhaps, retold it on set. Yet the media environment of silent film also exerts certain pressures on the problem of media *in* the story, particularly the relationship between two alphabetic "codes," one typographic and one manual.

When Keller experiences her epiphany in *Deliverance*, "water" is transcribed on-screen three times. Only one of these, the first, is in the Latin alphabet, as the word appears in an intertitle. In one extant production doc-

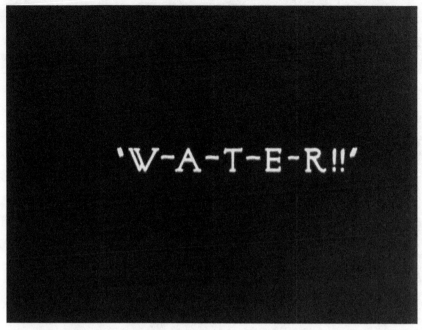

FIGURE 2.1 Title card in *Deliverance* (1919), dir. George Platt. Library of Congress, Motion Picture, Broadcasting, and Recorded Sound Division, http://loc.gov/item /mbrs00093858/.

ument, a draft list of all the title cards that would be used in the film, this one appears as number 51. The draft gives the word as "W-A-T-E-R," with quotation marks and a period after "R."[82] In the film, though, the word doesn't appear all at once. Over approximately seven seconds, it spells itself out one letter at a time. Each character is separated by a hyphen that looks like a shallow tilde, the slightest liquid waveform. First appears just the "W" (the letter accompanied by opening quotation marks on the left but none on the right, suggesting a speech act in progress), then another showing "W~A," and so on until finally, when "R" arrives, it's accompanied by two exclamation points inside closing quotation marks (fig. 2.1). As we return to live action, the word is then transcribed twice more, but now by the actors and in the manual rather than the Latin alphabet. First there's a close-up of the actors' hands, as Sullivan takes Keller's hands into her own and shows her how to shape the sequence of five letters (fig. 2.2). Then Keller spells it back into Sullivan's palm.

The intertitle that leads into these fingerspelling repetitions carries a pedagogical potential. It instructs the viewer who is literate in Latin but not

FIGURE 2.2 Learning "w" in the manual alphabet, in *Deliverance* (1919).

the manual alphabet, and who is attentive to the lesson, in how to translit-erate from one to the other. The scene of instruction can play out along two axes: from teacher to student and from film to viewer. That the film is not deeply committed to the latter pedagogy, though, is suggested by a follow-ing subtitle that takes a parallel form. Keller touches an infant, and then the intertitle spells out, letter by letter, "B~A~B~Y"; but there is no close-up on the corresponding manual transcription. The same title format is used again in the later scene of Oralist instruction, when Sarah Fuller of the Horace Mann School for the Deaf gives Keller speech lessons, but here the format is used to represent the temporality of vocalization rather than fingerspelling. The utterance *"I~~AM~~NOT~~DUMB~~NOW"* ap-pears one piece at a time, with the unit of the series now scaled up from the letter to the word.

Instead of pausing cinematic experience, these intertitles animate tran-scription. They position linguistic sequentiality as a figure for the optical illusion of the moving image itself. This takes on a sharp effect in the light of contemporaneous debates in film criticism about the perceptual effects of intertitles, particularly those used for representing dialogue rather than for narrative exposition. What was called the "spoken title" or "spoken subtitle" in the period (the term "subtitle" not yet having acquired the sense of a caption at the bottom of a moving-picture frame) was sometimes condemned as a stultifying force. Behind this criticism was a more fundamental position about the centrality of the visible body to cinematic art, in ways that were inseparable from arguments about cultural primitivity and elevation. When in 1915 Walter Richard Eaton of the *Boston Transcript* complained of film pantomime that filmmakers seemed naively to think "we can go back to what amounts to sign language at this stage of civilization," Henry McMahon of the *New York Times* responded, "How about the 'sign language' of pure music? The 'sign language' of sculpture? The 'sign language' of painting?"[83] Days before the premiere of *Deliverance* in 1919, another *Times* film column similarly insisted on the primacy of pantomime over the combination of "silent conversational motions" and subtitles, approvingly quoting director Oscar Apfel's complaint that filmmakers "do not give the public credit for enough intelligence and consequently load a picture with hundreds of feet of titles that could better be devoted to action."[84] A few years later, the *Times* critic returns to the same theme of cognitive demand: spoken titles "permit lazy, incompetent and mentally dumb people to make photoplays, and, what is worse, they encourage people who can work and have ability and imagination to loaf on the job." Meanwhile, the viewer's "mind takes a day off": knowing that any ambiguity will be explained momentarily, they don't have to worry about what characters might be saying to each other, and then when the title appears—"a simple sentence which any one can grasp with his mind functioning only as a passive recording machine"—it will hardly require much attention either.[85] For such critics, overuse of titles violates an aesthetic investment in perceptual renewal framed in terms of the artist's cognitive ability (tied to speech in the semantic overlap of "mentally *dumb*") and the audience's interpretive labor.

The well-pump scene provides a charged site for these concerns, since the same violation sounds something like the outcome of Keller's revelation, as it's often represented. Indeed, her own status as a "passive recording machine" was sometimes associated with the manual alphabet: John Wright, advocate for Oralist education, claimed that during the years when Keller was primarily communicating with the manual alphabet, "to tell her something was like writing it in a book. When you wished the fact again months or even years afterward, you had only to ask for it"—though, according to

Wright, this effect diminished as she gained competency in other linguistic modalities.[86] In Keller's own telling, what she learns at the well pump is not how to renew or estrange her experience of the water as a particularized, *watery* object of attention but how to make perception more efficient by naming the element in the abstract.[87] Of course, that realization involves a higher-order estrangement of the media of transcription itself. For the character of young Keller on-screen, there is a shifting sense of the semantic possibilities of the manual alphabet (and, in the later scene of vocalization, of the syntactic possibilities of the voice). At the same time, for the viewer, there is the unusual degree of perceptual attention, both to text and to performance, that first the animated intertitle and then the repeated fingerspellings call for. As each letter is given in sequence, the Latin alphabet bends toward the manual alphabet, both operating with the kind of linearity often identified as a key feature distinguishing fingerspelling from sign languages (with their greater degree of simultaneity).[88]

The production documents don't make it clear who authored these titles in their final form—who was responsible, for instance, for transforming the draft of the card that read simply "W-A-T-E-R" to one where that word prints itself on-screen.[89] But this is not the most significant change that happens to the titles' design. The screenwriter, Miller, had originally imagined that they would all be written in Keller's handwriting. His synopsis had proposed that "Helen Keller (in her blindness) will write the titles herself." Miller also suggested that she would "write a signed letter to the people as an introduction to our drama, verifying the astounding fact that every incident in the drama is absolutely true."[90]

Neither idea—the handwritten titles, the letter of attestation—ends up getting carried out as Miller planned. They are complexly synthesized, though, in one moment of the completed film. A few minutes after the well-pump scene, the film offers a still shot of Keller's own handwriting as a child. This moment evokes the medium of the title card in its format. The camera hovers over a block of text, isolated from the action of the film. Yet it also offers a documentarian touch of the real. The handwritten document is not a prop created for the film but an actual autographic specimen. Anticipating the later entrance into the film of the biographical subject's own body, the shot serves not only as verification of Keller's literacy but also as a kind of authenticating supplement to the film's scenes of historical reenactment.

To fully understand the effects of this document's appearance in the film, though, it helps to track the brief sequence that takes us from the well pump to the autograph. After the epiphany, the film moves briskly through a few exterior locations. Keller tries to teach her dog the manual alphabet; then she plays in the chicken coop and the barnyard with three other children. One is Martha Washington (played by Jenny Lind, a young actor who shares the name of the nineteenth-century opera star). Washington is described by Keller in *The Story of My Life* as "a little coloured girl, . . . the child of our cook," who enjoyed a similar brand of mischief, who "understood my signs"—that is, the idiolectal gestures Keller used before learning the manual alphabet—and who "generally submitted to my tyranny."[91] In the memoir, Washington is only mentioned in the years predating Keller's study with Sullivan, but *Deliverance* shifts the representation of this tyrannical friendship later chronologically, interweaving it with the scenes of Keller's acquisition of literacy. Also present in these early scenes of the film are two white children, an unnamed boy and a girl named Nadja (a fictional character, not drawn from the biographical material). Nadja dismisses and resents Keller, saying to the other children in the yard, "She cain't see . . . or hear . . . or even talk. . . . She cain't never know nothin'. . . . Or be smart like us." Note the stereotypical markers of dialectal speech: the diphthong "cain't," the dropped *g*, the double negative. These cues ask the viewer to read Nadja's insults back against herself—with the theme of literacy underscored by the fact that she and the other able white child have, at this point in the scene, gathered up their books, evidently headed to school. Even this other child, Nadja's unnamed boy friend, standing close at her side, seems to shift affections: impressed by Keller, he takes her hand in what amounts, the titles tell us, to a "little romance," drawing Keller's attention away from Washington (who laughs in response) and making Nadja jealous (fig. 2.3). Through early sections of the film, Nadja will represent a kind of small-minded stubbornness indexed by literary dialect, but in the larger arc, the film positions her as Keller's foil precisely in order to unite them later in life, across differences of class and national descent (Nadja's family having immigrated) in the cause of advocacy for the blind.[92] There is, as her name indicates, "hope" even for Nadja.

Washington, absent from those later acts of the film, does not play as central a role. She is crucial, though, to the early scenes of literacy acquisition. Nadja and the boy run off after the moment of "romance" in the yard, but the scene that follows reiterates the linguistic dynamics of that interaction—representing dialectal speech in the text of the titles as a foil for scenes of linguistic development—while reframing those dynamics in racial contrast. We cut from the children to an interior scene. Sullivan, seated, reads alone.

FIGURE 2.3 Helen Keller (second from left, played by Etna Ross) and friends, in *Deliverance* (1919).

Keller and Washington enter. Keller pulls at her friend's hair. Washington winces in pain. (Here *Deliverance* tweaks early passages of Keller's memoir about cutting off her "friend's little bunches of fuzzy hair," distinguished from her own "long golden curls.")[93] Standing behind the kneeling Washington, both facing the seated Sullivan, Keller raises Washington's hands and, through touches that only Washington seems to understand, gets her to wiggle her fingers. Washington laughs and plays along. Highly amused, Sullivan asks (per the spoken title), "Martha Washington . . . what on earth are you trying to say?" Washington's response is represented with some typical orthographic substitutions for the dialect writing of the period: "De dog's got chickens . . . de cat's got puppies . . .'n de hens got kittens! De whole world's done gone crazy with young 'uns." The three of them laugh. Sullivan touches Washington lightly at the elbow to direct her out of the room, bringing Keller onto her lap. Keller begins to fingerspell with apparent fluency. Instead of a spoken title giving us the content of their communication, though, the intertitle that immediately follows is expository. It turns us from the manual alphabet to the Latin, not only at the level of the medium represented visually on the screen but also at the level of the story:

"Within three months after the first word is spelled in her hand, Helen conquers another world—the written word." Here is where we get the still shot of the note itself, a well-known sample of Keller's earliest handwriting. (It had been printed as an inset illustration, for instance, in a 1906 issue of *American Anthropologist*.) Dated June 17, 1887, it reads, "helen write anna george will give helen apple simpson will shoot bird jack will give helen stick of candy doctor will give mildred medicine mother will make mildred new dress."[94]

The film positions the broken syntax of Keller's handwriting in proximity to the "broken symbols of speech" of the episode's racialized dialect. While the former serves in the narrative as a sign of dawning literacy, the latter indexes a world of illiteracy and gesture away from which Keller's education will, ostensibly, take her. This contrast is clarified in the scene that (in the film, if not in life) directly catalyzes the decision that Keller and Sullivan should leave Alabama for the Perkins School. At the Keller household one day, distracted in a book, Sullivan is alarmed to realize that she has lost track of Keller's whereabouts. But Washington quickly runs off to find Keller at the schoolhouse. Nadja is there, at her desk, among the other students; the camera comes in close to show her holding but conspicuously not reading a book (fig. 2.4).

This book is no randomly selected prop. *Monroe's Fourth Reader*, its cover reads. First published in 1872 (the year before Lewis B. Monroe founded the Boston University School of Oratory), then reprinted and revised into the early twentieth century, the *Reader* focuses on the pedagogy of proper speech. The first paragraph of Monroe's preface addresses the importance of teaching "articulation and pronunciation," particularly given "the constant influx into this country of foreigners," which "has a tendency to corrupt our speech." (The second paragraph thanks Alexander Graham Bell for his consultation and points interested readers to *Visible Speech* for a more precise reference on physiology and phonetics.)[95] A similar anxiety about linguistic norms is no doubt relevant to the film's representations of dialect in the speech of Nadja and Washington, but it isn't expressed primarily as nativism; indeed, to the extent that Keller was able to influence the content of the film, that would be surprising given her internationalist politics. Instead, "nonstandard" speech marks and crosses lines of race and class. When Washington comes to the schoolhouse to find Keller, a title gives us Washington's explanation of how she knew where to find her: "She's always wantin' to come to school . . . wantin' to learn something what I can't tell her." Setting Keller's desire to learn against the willful ignorance of Nadja,

FIGURE 2.4 Nadja (played by Tula Belle) not reading *Monroe's Fourth Reader*, in *Deliverance* (1919).

the scene frames Washington's friendship as both necessary for and incommensurate with the desire for education. Racial marking works prosthetically here. Blackness serves in the film as a metonym for disability, precluding Washington's presence in the subsequent narrative of literate overcoming that will, later in the twentieth century, be projected back in time as a cry.[96] The next section will consider the negotiations of this metonymy in the compositional history of a text to whose making Keller is vital—not as its author but as its intended reader.

Made to Speak

If you ever have occasion to write a tribute to Helen Keller, there's a template you can use. The key idea to touch on is that, even in her sensory impairments, she can see what the sighted can't, hear that to which the hearing are deaf, while her disability itself figures somebody else's spiritual or ethical lack. Ask Langston Hughes, "She, / In the dark, / Found light / Brighter than many ever see."[97] This template is a version of the fraught "blind seer" archetype, though often with special emphasis on moral innocence and often with a mixture of sensory metaphors.[98] Ask Jane A. Roulston: "You sit in silence, beautiful, serene, / Untrammeled by the fleeting lights that screen / Our fettered eyes."[99] Ask Arthur Spingarn: "Those with sharpest eyes hear least of Truth."[100]

These examples are all from the 1931 volume *Double Blossoms: Helen Keller Anthology*, edited by Edna Porter. An actor and organizer for the Actors' Equity Association, she had known Keller since at least 1919 (plausibly earlier, given their common involvement in socialist political circles in New York during the 1910s).[101] When *Deliverance* premiered in the summer of 1919, Keller was preparing to speak at a screening, only to learn that there was an ongoing strike in the theater business. She canceled her plans. Her announcement—"I would rather have my picture fail . . . than not be with the actors and the Actors' Equity Association in this glorious fight"—was relayed to the press by Porter.[102] In a meeting at the Lexington Theater, "Helen Keller, the blind and dumb woman who has gone into the movies, was on the programme as the chief speaker to urge the multitude of striking actors to keep their strike enthusiasm at fever pitch."[103] A decade later, when Porter wrote a review of *My Religion*, she recalled Keller's steadfastness: "She was Equity's friend!"[104]

Around 1927, Porter began soliciting poets, public figures, and friends of Keller to contribute to an anthology in her honor. It would be published several years later as *Double Blossoms*. When Keller was presented with an honorary degree at the Royal Institute in Glasgow in 1932, James Kerr Love, holding a copy of the anthology, wondered aloud "whether such a tribute has ever been given to a living author."[105] Having the living Keller in mind as the principal reader, Porter herself created a copy of the text in Braille. She intended to finish this in 1928, as a tribute to Keller originally intended for her forty-eighth birthday (presumably in reference to 1848, the year of revolutions). But Porter continued gathering contributions, and three years later, in October 1931, the book was printed in quantity, typeset in the Latin alphabet. A revised edition then appeared in December with a few late additions.[106] A review in the *Brooklyn Eagle* notes that Clarence Darrow, the celebrated Scopes Trial lawyer, "wrote the only piece of prose in the book," but even not counting Porter's preface (and, in the second edition only, a perfunctory appreciation from Rabindranath Tagore), this isn't the case; another piece in prose, appearing midway through the volume, is contributed by W. E. B. Du Bois.[107]

Du Bois's paragraph, titled simply "Helen Keller," has often been cited as evidence either of a long-standing alignment in the two figures' political purposes or of surprising affinities across intellectual histories associated with their careers and with that of William James (whom Du Bois briefly mentions). My account will differ in two ways: first, by reckoning with the text less as a documentation of historical fact than as a dynamic, inchoate navigation of the question of analogy and intersection across constructions of race and disability; second, by noting the most basic oddity of this document's form—the fact that it isn't a poem. Part of the reason that this formal feature hasn't been previously addressed is that, given a normative linguistic default to prose (as opposed to the abnormality of verse) in modern historiography, its status here as an exception is only evident in local contrast.[108] This contrast is glaring in both 1931 editions of *Double Blossoms* (for any reader more attentive than the *Eagle* reviewer, at least) but disappears in the version universally cited in recent commentary, a later collection of Du Bois's prose.[109] Another reason for critical inattention to this formal contrast is that its political consequences play out most dramatically only backstage, in the interaction between the content of the text and the terms of its editorial solicitation.

Du Bois's paragraph is worth quoting in full:

> When I was studying philosophy at Harvard under William James, we made an excursion one day out to Roxbury. We stopped at the Blind Asylum and saw a young girl who was blind and deaf and dumb, and yet who, by infinite pains and loving sympathy, had been made to speak without words and to understand without sounds. She was Helen Keller. Perhaps because she was blind to color differences in this world, I became intensely interested in her, and all through my life I have followed her career. Finally, there came the thing which I somehow sensed would come; Helen Keller was in her own state, Alabama, being feted and made much of by her fellow citizens. And yet courageously and frankly she spoke out on the iniquity and foolishness of the color line. It cost her something to speak. They wanted her to retract, but she sat serene in the consciousness of the truth that she had uttered. And so it was proven, as I knew it would be, that this woman who sits in darkness has a spiritual insight clearer than that of many wide-eyed people who stare uncomprehendingly at this prejudiced world.[110]

Let me first gloss the biographical references here. When Du Bois refers to the "Blind Asylum," he means the Perkins Institute (now located in Watertown but then in Roxbury). Some accounts of this first meeting indicate that

James brought Du Bois alone to visit Keller, others that there was an entire class of students. The chronology is murky, too. Most accounts place this meeting in 1892, but when Du Bois inscribed a Braille copy of *Darkwater* to Keller in 1925, his own inscription—"I have known you, unknown, since 1890"—raises the possibility of an earlier date.[111]

Du Bois's reference to Alabama, meanwhile, involves a sequence of events in 1916 that begins with Keller donating one hundred dollars to the NAACP, enclosed with a letter of solidarity that was then printed in *The Crisis*.[112] Keller was scheduled to speak in Alabama soon after, and the *Selma Journal*, having found Keller's letter in Du Bois's magazine, reprinted it with a vitriolic editorial. She must have been "poisoned," the *Journal* complained, "against her own people."[113] Although Du Bois later appreciates that she did not, in response, "retract," Keller did provide a statement to the *Selma Times* insisting that her words had been misinterpreted, that her letter had advocated "the equality of all men before the law," not "the social equality of white people and negroes, so repugnant to all."[114] While *The Crisis* reprinted this response under the headline "Sassing Back," a letter printed just below Keller's response in the *Times* took the same text to indicate that "the white man is the heaven-endowed leader of the forces of progress and civilization."[115] For Du Bois, recalling the episode over a decade later for *Double Blossoms*, the general consistency of Keller's progressive commitments may have led to his generous summation of a response that also happened to prove amenable to avowed white supremacists.[116]

Yet there may also be a certain theoretical pressure, an idea of disability, shaping the recollections that he sends to Porter for *Double Blossoms*. The template I described earlier is certainly present there, accompanied by a note of "loving sympathy" that cues a sentimentalist framing of disability as dependency. But note too how Du Bois's interest in Keller's career and his premonitions ("somehow I sensed") about the political struggles she would face derive potentially ("perhaps") from an identification of Keller as "blind to color differences in this world." In this context, the phrasing "color differences" could suggest either differences within the social order (economic inequality, unequal protection before the law, Jim Crow divisions of space) or the visible differences of skin color. Given that there is nothing to prevent Keller from understanding the former, though, it would seem, for Du Bois, to be the latter that is key here: the fact that she cannot physically sense color. (This "fact" was not always taken for granted during her life: on her visit to Glasgow in 1932, when asked if she could distinguish colors, she answered, "the waves seem to travel too fast for my sense of touch.")[117] Du Bois tilts the phrase in this sensory direction in a revision he makes to the first typescript draft of the paragraph. The first version reads "colored differences." He then deletes the "-ed," quieting without silencing the racial connotations of the phrase.[118] This could be Du Bois's revision of his own wording or his correction of a transcription from his dictation (the added "-ed" sound perhaps, in a typist's hearing, a back-formation from the following "d" of "differences," a phantom participle made probable by topical relevance). In either case, Du Bois's correction locates the source of Keller's status as an ally in her body. The fact that she can't see color is imagined to immunize her from prejudice.[119] Her body makes her innocent.

That logic reads differently, though, when we track the exchanges that led to Du Bois writing the piece. Porter contacts him in May 1927 to describe the project and solicit his contribution.[120] He writes back a few weeks later with a copy of the paragraph.[121] But Porter then has to awkwardly explain that this isn't what she's looking for: "You'll want to box my ears/when I tell you that I am collecting a volume of VERSE." She reassures him that he could "take all summer" to send a poem, explaining why she had asked him first: "I wanted something from you more than from the others; but now I shall send out the letters I had in mind to James Weldon Johnson, Jesse Fauset, Countee Cullen, Langston Hughes, and Claude McKay as I have already done their poems in braille for Helen Keller. If there is any other Negro poet you think I should include please let me know. And don't forget yours!"[122] From the summer of 1927 to the spring of 1928, Porter will ask three more times, mentioning again at one point that "colored poets" including Cullen and Hughes will contribute.[123] While Du Bois is responsive regarding other small items of business that he and Porter have to conduct (sending copies of The Crisis, for instance), he only acknowledges the queries about the anthology once, reservedly committing to "try and send [her] something."[124] But he never does send the "lyrical lines" that Porter keeps asking for.[125] In July 1928, she admits editorial defeat: "For the Brailled Helen Keller Anthology I used the message you sent me over a year ago. It seemed a relief amongst the many poems."[126]

Du Bois was, no doubt, busy. During 1927 and early 1928, he was (among other responsibilities) editing the financially struggling Crisis, coordinating the fourth Pan-Africanist Conference in New York, and preparing his novel The Dark Princess for publication. But he did, in his career, sometimes write poetry, and a few lines, fewer than he wrote to Porter in prose in their correspondence during this period, would have done the trick. It seems probable, in other words, that his de facto refusal to revise and resubmit was not only an incidental effect of practical circumstances. It may have been a response to the framing of the request: to her joke about his potential violence, "you'll want to box my ears"; to Porter casting him as foremost among "the others" of African American poetry. A year earlier, Du Bois had delivered a speech at an NAACP convention that then appeared in *The Crisis* as "Criteria of Negro Art." In his address, Du Bois surmised that some of the recent recognition of "younger Negro writers" was, if not a "conspiracy," then a convenient way to avoid the "agitation of the Negro question." He sardonically ventriloquizes this kind of bad-faith appreciation: "The recognition accorded Cullen, Hughes, Fauset, White and others shows there is no real color line. Keep quiet! Don't complain! Work! All will be well!"[127] While Porter's labor politics were aligned with Du Bois's argument here in important ways, her solicitation—dropping almost the same list of names—risked invoking what he considered to be a mystification, an elective blindness to the real color differences of Jim Crow.

Du Bois's reticence may also have involved a response to the meanings that "poetry" came to carry in the exchange. Of course, there are many reasons not to write a poem. There are surely incidental histories here that are forever unavailable to us. But a particular figurative movement in Porter's first two letters (the initial solicitation and the follow-up clarification) does begin to suggest a rhetorical context in which Du Bois may have preferred not to rewrite his prose as verse. "Please do not let this letter get too deep in the pile of the unanswered," Porter writes in her first letter, "and some fine day, when the spirit moves you, just pour out the blackness of your pen to a soul in a still blacker setting."[128] Nodding to two key terms ("soul" and "black") of Du Bois's most famous book title, the line also disarticulates them, linking blackness with the visual materiality of text and with sensory impairment. While the "spirit" may move Du Bois, here the "soul" is Keller's. Then, in Porter's follow-up letter, we move from the blackness of ink to the visual distinction of lineated text. This distinction is efficiently transmuted in her use of all caps: "VERSE," and, in the context of both letters, comes across as inseparable from the visibility of the racially marked person. To carry out Porter's request—to supply a text genre evidently imagined by the editor as analogous, in its visual exceptionalism, with the author's own marked person—might have meant to satisfy the kind of vision that Du Bois's paragraph had celebrated Keller for lacking. In other words, it may have become clear that this request did not meet his own criteria for art as "propaganda for gaining the right of black folk to love and enjoy," and that it would instead involve a kind of autographic spectacle.[129] In response, Du

Bois would not be, to repurpose a phrase from the text that he *did* send (and did not retract), "made to speak"—not, at least, to versify.

This brings us back to a dominant motif of Du Bois's tribute to Keller: vocalization as a trope for political expression. "She spoke out. . . . It cost her something to speak . . . the truth she had uttered." Just as Keller's antiracism is framed as a potential effect of her blindness, so is this trope tied, in Du Bois's paragraph, to the body: the audist implications of the metaphor in which proper political subjectivity is enacted only vocally and aurally (speaking out and being heard, versus the silencing of exclusion) are literalized in association with the speech training of Oralist education. If Du Bois and James had indeed visited in the summer of 1890, it would have been just after Keller started to work with Fuller; if it was in 1892, she would have been more practiced in the method. Du Bois writes that, though "deaf and dumb," Keller "had been made to speak without words and to understand without sound." This is one of the few places that Du Bois revises before sending to Porter, with the line initially reading, "made to speak *slowly* and to understand," with a period after "understand."[130] Whereas "slowly" may have seemed, in a second pass through the text, slightly negative for an encomium, "without words" makes Keller's speech a kind of paradoxical miracle. Adding "without sound" after "understand" then creates an evocative parallel. But both phrasings fit uneasily with the facts as Keller might have described them. "The word" was often, in Keller's own writing— in her recollections of the well-pump epiphany, most familiarly—specifically identified as the very basis of reason and imagination. And she did not generally describe her deafness as preventing her access to sound; to the contrary, she defined sound as accessible not only aurally but via multiple sense organs, as in the haptic experience of musical vibration—along with "the pop of a cork, the sputter of a flame, . . . and many other vibrations past computing."[131]

Contradiction, though, seems to be what Du Bois is after in these phrasings, as the right rhetorical mode to describe an empathetic "understanding" so radical as to verge on impossibility.[132] One of the key documents in the background of his tribute, Keller's 1916 letter to the NAACP, develops a comparable theme. She describes her shame at witnessing, in her "own beloved southland," the inheritance of "bondage" across generations of "suffering, toiling millions." Here disability signifies both moral impairment—"I pray that God may open the eyes of the blind and bring them by a way they know not to understanding and righteousness"—and the suffering of the oppressed: "My spirit groans with all the deaf and blind of the world. I feel their chains chafing my limbs. I am disenfranchised with every wage-slave. I am overthrown, hurt, oppressed, beaten to the earth by the strong ruthless ones who have taken away their inheritance."[133] In descriptions of Keller's disability, including her own, bondage often appears as a figure for impairment.[134] Here, the tenor and vehicle of the metaphor oscillate. First, blindness represents the ethical failing of the prejudiced, as in the common template of tributes to Keller. But then, within the space of a couple of lines, "the deaf and blind" comes to name those subjected to oppression in the post-Reconstruction "southland" of her early childhood.

These slippery figurations share a premise. They call on deafness and blindness as conditions to be overcome, whether in the moral redemption of the racist or in the economic uplift of those who are living under wage slavery. That metaphorical premise of impairment overcome is, of course, over the long twentieth century, reenacted nowhere more conspicuously than in representations of the "almost incredible" fact that Keller could write—even as *what* she wrote did not always serve to reproduce but also often to expose and particularize these patterns of talking about seeing and hearing.

Another poet's autograph, to close: in the summer of 1891 or 1892—around the same time, that is, that Du Bois and William James visited Keller—she and Sullivan visited the famed abolitionist poet John Greenleaf Whittier.[135] His "Howard at Atlanta" (1868), an excerpt from which Du Bois cites as an epigraph in *Souls of Black Folk*, describes the education of people "with freedom newly dowered" as a miraculous cure: "the dumb lips speaking, / the blind eyes seeing!"[136] In Whittier's "Laus Deo!" (1865), too—which Keller recited for the poet during her visit—the sound of the ringing bells that announce the passage of the Thirteenth Amendment is imagined to "give the dumb a voice."[137] Keller's performance of this text was a self-reflexive choice. Her audience, the poem's author, took the idea behind that choice and ran with it. After her recitation, Keller recalled, Whittier "placed in my hands a statue of a slave from whose crouching figure the fetters were falling."[138] Her description suggests that this may have been a replica of Thomas Ball's Emancipation Group, with Lincoln standing tall next to a man on one knee, implicitly a formerly enslaved person.[139] (The racially paternalistic statue was installed, with Whittier reciting a poem at the dedication, in Boston in 1879 and was removed to storage following the Black Lives Matter protests of 2020.) Decades after Keller's meeting with Whittier, she will write that, when he held the small statue with her, he referred to Sullivan as "thy spiritual liberator"—the Lincoln of the relationship—and told Keller that her teacher's work had reinforced his "faith that some day all fetters shall be broken which keep the minds and hearts of men in bondage.'"[140] A description of the same meeting in *The Story of My Life* quotes Whittier slightly differently—but still with reference to "bondage"—in a note that transcribes not a sentence he said aloud but an inscription he wrote as "an autograph for [Keller's] teacher": "With great admiration of thy noble work in releasing from bondage the mind of thy dear pupil."[141] This autograph gets its aura from the discursive intersection of deaf education with the histories of inequity—of chattel and wage slavery, of unequal educational access—that are simultaneously denounced and reproduced by the statue that mediates these hands' touch. That same logic explains, in part, both why Helen Keller's autograph is ubiquitous in print and why Du Bois's poem about her doesn't exist.

3 Gatsby's Tattoo

Music and Motor Habit

• •

As F. Scott Fitzgerald was trying to get his third novel into shape for publication, he put down the following line in an even, loopy hand: "Gatsby's foot
beat a short restless tatoo and, struck by an idea, Tom turned toward him."[1]
The setting of the action is the Plaza Hotel in New York. It's late in the summer, late on a sweaty afternoon, and late in the novel. If Tom Buchanan already has a pretty good idea about the affair between his wife Daisy and
Jay Gatsby, at this moment that intuition cascades into a scene of accusa-
tion, betrayal, racial panic, and, on the way home to Long Island, vehicular
manslaughter. The turn of Tom's body entails a pivot in the narrative, some
sort of recognition having been provoked by the restless tapping in earshot.

The content of Tom's "idea," though, is left without explicit explanation.
Gatsby's foot-tapping is not attended by the kind of deep backstory that follows, for instance, the moment in the *Odyssey* when Euryclea has a flash of
recognition upon touching the scar on Odysseus's ankle.[2] So what is it about
this action that causes Tom to turn and bring Gatsby's body into his field of
vision? Is a reader even warranted to find causation in this abrupt little
dance of noise, nerves, rhythm, and gaze? Exploring such questions in
Fitzgerald's fiction and in the anthropology of motor habit, this chapter
turns to the textual and graphic representation of bodily cues that, not belonging to a sign language or other formalized repertoire, sit on the mar-
gins of the discursive—a wink to nobody in particular, a stylish stride, a
gesticulation knotted in the air—but that nevertheless can tell us a lot about
the languages of American identification and the contours of assimilatory
rhetoric.

The line I just quoted—more specifically, a detail of this line's editorial
history—offers a point of entry to all this. This moment in the Plaza Hotel
isn't choreographed in quite the same way in the version of *The Great Gatsby*
that Fitzgerald's publisher, Charles Scribner's Sons, will release on April 10,
1925. The sentence as it appears above exists only as an ephemeral construction in pencil (like Hellen Keller, Fitzgerald avoided pen), entertained by
the author while working on the manuscript of a novel whose title was still

in flux. Several small aspects of the line will come to change, as I'll discuss later in this chapter. The one alteration I want to note at the outset was made not by the author but by the press. By the time the book appears, another *t* has been added to the word "tatoo."[3] The Scribner's staff could have felt confident in introducing this silent correction during production not only because Fitzgerald had, due to his excessive revisions of the galleys, forfeited his chance to review final proofs but also because, by the early twentieth century, this spelling was standard for both of the word's primary senses: as an ink inscription in the skin and as a staccato pattern of percussive sound.[4]

This is an orthographic convergence of distinct etymological lines. The sense of "tattoo" as patterning, imagery, or writing on the body not by branding or scarification but by means of inked "punctuation"—the term often used in the eighteenth-century travel writings that brought the term to English—derives from Polynesian words including the Samoan *tatau*.[5] The noisy sense of the word derives separately from a Dutch phrase for the military signal, played by drum or bugle toward the end of the evening, that it is time to close the taps (*doe den tap toe*) of the beer kegs and return to barracks.[6] From there, speakers generate a range of usages including both the tattoo of rain against a window—where the word's two voiceless stop consonants become onomatopoetic—and the tattoo of a grand military display of pageantry and armament. In Fitzgerald's favorite Dickens novel, *Bleak House*, it seems an apt echo of these origins when it's the stoic veteran trooper Mr. George who "beats a tattoo on the ground" as a sign of his displeasure with a conversational direction.[7] But in the one other instance of the word in *Bleak House*, it is Richard Carstone, verging perpetually on financial and personal dissipation, who beats "the Devil's Tattoo with his boot on the patternless carpet."[8] Here, while the detail of the carpet's patternlessness indicates a class status, it also allows the action's nervous rhythm—quietly pathologized as behavior not suited to the able body—to find its formal expression against a surface as blank as paper. Or, in certain formulations of the racial imaginary of Anglophone empire, as blank as whiteness.[9] This "tattoo" is shadowed by its homonym.

So is Gatsby's. When he drums his foot on the floor of the Plaza Hotel, it is obviously the sonic sense of "tattoo" that is dictated by the semantic surround. This usage doesn't feel like a pun. Still, the sound of this fictional event takes up its meanings in response to discursive histories that also surround the figure of the inscribed body, especially as this figure is linked with anthropological alterity. What this chapter will elaborate, then, is not the theme of body art itself (though that theme will be relevant on occasion). It is instead the matrix of ideas of the body—including the fluctuating constructions of white masculinity—in which it makes sense for Fitzgerald to locate a narrative climax in the event of a tattoo that is both aural and visual. This event plays out along those dual sensory axes not just because of a homonym that may or may not have crossed the author's mind but also, and more to the point, because it is performed as a sonic improvisation only to elicit a visual response—a response that, as in a sound-blind transcription, may miss some of the small differences that matter most.

As a novelist, Fitzgerald sustains an unmistakable interest in the embodied pragmatics of conversation. To recognize this interest is hardly to label a scene like the one he imagines in the Plaza as an exceptional instance of literary representation. Dickens wrote the body into dialogue, too.[10] But it does help us begin to plot common ground between his fiction and empirical research on gesture. This was a significant topic of anthropological study during the span of his career, for several reasons. One was technological. Photography and film offered new possibilities for the recording and analysis of gesture, even if these media were still understood as auxiliary to print in journals and monographs. Another was institutional. At the moment when anthropology in North America was being remade as a field for professional academics (gradually coming to exclude the amateur, the travel writer, the missionary, the dilettante folklorist), the study of gesture suited the needs of discipline formation; what that transformation needed were techniques that affirmed anthropologists' scientific authority, and gesture was one object around which that authority could be effectively fashioned. While a gesture may be ephemeral, its framing in terms of motor habit—implying recursion and causation—affirms the predictive strength of a scientific observation about social patterning. And while a gesture may be semantically ambiguous, difficult to translate into text, the fact that it is still amenable to visual observation and representation carries weight in an epistemological world where sight works as a trope for knowledge in general. For the same Boasians who were accruing institutional power, there was also a political, even moral, motivation for the ethnographic turn to gesture. In theories of linguistic evolution, gesture may have been located at the primordial origin point of communication (an idea that lurked in narratives of Keller's alphabetic education, as chapter 2 argued), but for historical particularists, it offered a unique site for inquiries about the body that could subvert the determinisms of racial heredity. Focusing on the axis of environmental influence and human response, the study of gesture could ideally show that the practices of the body take shape independently of the "types" of the body.

Yet these lines of research, privileging visual observation, could hardly develop in isolation from the ideas and expressions of racial and gendered visibility that have so profoundly defined the spaces in which American bodies move—in which, more precisely, the movement of bodies conditions their imagination as American.[11] Fitzgerald's work is preoccupied with that imagination and those movements. The first two sections of this chapter, setting his fiction against and within the history of gestural studies—with a particular focus, in the middle of the chapter, on an extensive ethnographic project carried out by David Efron, with Boas's guidance—will to some degree reflect the privilege accorded to the visual within that body of knowledge. But if gesture, in its ostensible silence as a visible communication channel, is often imagined by audists as "the next step away from the nothingness of nonspeech," the question of what's communicated in the tattoo's beating sound needs to be reckoned with as well.[12] Questions of aural and haptic experience will move back toward the center, then, as the chapter returns to that event and its more immediate narrative surround. This surround is shaped, as Fitzgerald's manuscript revisions help to show, by an idea of improvisation tied to Black musical traditions at a historical moment of heightened, and often reactionary, focus on the aesthetic and social dimensions of jazz. Compelling recent studies of jazz have opened up the interplay between embodiment and textuality in improvisatory performance.[13] To follow the tattoo in both its inscription and its ephemeral audibility is likewise to ask what it means to nest the textual within the gestural.

The premise here is not that Fitzgerald, that "jazz age" popularizer, held a particularly deep knowledge of jazz. Nor is it that he was clued in to professional anthropology's emergent paradigms. What John M. Oskison occasionally satirized as the vague chatter of these scientists, Fitzgerald largely ignored.[14] The ethnographers discussed in this chapter are much more likely to have known of his work than vice versa. But I'm not primarily after a claim of influence in either direction. What interests me here are the ways that lines of artistic and scientific research mesh around certain conceptual distinctions (gesture and tic, habit and style, movement and noise) and in particular historical formations ("Nordicist" and white-supremacist discourse in the context of immigration restrictions; the migratory spaces of New York in the interwar years). Moving through the spaces that link the empirical study of gesture and Fitzgerald's writing—in its descriptive subtleties, its normative anxieties, its compositional processes—can, too, help delineate a powerful contradiction. As ideas of *culture* and *gesture* become neatly reciprocal—each act of gesture given meaning by the semiotic system of a particular cultural location; each culture constituted historically through the contingent, iterated gestures of human practice—their overlap in the body also keeps them in restless proximity to the concepts to which they are so often opposed: race and nature; noise and tic.[15] Those proximities manifest themselves in everyday behavior, in the way, for instance, that the movement of a tapping foot or a writing hand can simultaneously index musical traditions, class precarities, and the forms of loss, continuity, and improvisation that open within the histories of diaspora.[16] The questions and methods of this chapter are thus caught by, caught up with, a line from Nick Carraway, *Gatsby*'s narrator, as he describes the first party he attends at his neighbor's house: "The groups change more swiftly, swell with new arrivals, dissolve and form in the same breath" (40).

One more compositional note as prelude. Later at that same party, just before a big-band performance, "there was the boom of a bass drum, and the voice of the orchestra leader rang out suddenly above the echolalia of the garden" (50). Fitzgerald wrote "echolalia" here only after the novel was published, annotating his own copy of the bound book. It's a postpublication revision that has been subsequently incorporated by many an edition. "Chatter" was what he had first written here (in the same galley revisions that introduced the "tatoo"), and "chatter" was still present in the first edition in 1925. This wording had neatly conveyed the social frivolity and skittering noise of small talk. "Echolalia," though, quietly reconfigures the relation between discourse and sound. If the prefix *echo-* invokes the idea of sonic repetition with a difference, the rest of the word, *-lalia*, then flirts with just such an echo in its near-doubled form. As if taking a cue from the musical "boom" of the percussion, it evokes the voice in song: *la, la*. But if "echolalia" aestheticizes the small talk at the party, it also suggests a concern with the loss of able-bodied control that recurs across Fitzgerald's work. It mingles, in other words—as does Gatsby's tattoo—the registers of the musical and the medical. The latter is where I'll start.

Walking on Paper

Take a very long sheet of cheap, light-colored wallpaper; lay it along the floor of a hallway; coat the soles of the patient's bare feet with a fine red dust; direct them to walk the length of the paper in one direction; and then outline, photograph, and measure the prints left behind. This was Georges Gilles de la Tourette's method in a study whose results were published in an 1886 essay, "Clinical and Physiological Studies of the Stride: The Stride in Nervous System Disorders, Studied with the Imprint Method (With 31 Figures)."[17] It isn't incidental that "31 Figures" makes it onto the title page of Gilles de la Tourette's pamphlet. The study is crowded with line drawings. Most of these thirty-one figures include the same graphic element. A vertical line divides the alternating footprints of each subject. This bold line is meant to fade into the discursive background, a representational device against which the marks of the human foot, and the patterning of their distribution—each stride's angle of strike, its lateral movement, its forward travel—can be more clearly compared (fig. 3.1). The form of the line is far from neutral, though, in a study of motor control. Between those wayward footprints, this form announces the true path of the scientific hand. Of course, these lines are obviously made with the prosthetic aid of a straight edge. What they indicate to the reader has less to do with any particular researcher's gestural ability than with the employment of a representational method that can be readily adopted by others, anonymous in their draftsmanship. These lines, in other words, help the study announce its reproducibility. The text itself clarifies this principle; Gilles de la Tourette insists that the ease of the study's design for future replication is just as important a contribution as any of its results.[18] His method can be yours, too.

The study clearly identifies its primary object: the afflicted stride. As the first line of the preface states, many nervous disorders affect how one walks, and simply observing these effects can sometimes suffice for a diagnosis of the disorder that causes them.[19] The purpose of the study's assessment of "la marche normale" (the normal stride) is to provide a controlled metric for the analysis of other, less "common" forms of walking—dragging feet, asymmetrical strides, and other locomotive deviations that might be taken as physiological and neurological symptoms (fig. 3.2). As historians of medicine have observed, the study is thus related to another (and now more familiar) of Gilles de la Tourette's reports, published the previous year as "A Study of a Nervous Affection Characterized by Motor Incoordination Accompanied by Echolalia and Coprolalia (Jumping Latah Myriachit)."[20] In this account of the *maladie des tics* that would later be renamed (in a truncation of his surname) Tourette syndrome, the physician describes several patients exhibiting involuntary physical behavior across a wide spectrum of behavioral genres, including the imitative vocal reflexes known as echolalia.

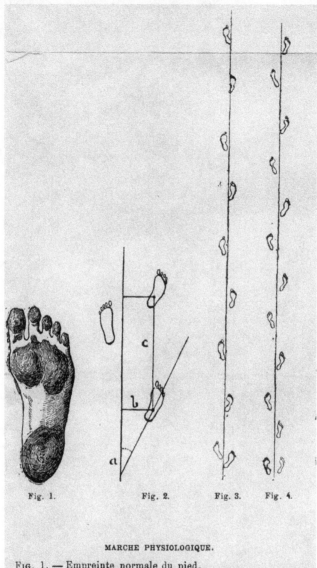

MARCHE PHYSIOLOGIQUE.

Fig. 1. — Empreinte normale du pied.
Fig. 2. — Schéma destiné à montrer comment sont obtenues
les valeurs des divers actes qui constituent le pas.
Fig. 3. — Marche normale, homme.
Fig. 4. — Marche normale, femme.

FIGURE 3.1 The "normal" stride. Partial view of "Genres de
Marches," foldout diagram in Gilles de la Tourette, *Études
cliniques et physiologiques sur la marche* (1886).

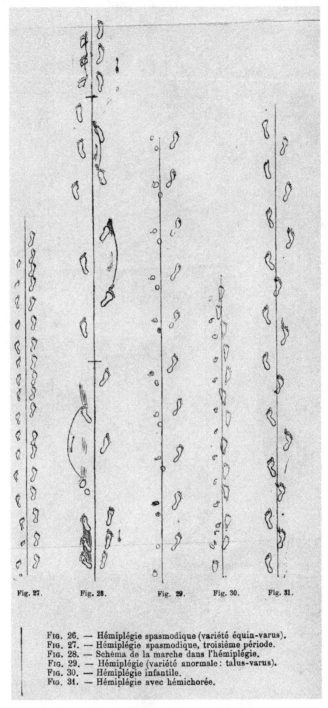

Fig. 27.   Fig. 28.   Fig. 29.   Fig. 30.   Fig. 31.

Fɪɢ. 26. — Hémiplégie spasmodique (variété équin-varus).
Fɪɢ. 27. — Hémiplégie spasmodique, troisième période.
Fɪɢ. 28. — Schéma de la marche dans l'hémiplégie.
Fɪɢ. 29. — Hémiplégie (variété anormale : talus-varus).
Fɪɢ. 30. — Hémiplégie infantile.
Fɪɢ. 31. — Hémiplégie avec hémichorée.

FIGURE 3.2 Afflicted strides. Partial view of "Genres de Marches," foldout diagram in Gilles de la Tourette, *Études cliniques et physiologiques sur la marche* (1886).

Yet if the focus of the walking study was, similarly, on the involuntary deviation, what was taken away from it in the American press were its revelations about the "normal" stride. In December 1886, a capsule summary of its findings was published in both *Scientific American* and *Science*, weeks before Franz Boas accepted a position as assistant editor at the latter, and was then reprinted in a number of American newspapers.[21] (This study followed a print trajectory quite similar, in other words, to that of J. C. Tarver's story about sound-blindness a year later, as I discussed in the introduction.) In subsequent years, news would occasionally travel to the United States of other research by Gilles de la Tourette—his invention of a "vibrating cap" meant to aid sleep in "this age of 'nerves' and overpressure," for instance, and his method for diagnosing the health of the brain by striking the head with a hammer and listening for any "peculiar sound" that might reveal "disease or fracture." Don't forget: "the skull of a child gives out a higher pitch than that of a man."[22] By contrast, reports of the walking study were on the dry side. They generally included no mention at all of "afflicted" strides, only a report of the gendered mean: "The average step of a man, according to Dr. Gilles de la Tourette, is twenty-five inches; of a woman, twenty inches. The reach with the right foot is usually a little longer than with the left."[23] Still, the news of the quantification of a behavior rarely noticed was sufficiently curious to circulate widely.

I've spent a few moments with the story of this study for three reasons that ought to be underscored: first, that its visual rhetoric not only compares the behaviors of observed subjects but also implicitly contrasts them with those of the observer; second, that it identifies as its chosen behavioral field the rhythms of feet making contact with the ground, some of these rhythms being four-on-the-floor, others syncopated; third, that as we move from the study itself into the paraphrased findings of its wider circulation, we find those syncopations and "abnormalities" churned into the report of an able body whose ostensible universality is not so much disrupted as managed in the math of gender. These three themes—the self-reflexivity of gestural representation, the feeling of having your feet on the ground, the blank and gendered subject—will braid through what follows.

Whether there exists a universal norm of the human stride remained an open question during Fitzgerald's lifetime. Marcel Mauss will emphasize in 1934 that "there exists an education in walking," but this was not a self-evident way of thinking about locomotion in the social-scientific discourse of the early twentieth century.[24] Edward Sapir, for example—linguist, poet, and Boas's student—wrote in 1921 that, unlike the "cultural" practice of speech, "walking is an inherent, biological function," an "instinctual" behavior that "varies only within circumscribed limits as we pass from individual to individual."[25]

Fitzgerald enters the conversation, in a fashion, six years earlier. Writing to his younger sister, Annabel, in 1915, he comments on her stride, urging her to walk with greater grace. "Look what stylish walk Eleanor and Grace and Betty have," Fitzgerald writes, "and what a homely walk Marie and Alice have. Just because the first three deliberately practised every where until now it's so natural to them that they cant be ungraceful—This is true about every gesture." The contents of the letter—or, better, memorandum—are outlined alphanumerically and under section headings including *"The General Subject of Conversation," "Poise: Carriage: Dancing: Expression,"* and *"Dress and Personality."* Managing to both burlesque and affirm the conventions of the etiquette manual, the note combines private cruelty and sociological ambition. "I noticed last Saturday that your gestures are awkward and so unnatural as to seem affected," Fitzgerald writes, but—while the situation is hopeless for himself and their mother—Annabel still has a chance.[26] Rather than reiterate a common story of alienated modernity in which the "natural" is lost in the past, the letter positions it as waiting ahead for the eager taker, potential, through imitation and repetition, in what William James described as the "second nature" of habit.[27] *"Practise anywhere,"* Fitzgerald counsels Annabel. *"Practise now."*[28]

In a short story published five years after the letter to his sister, "Bernice Bobs Her Hair" (1920), Fitzgerald loosely reworks the content of his advice into a plot. (At some later date, in organizing his papers, he will write "basis of Bernice" in the header of the correspondence.)[29] Self-presentation remains the predominant theme. Late in the story, he introduces a variation on it. The protagonist is dancing at a party. Another character, the college boy Warren McIntyre, "regarded her intently. She had that look that no woman, however histrionically proficient, can successfully counterfeit—she looked as if she were having a good time."[30] It is unclear whether it's the narrator or Warren who imagines this limit to physical "counterfeit." In either case, and regardless of whether Bernice is in fact having a good time, the judgment's premises should probably be read as false—at any rate, in contradiction with the author's advice to his sister that she should make her face "almost like a mask so that she'd have perfect control of any expression."[31]

In *Gatsby*, published another five years on from "Bernice," the titular character might seem to represent the achievement of such control. That smile: the soul of fellow feeling. When Gatsby was young, we learn late in the novel, he created a schedule of self-fashioning that seems to merge the letter to Annabel and Benjamin Franklin's autobiography: "Dumbbell exercise. . . . Practice elocution, poise. . . . Study needed inventions" (174). But as an adult, he's hardly the model of perfect self-presentation. In a novel preoccupied with money and falseness, the word "counterfeit" appears only once. As it does in "Bernice Bobs Her Hair," the word again refers to the performance of a "look," though in this case one that aims for the natural and misses. Nick Carraway has arranged for the reunion of Gatsby and Daisy in his living room. Aflutter at encountering his old flame, Gatsby "was reclining against the mantelpiece in a strained counterfeit of perfect ease, even boredom" (87). (Fitzgerald advised Annabel that affecting boredom is "hard to do . . . gracefully.")[32] An earlier version of this line, before Fitzgerald rewrote it, was more explicit about the mechanics of body language; "in [a] strained *posture that was evidently meant to suggest* perfect ease," it read.[33] While posture is often understood as asemantic (as opposed to the meaningful acts of gesture), it's long been argued that in fact the forms of posture are similarly ritualized and significant. Paradigmatic examples include military protocols for standing "at ease," which, despite the implication of laxity, involve specific forms determined in contrast with those of "attention."[34] This may seem a narrow field of examples for a generalized argument about the cultivation of postural (like gestural) forms, but of course in *Gatsby* military decorum informs both the gaze of the narrator— who desires a world "in uniform and at a sort of moral attention forever" (2) and who admires Jordan Baker's way of "throwing her body backward at the shoulders like a young cadet" (11)—and the habit of the character, Gatsby, who, like Nick, is a veteran of the Great War. While Daisy sits "frightened but graceful" in Nick's living room, Gatsby stands at such strained ease that he knocks over a clock with the back of his head (87).

For those whose physical composure tends to such awkwardness and evident counterfeit, Fitzgerald counsels Annabel in his letter—and if Gatsby at least has his winning smile, hers is "on one side which is *absolutely wrong*"—every opportunity to practice must be seized at a young age. "Cultivate deliberate physical grace," Fitzgerald exhorts his sister. "You'll never have it if you don't."[35] The threat derives from a developmental limit. Youth is imagined here as that peculiar condition in which habit has yet to calcify. The older brother mentions that it's already too late for himself and for their mother, as an additional incitement for his sister to get started; but of course, this is a losing game no matter when one begins to play it. Even if you start early enough, the etiquette manual that defined grace in one year may need revising for the next.[36] Then the gap between habit and convention will open beneath your feet.

Both the thesis that motor habits are cultivated (not inherited) and the question of how social environments of habit change over time are popular topics of anthropological discourse in the first half of the twentieth century. Consider an article by Flora Bailey—anthropologist, physical education teacher, and children's book author—on Diné (Navajo) motor habit. The piece organizes itself, "for ease of reference," around categories like those that structure Fitzgerald's letter to his sister, with motor habits "grouped arbitrarily under such headings as Personal Habits, Social Habits, Work Habits, and the like."[37] Bailey primarily operates in a descriptive mode but occasionally takes an evaluative turn. Among the broad range of physical behaviors she describes is the style of the Diné gait. "The effect is that of ease, relaxation, and control in the walk," she writes. "Especially in the women, aided no doubt by the graceful swing of a long, full skirt, it is most pleasing. It contrasts decidedly with the gait of the Pueblo woman which, viewed from the rear, is a waddle from side to side."[38]

The ethnographer's pleasure and distaste, her sense of the "graceful," echo Fitzgerald's evaluation of "stylish" and "homely" walks. What, though, does this echo illustrate? There are of course ineradicable differences between the young writer's interest in norms of Anglo teenage socialization and the social scientist's interest in variations of Indigenous motor habit. Observing a similarity between these accounts, taking them both as examples of a particular kind of settler gaze, might seem to confuse the matter of stylistic competency within a given social world with that of stylistic convention across such worlds. It might seem to confuse the performance of class with the embodiment of ethnicity. But in Fitzgerald's work, such confusion is a narrative engine. The aspirational premise that behavioral cultivation is the way to access a given social milieu has as its flip side the awareness of its porousness to other outsiders—an awareness that proves to be fertile soil both for the anxieties of whiteness and for the making of plot.

Take "Bernice Bobs Her Hair" again. When the popular Marjorie Harvey's cousin Bernice arrives in town, she's awkward and reticent. Warren describes her as "sorta dopeless," while Marjorie contemptuously suggests that Bernice's social hopelessness may be due to her "crazy Indian blood."[39] Her mother, Mrs. Harvey, dismisses the connection between blood quantum and socialization. But in the act that closes the story, Bernice herself seems to put such connections into play. Having gotten her own hair cut short earlier in the day, she sneaks up on the sleeping Marjorie with a pair of scissors, cuts off the blond braids that remind her of "a delicate painting of some Saxon princess," and skips town, shouting in the street, "Scalp the selfish thing!"[40] In the phrase, she resignifies her cousin's racist taxonomies in a mocking exhortation.[41] Her own rape-of-the-lock moment, meanwhile, comes across not as a sign of blood but as a sign that she is no longer dopeless, having cultivated the stylish norms of flapper impertinence that would make it perfectly natural to give your uptight cousin an unwanted bob.

That attitudinal transformation is represented less in an interior experience than in a ripple of the ocular musculature. When Bernice decides, earlier in the day, to get her own hair bobbed—an act that shocks the town's stylistic norms—her determination is hardly articulated (by herself or the narration) except as a "narrowing of the eyes."[42] Then, later at night, when the idea comes to turn the scissors on Marjorie, "an expression flashed into her eyes that a practiced character reader might have connected vaguely with the set look she had worn in the barber's chair—somehow a development of it. It was quite a new look for Bernice—and it carried consequences."[43] The mention of a "practiced character reader" may remind us in retrospect of Virginia Woolf's reflections, a few years later, on the necessity of "practis[ing] character reading," but there is an earlier point of reference.[44] Fitzgerald is probably alluding to L. A. Vaught's *Practical Character Reader* (1902), a popular study in phrenology (and the predecessor of the methods of grapho-analytical character reading I referenced in chapter 2). Vaught's thesis, supposedly founded on "at least fifty thousand careful examinations" and then confirmed by "more than a million observations," is that "individual character is a particular combination" of "elements that are unchangeable in their nature and the same the world over." For Vaught, in the assessment of personality types, "heads, faces, and bodies tell the story."[45] The turn to the exteriorized identity would surely seem to hold a certain appeal to Fitzgerald, but, in the chase of physiognomic "character reading," this appeal offers at best a "vague" account of what drives Bernice's looks. What's key about those looks is a formal variation not reducible to physiognomic structure. The "new look" that flashes into Bernice's eyes is "somehow a development" of her earlier expression, its novelty registering a profound shift in her affective relation to the racially exclusionary community of style in which (and then out of which) she finds herself. So while the scene of Bernice's rebellion gives an allusive nod to Vaught's physiognomy, the emphases of narrative report themselves suggest a stronger affinity with an ethnographic imagination like Bailey's.

With Boas's, too. The first citation in Bailey's study of motor habit points to a span of pages in Boas's *Primitive Art* (1927) that treats the relationship between gestural habit and aesthetic novelty—asking how a "new look" comes about—though with an emphasis on material and visual culture. Boas suggests that "fixed motor habits" can in fact shape the aesthetic principles of a "people" by placing certain functional limits on the design of implements of all kinds: "even if a variation should appeal to the eye, it will not be adopted if it should require a new adjustment of the hands," so that gestural convention sets conservative parameters for design in ways likely to ramify out into others kinds of patterning and artistic practice.[46] Yet the fixity of motor habits, as the generalized source of aesthetic conservatism, is not absolute for Boas. It is, instead, a function of development. In the book that Boas publishes the following year, *Anthropology and Modern Life* (1928)—a book intended to present his critique of racial thinking for a broad audience—he argues that while habits are relatively plastic in early youth, they then tend to become fixed in adulthood.[47] Making an analogy with the difficulty of learning a new language—"the demands of everyday life compel [the adult] to use speech, and the articulating organs follow the automatic fixed habits of [their] childhood"—Boas remarks that for grown people, "to change one's gait, to acquire a new style of handwriting, to change the play of the muscles of the face in response to emotion is a task that can never be accomplished satisfactorily."[48] This thought expands on a point in "On Alternating Sounds," where Boas, discussing children's linguistic development, had noted that in order to express certain sounds, "we learn by practice to place our organs in certain positions."[49] But in the 1928 text, the example of the "articulating organs," offered as a synecdoche for all physical movement, has less to do with orality than with nonverbal habit. More precisely, the former is brought under the umbrella of the latter. In the tissues of facial musculature, this synecdoche (speech as part of a gestural whole so expansive as to include the behavior of walking) enjoys a snug physical connection.

The difficulty of changing "the play of the muscles of the face" underscores the unrealistic hyperbole of Fitzgerald's advice to Annabel that she should strive for such fine-tuned control that her face becomes "almost like a mask." It also draws out something deeply odd about that simile. A mask is not generally understood to allow subtle modulations. Once applied, the look is set. The confusions of this trope carry a question, animating in its irresolution, that runs through the anthropology of gesture. On the one hand, the act of situating gesture within the sphere of discourse and learned convention works to liberate the interpretation of behavior from the determinisms of heredity. On the other, this view can entail a phenomenology of foreclosure and stasis, in the "conformity" produced by the strong influence of social environment. "Culturally acquired automatic habits," Boas writes in *Anthropology and Modern Life*, "are among the most important sources of conservatism."[50] Part of what his account of the gestural plasticity of early childhood attempts to do, rhetorically—and a similar move is inchoately at work in Fitzgerald's letter to Annabel—is to mediate this tension between plasticity and foreclosure, reproducing it not as a synchronic feature of culture but as a diachronic story of individuals.[51] Other moments in that developmental (and eventually, for all of us except Benjamin Button, degenerative) story work in like fashion. Boas writes that when adults do attempt, too late, to change long-held habits, these changes are generally imperfect, and they do not last forever: "unwonted movements reappear when, due to disease, the control of the nervous systems breaks down."[52] The mask will slip. The foot will drag. Practice anywhere. Practice now.

Stepping away from Fitzgerald's fiction, the next section will focus on one major ethnographic study of the cultural transmission of "automatic habits." The ethnographic emphasis on localized meaning and convention diverges profoundly, of course, from the medicalized analysis of impaired strides in Gilles de la Tourette's research, a divergence nameable in the distinction between gesture and tic. But two factors compel me to keep these lines of thought in conversation. One is the tenuousness of the gesture-tic distinction. The other is that these radically different approaches to the study of kinetic behavior share an unnamed methodological recursion: they not only represent but also involve the movements of the body, in, for instance, the graphic material presented as a key means of empirical grounding in the sensory worlds of everyday life. Fitzgerald's work may not involve such illustrations, but it is informed by this recursion, in his sense of motor habit as the opposite and source of the music of fiction.

Assimilation, Illustration, Notation

Frank Thone, staff writer for the *Science News Letter*, opens an article in the periodical's September 5, 1936, issue with a question: "Do you talk with your hands?"[53] The answer to Thone's question is yes, you do, and more than you think. The "you" here is not the generic second person, and the rhetorical upshot of this opening move is not the generalized claim that one talks with one's hands. It is rather that the particular reader whom Thone more than once invokes, the "typical average American," is guilty of the same kinds of gesticulation that they tend to associate with "foreigners": Americans "talk with their hands a good deal more than they realize." Yet "we"— *you* becoming *they* and also *we*—"have become so used to our gestures that they 'don't count,'" which leads to a more fundamental, if implicit, point about the relationship between gesture and speech. The former does not only serve as an instrument that supports the latter; these modes are also structurally analogous. Gestures, Thone writes, "fit into the pattern of our lives as thoroughly as English speech fits in, or the habit of saying 'yeah' or 'uh-huh' instead of 'yes.'"[54] Like vernacular speech, gestural habits take shape independently of reflection.[55]

The occasion for this article is an ongoing ethnographic study, which Thone describes, of New York City immigrants' gestural habits. The study is conducted by David Efron (who authored the text of the eventual book publication, which was also his doctoral dissertation) and Stuyvesant Van Veen (who helped Efron with fieldwork and provided illustrations), under Boas's supervision.[56] Efron's overarching hypothesis is the primacy of "environmental" (historical and social) over racial contexts in shaping gestural behavior. He develops this claim through both qualitative and quantitative accounts of the differences between the habits of "traditional" and "assimilated" immigrant groups in New York City—specifically, "Eastern Jews" ("Eastern" meaning eastern European, with the study focusing on immigrants from Poland and Lithuania) and "Southern Italians" (from Naples and Sicily). Efron's analysis of the data reveals that the behaviors of both of the assimilated groups within these ethnicities "(a) *appear to differ greatly from their respective traditional groups*, and (b) *appear to resemble each other*." Together, these patterns support the conclusion that "that gestural behavior, or the absence of it is, to some extent at least, conditioned by factors of a socio-psychological nature" rather than "by biological descent."[57] In the text's foreword, Boas frames the study as supporting the bolder claim that in "sub-divisions of the White race, the genetic element may be ruled out entirely or almost entirely."[58]

Efron imagined his work within a large intellectual-historical horizon. His research involved generating an enormous, unalphabetized, working bibliography of gesture-related writing. The 1934 essay in which Mauss describes the acculturation of the stride features as the first entry in the bibliography, but Efron's list is far from exclusively social-scientific; it includes numerous philosophical and literary works, from Pope's *Dunciad* to Keller's

Story of My Life (with an annotation for the latter entry that specifies the pages referring to the manual alphabet).[59] By the time Efron publishes the study as *Gesture and Environment* in 1941, this wide-ranging reading has turned toward a polemically specific intervention, contradicting Nazi theories of physical expression. Efron, from an Argentinian Jewish family, was as engaged in political science as in anthropology, securing a teaching position at Sarah Lawrence in 1936. In the late 1930s, while completing the gesture study, he made headlines more than once by arguing at political conventions that Axis powers had begun to secure footholds in South America and that the time for pacifism was over.[60] At Vassar in August 1938 (the same year that Frances "Scottie" Fitzgerald, the author's daughter, arrived at the college), Efron joined the World Youth Congress and "organized national anti-fascist committees from each Latin American nation."[61] Also in attendance there, as a rare photograph of Efron reveals, was his sister, Paloma Efron, a Bueno Aires–based jazz singer and, later, media personality and producer (fig. 3.3). In the late 1930s, she studied ethnomusicology at Columbia (working with Boas's colleagues) and then at Tuskegee; as a performer, she used the nickname "Blackie," given to her in 1934 by the listeners of a Buenos Aires radio station after a particularly impressive on-air performance of "Stormy Weather."[62] The photograph at Vassar shows her brother, the ethnographer, in relaxed pose, his right elbow over the back of an auditorium bench, a newspaper folded against his leg, eyes brightly attentive to the Italian delegate as he listens to live linguistic interpretation through headphones whose wiring can be seen snaking along the floor.[63]

The escalation of the war seems to have played a part in the sense of urgency that Boas felt about publication. He wrote to Van Veen in April 1939, "it is absolutely essential that I get the gesture book completed now." By "I," he meant "you," summoning Van Veen and Efron to his office.[64] When *Gesture and Environment* is indeed completed and published in 1941, the data about "Americanization" emphasized in Boas's conversation with Thone five years earlier remains the primary empirical contribution of the book. But this material is now framed by an extended introduction in which Efron carefully skewers the biological vitalism of "spiritualist-racist" arguments for Nordic superiority. "All these writers"—Hans Günther, Fritz Lenz, L. F. Clauss, and other Third Reich scientists—seem, Efron writes, to have no regard, in their comments on physiology and habit, for "the elementary question of empirical evidence" (9). Even the styles in which these Nordicist arguments are developed serve, according to Efron, as evidence against their theses, in that their metaphorical excesses—musings about "elliptical

FIGURE 3.3 From left: José Stuera, Paloma Efron, Juan Marinello, and David Efron. World Youth Congress at Vassar College, August 18, 1938. Photograph: Acme Newspictures.

souls" and the "racial" essences of household objects—contradict a sense of "Teutonic" discipline and restraint. "One is bound to wonder whether these authors might not have been a bit more convincing," Efron writes drily (a dryness that makes a point, by stylistic contrast) "had they managed to remain faithful to the 'racial taciturnity' which their fancy has ascribed to the ethnic group to which they happen to belong" (15).

However frustrating to the senior anthropologist, the interval between fieldwork and publication enabled the ordering and analysis of an immense amount of documentation (if not quite up to Vaught's claim of a million-plus observations). Efron and Van Veen had developed a labor-intensive and technically inventive process involving "(1) direct observation of gestural behavior in natural situations, (2) sketches drawn from life . . . , (3) rough counting [of number of gestural unit-motions over time], (4) motion pictures

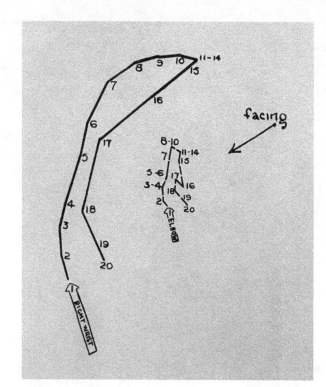

FIGURE 3.4
A gesture broken
down. Illustration
by Stuyvesant Van
Veen. David Efron,
*Gesture and
Environment* (1941),
142, fig. 12.

studied by (a) observations and judgments of naive observers, and (b) graphs
and charts, together with measurements and tabulations of the same" (41).[65]
The "measurements and tabulations" of these filmed gestures were generated by moving frame by frame through recordings of a given movement,
transferring the key points of the gesturing limb onto chart paper, iterating
the same process for multiple recordings of the same genre of gesture, and
then (adjusting data for relative size and position, to make measurements
commensurable) producing an aggregate representation (44) (fig. 3.4).

While the analysis of filmed gestures allowed Efron and Van Veen to develop quantitative comparisons of motion—the distance of elbow from trunk,
the range and speed of the hand's movement—they also arrived at qualitative
claims about group variation in gestural function. These differences were, in
conformity with the study's hypothesis, found to be more pronounced
in less assimilated populations. The most fundamental such distinction had
to do with how "traditional" Italians and "ghetto" Jews construct relations
between speech and gesture. The former, Efron claims, tended to use gestures

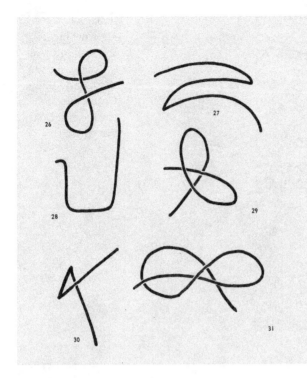

FIGURE 3.5
Original caption: "Ghetto Jews: logico-topographical gestures (gestures = syllogisms)." Illustrations by Stuyvesant Van Veen. David Efron, *Gesture and Environment* (1941), 145, figs. 26–31.

quasi-pictorially, sketching iconic representations—sometimes pantomimic—of the content of their speech. The latter more often used a kind of gesture reflecting the structure of an argument as it proceeds from one idea to the next. In an analogy with visual technologies, Efron refers to "the gestural 'slides' of the Italian versus the gestural 'maps' of the Jew": "the former is more likely to give an *illustration*," while "the latter is more apt to give a gestural *notation* of the logical features of discourse" (101).[66]

Van Veen's representations of gestural "notation," of the metadiscursive gestures associated with conversation among nonassimilated Jewish people, include the study's most stylized formal reductions of behavior (fig. 3.5). As if mimetic of the abstractions of these gestures' content, they approach the graphic register of mathematical notation, even while creating a methodological contrast with the calculations of the film analysis. This register carries through in the caption of one such diagram: "gestures = syllogisms." But the diagram's visual forms—creating their own kind of contrast with the punctuated line segments of the aggregated gesture charts—also equally seem to suggest the flowing line of a knot diagram. At points of intersection, the lines are drawn with gaps to indicate which part of the loop is in the foreground. It's as if, for each gesture, a thread has been let down onto the page and carefully looped back over itself, so as to represent spatial movement in a way that maintains temporal linearity.[67] If one actually tries to follow these threads from one end to another, though, this effect breaks down. The lines in the illustrations numbered 29 and 31 loop both over and then *under* themselves. The gaps in these forms have less to do with the space-time of the gestures than with the aesthetics of the illustrator.

"Illustration" and "notation" may have presented themselves as apt classifications of gestural genres because they also named aspects of the study's own method. In addition to working with the charting and measurement of filmed gestures, Van Veen was making sketches in the "field" (especially but not only in Manhattan's Jewish and Italian neighborhoods). He was increasingly conducting interviews and jotting down his own speculations, supplementing illustration with notation. In the publication, Efron sometimes quotes directly from Van Veen's notes, often setting them apart from the main text as block quotes. While grounding the research in street-level practice (as opposed to the armchair ethnology critiqued in Efron's introduction), the artist's notes also allow the study to include, without staking its scientific authority on, more speculative hypotheses. Sometimes when quoting one of Van Veen's assertions, Efron frames it with an affirmation or a disagreement; sometimes he leaves it without comment. In one of the longer notes that Efron quotes, Van Veen writes that "Americanized" Jewish people tend to have a greater "expansiveness" of gesture than their recently arrived or more enclaved kin, and he attributes the difference to increased "social freedom": "The ghetto Jew . . . carries with him even into this country a sense of oppression and inhibition borne through centuries, and his physical aspect and bodily deportment betray this. The Americanized Eastern Jew, growing up in relative freedom, has a sense of well-being and expansiveness, which manifests itself in a broad, free gesticulation" (110). Efron, neither confirming nor denying Van Veen's reflections, does not make such a strong claim about the sources of gestural freedom.

Neither does Boas, when, the year after the book was published, he addressed a parallel question in the context of a presentation on Kwakwa̱ka̱'wakw (Kwakiutl) dance, for a study of which he had also hired Van Veen to make illustrations. The context of his talk was a series of seminars hosted by his daughter, Franziska Boas, the anthropologist, dancer, and percussionist, among other roles in a varied career. She would later publish a volume of the presentations and ensuing discussions. In the discussion following Boas's talk, an audience member, their name unrecorded in the published transcript, asks the elder Boas about "the relation of ordinary movement in everyday activity to the movements of the dance." Remarking that it is "a very difficult question," Boas begins with common ground: "everyone will agree that when you see an Indian of one tribe walk, you realize it is an entirely different gait from that of another." Then, while disclaiming that he "cannot prove it," Boas affirms the questioner's intuition that differences in style of dance probably "have to do also with the general habit of walking." If Boas's comments echo Flora Bailey, whose article was published in *American Anthropologist* the same year, the next anonymous questioner comes even closer, noting that "the Navajo behave in a manner contrasting to the Pueblo" and that the difference involves a tendency toward "relaxation." This questioner is interested in the effects of canoe handling on general motor habit and therefore on dance forms, and Boas again offers a formal distinction but hedges his bets about the source of variation. "Some people have free gesture-motions and others have restricted gestures, and these are generally determined by social environment," he answers, "but the actual reason is very difficult to determine."[68] The expressive movements of the dancing body both tempt and refuse a causal account of aesthetic influence.

When Van Veen, quoted in *Gesture and Environment*, makes the kind of claim about causation that Boas won't—suggesting that what he observes as gestural freedom among Jewish Americans is an index of their increased social freedom—Efron, without engaging with the substance of that claim, does point the reader to two sketches in the book's appendix that illustrate the formal variation at issue (110). One depicts a "ghetto Jew" exhibiting "confined gestural radius" (140), the other an "Americanized Jew." "Note the unrestricted manner," per the caption, "the free broad gesture, and complete absence of Jewish tempo" (150)—the latter a reference to observations of comparatively rapid gestural repetitions. There's another asymmetry between the two figures, though, not in the gestures depicted but in the logic of depiction: while the first subject is shown from the front with certain conventional markers of ethnic presentation visible (beard, hat), that of the "assimilated" subject is depicted from over the shoulder, face hidden from view. Many of Van Veen's figurative sketches (that is, those that include representations of flesh and clothing in addition to the abstracted lines of kinetic action) blank out facial features even when the subject is viewed from the front, as if to imply that these elements are irrelevant to the depiction of the gesture. Faces are blanked out slightly more often for assimilated subjects, although this is not perfectly consistent. The most extreme

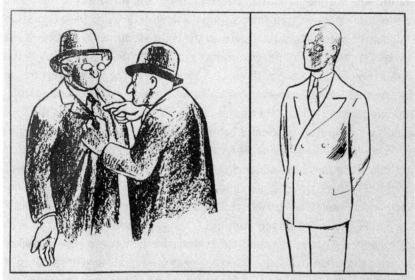

CONTRASTS

At the left you see "buttonholing," a characteristically Jewish gesture though by no means confined to that race. Note the slumped shoulders of the argumentative one. At the right, 100 per cent American? Surely. Yet this upstanding, gestureless gentlemen is also a Jew. His family, of German origin, have lived in the South for several generations.

FIGURE 3.6 Illustrations by Stuyvesant Van Veen, as captioned in the *Science News Letter*. Frank Thone, "Do You Talk with Your Hands?" (1936), 154.

instances of this method's application carry the eerie menace of "The Blank," aka Frank "Faceless" Redrum, the cheese-cloth-wearing villain introduced to Chester Gould's *Dick Tracy* comic strip in 1937.[69]

A subtler instance, but one that reflects consistent elements of Van Veen's style—and that will begin to bring us back toward Fitzgerald—can be found in a diptych of two illustrations included in Thone's 1936 article for the *Science News Letter* (fig. 3.6). On the left side of the figure, "traditional" subjects gesticulate in conversation. The image in this panel is reproduced in both book versions of the study and is even singled out to be embossed, in a slightly modified version, on the front cover of *Gesture and Environment*. In the right-hand panel, a sketch that does not appear in Efron's book, an "assimilated" subject does nothing but stand—or stand *against,* per its caption heading: "CONTRASTS," from *con-trare,* "standing against."

The juxtaposition across the two panels aims to visualize the overarching thesis of environmental influence.[70] Yet it can only make this point with the help of the caption, explaining that both the "characteristically Jewish gesture" of "buttonholing" depicted on the left and the stock-straight pose seen on the right are performed by men of Jewish descent. In the question and answer posed about the figure on the right—"100 per cent American? Surely. Yet this upstanding, gestureless gentlemen [*sic*] is also a Jew"—the caption repeats the move with which Thone opened the essay, overturning the assumed reader's expectations about the "typical average American."[71] But note that the traditional figures at left are in dialogue, while the "upstanding, gestureless gentlemen" stands—as far as the viewer knows, and typo notwithstanding—alone. For a more commensurable contrast, one that minimized the variables influencing the data, it would seem that the viewer should have been offered a second pair of interlocutors. Why depict the "100 per cent American" in isolation? Does assimilation entail estrangement? More likely, for the diptych's designer, it signals individuation and self-sufficiency: the use of "upstanding" to describe the figure's posture makes the same play that, in *Gatsby*, Nick Carraway does in his idea of standing at "moral attention," associating moral with spinal rectitude (even if the language of US military posture might call this "ease" instead of attention).[72]

This raises another question, though. Why is the face of this upstanding American cast in shadow? Given the way that the rest of his body is shaded, minimally as it is, the dark patch of line shading across his face seems gratuitous. Taken together with the only other significant shadow, on his left torso (there are also hints of shading along his arms and where jacket falls against pants), it's hard to imagine a consistent light source here. That wouldn't be so strange in a photorealist representation of a scene with natural lighting. Shadows fall "inconsistently" all the time. But in the cartoonish, outline-dominant visual style of the drawing on the right, the facial shadow seems out of place. And it's surprisingly textural—roughly cross-hatched, as opposed to the clean contour lines of the large shadow on the side of the suit jacket.

By contrast to this obscured face, consider the faces of the "traditional" Jewish figures on the left. Even as the inky shadows of their coats and the bodies beneath them dissolve into the blank of the lower frame (indeed, they are separated by a gap of white space) and even as their eyes are hidden by angle and eyewear, Van Veen takes care to outline the racial stereotype of what Nick, in the antisemitic characterization of Meyer Wolfshiem, calls the "expressive nose" (*Gatsby*, 70). In the drawing, if noses are expressive, what they express is heredity. Linguistic expression, meanwhile, is not tied to mouths (unnecessary, left blank) but to hands. In the right panel, both face and hands, imagined in the logic of the illustration as the respective sites of "race" and "culture," are secreted away—in a version of the racial "color-blindness" that might ostensibly be produced by the blankness of assimilated figures' faces in other sketches, except that, in this case, that blankness has a rough graphic texture. It's as if the signs of heredity need to be hidden in shadow in order for this person to pass, with his gestural practice or his lack of it, as the "typical average American" and so to stand synecdochically for a whole category of blank "gentlemen."[73] Yet the particular ethnic designation in the caption matters here, too, in that, in the late nineteenth- and early twentieth-century United States, the category of Jewishness had come to function as "a racial tabula rasa" accepting various inscriptions of both color ("white," "black") and racial type ("Semitic," "Oriental," "European").[74] The reveal of this blank American's ethnic origins thus derives its rhetorical impact from the way that, in the period, Jewishness sits in a position of both proximity and alterity to whiteness, in the emergent sense that whiteness begins to hold as a kind of European consanguinity.[75]

The diptych gives a crosshatch of interwar racial inscriptions and projections, both in its rhetorical effects and in its graphic construction. Its structure—in which one side, dark with ink, frames the ethnically marked, and the other, left nearly white, the unmarked—mirrors the WHITE/COLORED diptych of the Jim Crow sign, even as the illustration's discursive content negates the essentialist premises of segregation.[76] The misplaced shadow on the figure on the right reverses that dynamic, though. Here, the Boasian critique of racial essentialism is tested by a visual logic that implies a viewer unable to think beyond phenotype (beyond, here, "sub-divisions of the White race"): only such a viewer would require the masking of the face in order to notice the difference in pose. The premise of the image's argument is that behavioral difference can only become visible when heredity is veiled, that color-blindness is only possible when it's literal. The shadow, meant to situate the figure in the unmarked position of a "typical average American," also reiterates his racialization.[77] His face is obscured in two senses: hidden and marked.[78]

In this way, Van Veen's assimilated man begins to take on the shape of Jay Gatsby, the character who initially impresses Nick, from a silent distance, by his "leisurely movements and the secure position of his feet" (*Gatsby*, 21) but who is rendered with such obscurity that "the reader's eyes can never quite focus upon him"—as editor Max Perkins wrote in November 1924 to the author.[79] In one section of Fitzgerald's manuscript, heavily revised before publication, what Perkins anticipates as a problem for the novel's reader had already been introduced as a problem for its characters. Nick, seeing Gatsby's face in despair, realizes he "can't describe . . . what he was intrinsically 'like'"; Tom insults Gatsby as "*nothing* . . . like a shadow"; and Gatsby himself projects the empty outline of his own persona into space: "his eyes were wide open and fixed as though apon [*sic*] an unoccupied human shape that was concievably [*sic*] his own shape."[80] It is no accident that this all occurs in a draft of the scene of confrontation at the Plaza Hotel, where the question of Gatsby's uneasy relation to the category of the "American"—a question bound up, as other scholars have suggested, with the sense that his social mobility may depend on an act of racial passing—comes to a head.[81] Just as the faces in Efron's gesture study must, it seems, be blanked out to accommodate ethnicity and "Americanization" at the same time, here perception bends around Gatsby's likeness.

While Fitzgerald agreed with Perkins's assessment of the problem of picturing Gatsby, he didn't solve it by sketching in the details of the character's face. But he did redirect the working of perception in the Plaza Hotel scene in ways that I will address in the next section, turning to the tattoo more directly. Studies of the racial imaginaries that jostle in Fitzgerald's fiction have sometimes commented on one of the very few other references that he makes, across his career, to a rhythmic "tattoo." This other tattoo appears in the manuscript of his last novel, *The Love of the Last Tycoon* (published posthumously in 1941). The film studio executive Monroe Stahr, in a moment of searching revelation, begins to imagine forms of "new music" that "would come in some such guise as the auto-horns from the Technicolor boulevards below or be barely audible, a tattoo on the muffled drum of the moon."[82] Occurring just after the film producer's eye-opening conversation about the vacuity of mass culture with a man he meets on the beach, Stahr's new attunement has been read as a sign of Fitzgerald's increasing openness to Black aesthetic traditions—and also as a demonstration of his idea of whiteness as an assimilatory horizon that extends to certain forms of Jewishness but not others.[83] It is no surprise that the moment resounds in ambivalence: urban noise and environmental hum; hyperreal electric light and celestial glow; an art said to intrude on the senses in false "guise" and to recede, "barely audible," to the threshold of perception. What draws my attention more particularly to the earlier novel, though, to *Gatsby*, is the way that the racial fantasies that eddy around the title character and all his guises take shape within the feedback produced by the gesture of notating gesture. The connection of that feedback to regimes of ethnological visibility is all but audible in Van Veen's crosshatching—so, too, in the writing of a foot drumming restlessly on the floor in a novel that is a study both of and in motion.

Tic Description

Sweaty and suspicious at the Plaza, Tom has begun to prod his rival by asking about Gatsby's constant use of the idiom "old sport" (*Gatsby*, 127). The implication is that Gatsby is trying to pass counterfeit linguistic coin, flashing some vague, chummy sign of Anglo elevation. But the confrontation doesn't yet escalate. Soon the sounds of a wedding drift up from downstairs in the lobby to the room they have taken for the afternoon. This brings conversation to "Blocks" Biloxi, who, as Jordan Baker reminds everybody, collapsed in the heat at the Buchanans' wedding. It only takes a few lines of dialogue to bring out the fact that he was an impostor. Jordan recalls that Biloxi had claimed to go to college with Tom and Nick:

> "He told me he was president of your class at Yale."
> Tom and I looked at each other blankly.
> "Biloxi?"
> "First place we didn't have any president——"
> Gatsby's foot beat a short, restless tattoo and Tom eyed him suddenly. (129)

The tattoo draws Tom's surveilling attention, and he now takes up in full earnest the effort to defame (that is, in another sense, to "tattoo") Gatsby.[84] The "blank" look that he and Nick give each other converts to a sharp eye. Tom begins by sarcastically comparing Gatsby's academic career to Biloxi's: "You must have gone [to Oxford] about the time Biloxi went to New Haven." When Gatsby explains that he spent a semester at Oxford through a GI program, Nick's faith in him is renewed (130). But Tom continues to press, and in the end, even Gatsby acknowledges that Tom made him look like a "cheap sharper" (152).

At the same time that Fitzgerald was beginning to develop *Gatsby*, he published a short story, "Dice, Brassknuckles & Guitar" (1923), that anticipates the novel's interests in the limits of self-fashioning.[85] Jim Powell, a young white man from Tarleton, Georgia, and Hugo, an adolescent Black "body-servant" whom Jim claims to have raised, drive to the New York area in a beat-up car to try their luck for the summer. When their initial plans for a taxi service fail, they open a school that trains well-to-do New Jersey teenagers in modern socializing: shooting dice, playing guitar, speaking in dialect, and fending off aggressive dates with "defensive brassknuckles, débutante's size." Students receive their "Bachelor of Jazz" degree.[86] The story of the school and its quick demise involves the class functions both of racial masquerade—whose function is complex here in the way that Hugo seems both to exemplify and to teach minstrelsy—and of segregation; the school is eventually shut down, with parents in a panic about the biracial space.

Much of this is already in play, near the beginning of the story, in an interaction between Jim and Amanthis Powell:

> Jim began to tap his foot rhythmically on the porch and in a moment Amanthis discovered that she was unconsciously doing the same thing.
> "Stop!" she commanded, "Don't make me do that."
> He looked down at his foot.
> "Excuse me," he said humbly. "I don't know—it's just something I do."[87]

Like the "typical average American" that Frank Thone imagined in the *Science News Letter*, Jim's body is more active than he realizes; like saying "'uh-huh' instead of 'yes,'" tapping his foot is just something he does, part of the pattern of his life. Still, this behavior resists the functional categorization in which Efron's ethnographic study of gesture is invested. Perhaps Jim, whose business card designates him as a "Jazz Master," is tapping out a beat.[88] But perhaps this foot tapping—compulsive, viral—is, instead, a momentary expression of Jim's precarious class position or his social uncertainty, both of which the story ties loosely to his regional dislocation and his traversal of racialized space.

Fitzgerald refers to the same action again in the 1931 essay "Echoes of the Jazz Age," as he looks back in a sociological register at the shifting mood of the previous decade. Here, foot-tapping does not appear as behavior but as simile: "By 1927 a widespread neurosis began to be evident, faintly signalled, like a nervous beating of the feet, by the popularity of cross-word puzzles."[89] The idea of the "signal" works in an unusual way here. What's "faintly signalled" in this line is something inadvertently revealed, whereas, more often, to signal is to communicate with intention, and as a noun, "signal" refers to what's meant to get transmitted despite any other informational noise in the channel. Fitzgerald's marking of the feet's beating as "nervous" calls up a different opposition, not *signal versus noise* but *signal versus symptom*.

In the late twentieth-century discourse around "thick description"—a common way of identifying the shared investment of literary criticism and ethnography in attending to the multiple, simultaneously operant levels of meaning that pertain to any given utterance or act—the same opposition, signal versus symptom, was influentially theorized in the distinction between a wink and an eye twitch. These forms of eyelid contraction are, at least in thought experiment, potentially indistinguishable from each other on the basis of their measurable physical qualities (on the basis, that is, of a "thin" description)—but they are crucially different in that only one of them means to signal something to an audience.[90] Of course, it's one thing to define the wink as a genre and quite another to identify one in the field. The perspectival effects of narrative fiction introduce further complications, including the way that a discursive report can itself, in the noise of its own signals, track the experience of observational uncertainty.

Let me concretize this point in an example from *Gatsby*. Early in the novel, we are given two eyelid contractions. They are minor notes in a well-known passage. When Nick goes to the Buchanans' for lunch early in the summer, Tom turns conversation to his recent reading, a book titled *The Rise of the Colored Empires*.

> "This fellow has worked out the whole thing. It's up to us, who are the dominant race, to watch out or these other races will have control of things."
>
> "We've got to beat them down," whispered Daisy, winking ferociously toward the fervent sun.
>
> "You ought to live in California——" began Miss Baker but Tom interrupted her by shifting heavily in his chair.
>
> "This idea is that we're Nordics. I am and you are and you are and——" After an infinitesimal hesitation he included Daisy with a slight nod and she winked at me again, "——and we've produced all the things that go to make civilization—oh, science and art and all that." (13–14)

As many scholars have noted, in Tom's reading, Fitzgerald alludes to another book released by his own publishing house, Lothrop Stoddard's *The Rising Tide of Color against White World-Supremacy* (1920). The sentence that Tom doesn't let Jordan finish ("You ought to live in California——") seems about to extend this connection in a specific direction: Stoddard's work was often invoked in discussions of the 1924 Johnson-Reed Immigration Act—legislation, Boas would write, that "discriminate[s] . . . against all people that are not considered as representatives of the 'Nordic' type."[91] Stoddard had argued that the need "for rigid Oriental exclusion is nowhere better exemplified than by the alarm felt to-day in California by the extraordinarily high birth-rate of its Japanese residents."[92] While we have a sense of where Tom stands, it is less clear where Jordan is headed—what kind of rhetorical inflection her comment is moving toward—and the immediate cause of this obscurity is simple: Tom moves his body. When he cuts off Jordan midsentence simply "by" (not, for instance, *while*) shifting in his chair, as when the sound of Gatsby's tapping foot interrupts the conversation in the Plaza, the text so emphasizes the discursive effects of gesture as to strain verisimilitude.[93] The conversation is as physical as verbal. What still needs attention in this scene, then, is how it asks us to think across scales of embodied social power: from the commonplaces of white-supremacist historiography to the small gestural cues—including those that the narration doesn't name, as in the physical indications that Tom must make when he says, "and you are and you are and . . ."—that facilitate and subvert those ideas' circulation.

This is where Daisy's two eyelid contractions come in. Each is labeled as a wink, rather than as, say, a blink or a twitch. First Daisy is "winking ferociously toward the fervent sun," and then she "winked at [Nick] again." From the start, these winks carry the potential of irony or flirtation. But it isn't clear that Nick takes the first one as a signal meant for his reception until his description of the second. Daisy may still be winking *toward* the sun but is now also winking *at* Nick (and, as "again" retroactively indicates, has been from the start). The first wink's intentionality remains indeterminate until, with the second, Nick's narration thickens. But it also thins, stylistically. The first wink was more lushly described ("ferociously . . . fervent"). Perhaps the increased formal density itself informs us about Nick's perceptual experience: uncertainty calls for heightened attention. As long as the wink's status as signal or symptom, gesture or tic, remains unknown, Daisy risks the unfortunate fate of those who have had one thing taken for another, and Nick risks missing the point.[94]

Yet those risks help the winks work. While Jordan's interjection gets barreled over, Daisy's winks make it across the room. They undercut Tom's Nordicist anthropology without drawing direct reaction. For Daisy, practiced in nonchalance, the motivation here may just be ridicule. If her whisper of racist violence is meant to ironically mock Tom's intelligence, it seems to be an easy joke for her to make.[95] The point I'm developing has less to do with character, though, than with the interplay of dialogue and narration.

As one voice—transcribed in direct discourse—attempts to inscribe an anthropological theory in the flesh of its auditors, that theory's force is also diverted by their bodies' pluralistic capacities and opacities, a diversion that is implicit in the quirks of a narrator's shifting attention.

Gatsby is not in the room for this scene. But when, a few chapters later, we get a description of his way of moving, the blur of symptom and signal that's in the background of Daisy's winks moves into the foreground. Gatsby carries himself "with that resourcefulness of movement that is so peculiarly American," which Nick traces to the freedoms of American youth and to "the formless grace of our nervous, sporadic games. This quality was continually breaking through [Gatsby's] punctilious manner in the shape of restlessness. He was never quite still; there was always a tapping foot somewhere or the impatient opening and closing of a hand" (*Gatsby*, 64). "A tapping foot *somewhere*"? This is restlessness as dismemberment—yet also as "resourcefulness," as a ludic style that's useful for living. Disorder is revalued here as an exceptional national aesthetic. In this, Fitzgerald echoes the neurologist George Beard's account (in an 1881 study known to Gilles de la Tourette) of the "pre-eminent and peculiar" quality of nervous behavior in the United States: "there are special expressions of this nervousness that are found here only; and the relative quantity of nervousness and of nervous diseases that spring out of nervousness, are far greater here than in any other nation of history, and it has a special quality."[96]

Gatsby's "peculiarly American" style, superimposing aestheticized gesture and pathologized tic, finds its special quality in the formal synthesis of continuity and punctuation. Notice how Gatsby's physical style is "*continually breaking through* his punctilious manner"; and the combination of constancy and interruption in the phrase "never quite still"; and the curious reference to "the shape of restlessness," whereas the restless would seem to be that which doesn't settle into a given shape. Evoking the structure of the cinematic moving image, this tension reverberates throughout *Gatsby*. It's there in the phrase "constant flicker," an oxymoron that Fitzgerald likes enough to use twice (57, 69). It's there in the "endless drill" of people who come to Gatsby's house in the end and in the "relentless beating heat" that makes Nick sweat (164, 124). It's there in the "intermittent beads" of said sweat, an intermittence that soon reappears in the "intermittent cries of 'Yea—ea—ea'" heard in the Plaza Hotel moments before Gatsby taps his foot (126, 128).[97] And it's there in the structure of that cry, "yea—ea—ea" instead of yes, expressing even in its internal punctuation the dialectic of duration and fracture to which Fitzgerald keeps looping back.[98]

This dialectic features even in the novel's most romantic description of Gatsby's subjectivity. Let me put it into print one more time: "If personality is an unbroken series of successful gestures, then there was something gorgeous about him, some heightened sensitivity to the promises of life, as if he were related to one of those intricate machines that register earthquakes ten thousand miles away" (2).[99] The line's sweeping affect may obscure how its sensory metaphors mutate. The reference to "something gorgeous" adopts the register of visual beauty to describe Gatsby, but then, in the comparison to the seismograph, this quality pivots toward his haptic receptivity. Gatsby's beauty becomes a function not of his performative or visible qualities but of the way that his body receives unseen environmental vibrations. This capacity is figured as mechanical, making of this body a recording device—the seismograph stylus, the phonograph, and the tattoo needle all hover around the figure—for movements that travel at frequencies below the audible through the earth and into the flesh. Near the end of this long line of kinetic transmission, from earthquake to sensitive subjectivity, is the point where that flesh makes contact with the ground: the soles of the feet.[100] It's a shadow version of the scene of Gatsby's tattoo. In each scene, the foot transmits vibrations passing between subject and ground. In the Plaza Hotel, though, that energy seems to pulse downward, into the floor, not up. This reversal is fitting. The tattoo provides a counterpoint to Nick's reflection on Gatsby's personality in more than one way. Its staccato interruption puts pressure on the tenuous continuity implied in an "unbroken series of successful gestures." But if the event of the tattoo, in its broken seriality, may enjoy a formal analogy with the musical expression that gives rise to and that inheres in the cries from below—if the sonic shape of the tattoo is like that of "Yea—ea—ea"—there is also a more direct connection here. Fitzgerald's revisions to the manuscript version of the Plaza Hotel scene suggest that what he is writing when he writes the tattoo is jazz under erasure.

When music is first mentioned in the scene, it's experienced as a kind of thermal transduction. It's a hot day, and Tom has picked up the phone to order some ice. "As Tom took up the receiver the compressed heat exploded into sound and we were listening to the portentous chords of Mendelssohn's Wedding March from the ballroom below" (*Gatsby*, 128). The explosion of heat into sound makes a certain sense given their common medium of transmission, the atmosphere (a commonality reinforced because it doesn't extend to the *other* channel of sonic transmission in the scene, the electrified wiring of the telephone).[101] The sounds of the wedding provide an audio surround, mentioned sparingly in the narration, for a simmering conflict related to fidelity. A few beats later in the scene, the ceremony downstairs gives way to a party, and the soundtrack shifts genres: "a long cheer floated in at the window, followed by intermittent cries of 'Yea—ea—ea!' and finally by a burst of jazz as the dancing began." Daisy says, "We're getting old. . . . If we were young we'd rise and dance" (128). There are a few more remarks about Biloxi, then the tattoo. The overhead cries from below (heard but not seen, in the story; seen but not heard, in the text) are in the mode of call and response. Ambiguating performance and reception, it is not clear whether they're vocalized by the musicians or the revelers.[102] Those who are in the room above—feeling old, says Daisy—demur to respond.

The manuscript tells a different story. These pages were written in the summer of 1924 (before being converted to galleys by the press and sent back to Fitzgerald, who, as I mentioned in the opening sentences of this chapter, then revised in the early weeks of 1925). In these draft pages, there was not yet any mention of Biloxi, nor the tattoo. There was, however, dancing: "A long cheer drifted in from the ballroom, followed by intermittent cries of 'Yea—ea—ea!' and finally by a burst of jazz as the dancing began. Hilariously we danced, Daisy and I, Gatsby and Jordan, while Tom at the telephone watched with unrestful eyes."[103] Perhaps, when he reworked the scene several months later in Rome, hilarious dancing on an oppressively hot afternoon struck the author as improbable. Earlier in the day, after all, Nick notes that in the heat "every extra gesture seemed an affront to the common stores of life" (*Gatsby*, 115). So Fitzgerald suppressed the hilarity.[104] But if this was a concession to realism, it also changes the exchange. With the revision, the extra gesture of Gatsby's tattoo provides a new focal point for Tom's vague contempt. What had been, in the manuscript, his "unrestful eyes" scanning a general bacchanal now come to rest, in the novel, on one restless foot.

Taken as the residue of the excised dance to the music drifting up from the lobby, the tattoo is not only an expression of momentary impatience or a characteristic tic. It is an improvisatory percussive response. The dancing that Fitzgerald deleted was undefined. We don't know how long it carried on or what form it took. We only know that it was hilarious. The tapping with which Fitzgerald replaces it is slightly more specific. Most obviously, it evokes tap dancing, a performance genre that distinctively aligns the heard and the seen. This evocation is indeterminate, but, like Daisy's winks, that indeterminacy is part of the pragmatics of the genre: intrinsic to tap is a constant question of performance or accident, in that what's often regarded as excessive to the situation of dance performance (in many genres of dance, you're supposed to see the dancing body but hear the music, not hear the sounds made by the movements) is made central to the act.[105]

Close-up on Gatsby's foot, cut to Tom's eyes, and cue his "impassioned gibberish"; when Daisy asks him to "control" himself, he spits on the idea: "Self-control! . . . I suppose the latest thing is to sit back and let Mr. Nobody from Nowhere make love to your wife. . . . next they'll throw everything overboard and have intermarriage between black and white" (*Gatsby*, 130). It's a reaction both to being cuckolded and to the Black aesthetic he deciphers in the tattoo—and a reaction that is itself overboard, a loss of control that flies the limits of a restraint defined, in the imagination that irrupts here, as masculine and Nordic.[106]

This reaction is part of the weight carried by the word "tattoo," with all the transoceanic histories of imperial knowledge making and all the disquietude about bodily autonomy that it might connote.[107] In the strange brew of ethnography, psychology, art history, and erotics that is the 1933 book *Tattoo: Secrets of a Strange Art as Practiced among the Natives of the United States*—a title that indulges the idea of ethnographic suspicion to the point of burlesque—Albert Parry writes that tattooing "relates itself to the artistic impulse but basically is born of sex," nearly echoing Fitzgerald's statement, published two years earlier, that jazz first meant "sex, then dancing, then music."[108] But Parry's description of the practical process of tattooing is even more germane here. He writes that new electric tattoo needles are "capable of making about three thousand jabs a minute as against one hundred and fifty to two hundred jabs of the hand tool." The artist makes a tracing on the skin by hand and then applies the machine's needle, "much in the manner of a sewing-machine needle, along the traced lines. . . . One saw only a shapeless spot or series of spots; the ink seemed to run all over the wound without following the lines of the design. In fact, the ink penetrated the skin only where the skin was punctured."[109] The continuous line of the artist's gestural trace is mediated through a process of serial puncturing that seems to lack expressive form, spilling across the skin in "a shapeless spot or series of spots." Then the ink resolves itself in design.

After the funeral at the conclusion of *Gatsby*, Nick finds himself looking westward, at and through Gatsby's mansion, in a melancholy projection of the land's supposedly untouched past, of the "vanished trees" that once stood on the "fresh, green breast of the new world." The novel's last line then converts this fantasy of the settler's experience of *terra nullius* into an expression of human desire and nostalgia: "So we beat on, boats against the current, borne back ceaselessly into the past" (182). Part of what might make the famous line so "gorgeous," to borrow Nick's term, is that even here, in the sentiment of a universal continuity, the formal principle that Fitzgerald invokes is a "relentless beating." A constant flicker. A restless looping iteration of the sort that attaches to the histories of diaspora just at the cut between subject and flesh: right at the site of the question of gesture's loss.

A Finish

From ink back to lead. In reading Fitzgerald's revisions, we might ask what it means that his pencil so often seems to worry over moments of looking and listening—why, in other words, his practice is so regularly caught up with, seemingly vexed by, the relationship between the visual and the aural. Partly it may be that these sensory modes felt like metonyms for a novelist's own capacities of attention.[110] But this metonymy itself also involves, I'd hazard, the way that popular musical expression during the early 1920s serves as a general figure for aesthetic expression, while also carrying very particular social valences.

The way that Tom hears Gatsby's tattoo—as a cue to look instead of listening; as an incitement to ethnographic suspicion—conforms with all sorts of contemporaneous discourse about jazz music in relation to nervousness, to pathology, to criminality, even to the sounds of militarism and the experience of shell shock. (In the late 1920s, Helen Keller will describe the "bombarding sensation" of jazz.)[111] Alongside accounts of the resistance of the music to notation, and of its prioritization of rhythm over melody, came press about its psychological threats. Although a popular topic for the entire decade, this discourse, with its thinly veiled anxieties about the status of whiteness, reached fever pitch in early 1925 due to the widely publicized trial of Dorothy Ellingson, matricidal teenage jazz fan. (It was Ellingson's case that inspired Fitzgerald, just after he finished *Gatsby*, to begin working on *Tender Is the Night*.) While most coverage identified Ellingson's ostensible jazz fanaticism as key to her corruption, H. L. Mencken took a contrarian position in response to the case. He dismissed the potential influence of jazz as overhyped, but not because he felt the genre had much else to recommend it: its "monotonous rhythms and puerile tones make it a sedative rather than a stimulant. If it is actually aphrodisiac, then the sound of riveting is also aphrodisiac."[112]

A few months later, Mencken publishes his review of *Gatsby*. Here too the aesthetics of jazz are at issue, though tacitly. For Mencken, the novel marks a turn for the novelist: "Fitzgerald, the stylist, arises to challenge Fitzgerald, the social historian." In constructing a trivial tragedy that deals only with the "glittering swinishness" of the rich, "the devil's dance that goes on at the top," Fitzgerald "does not go below the surface." But the figure of the surface also comes to carry a positive valence for Mencken: "The story, for all its basic triviality, has a fine texture, a careful and brilliant finish." And improvisation is what Fitzgerald must abandon to achieve this finish. Fitzgerald's earlier fiction "suggested, only too often, the improvisations of a pianist playing furiously by ear, but unable to read notes," but with *Gatsby*, he evidently "wrote, tore up, rewrote, tore up again. There are pages so artfully contrived that one can no more imagine improvising them than one can imagine improvising a fugue." Mencken's analogy assumes a musicological hierarchy within which the gestures of Fitzgerald's writing move from a racially coded stereotype of jazz improvisation to a sense of compositional rigor associated with European musicology, from a restless, compulsive aurality, "playing furiously by ear," to literacy, "read[ing] notes."[113]

We might hear some of the same stereotype in the "intermittent cries" in the Plaza lobby, with Fitzgerald's narration potentially figuring jazz aesthetics as random outburst.[114] That is not the only way Fitzgerald thought of improvisation, though. In "The Captured Shadow," a 1928 story for the *Saturday Evening Post*, the teenage playwright Basil Duke Lee envies the Yale freshman Andy Lockheart's ability "to play the piano by ear" (and Basil also spent a year trying to copy Lockheart's style of walking); in one scene, as Lockheart "began playing a succession of thoughtful chords, which resolved itself into the maxique, Evelyn fluently tapped out a circle with her heels around the floor."[115] Here, with "fluently" suggesting both physical grace and linguistic second nature, the tapping response to improvised music is not only a performance of the body moving in space; in "tapp[ing] out a circle," the response generates a kind of *description* of space—not walking on paper but writing on the floor.

But I'd like to stay even closer to the question that Mencken raises about Fitzgerald's own writing practices. The question of how this writer worked has been a motif of the critical reception from nearly the beginning. Hildegarde Hawthorne, reviewing Fitzgerald's *Tales of the Jazz Age* for the *New York Times* in October 1922, beats Mencken by a few years to some of the central themes of his review of *Gatsby*. She does so not in the rejection of jazz (for Hawthorne, if Fitzgerald "prefers to paint with startling vividness and virility the jazz aspect of the American scene, why not? It exists") but in the way that she describes the "finish" of his style. The book, Hawthorne writes, is, "as to its performance, a finished thing, each piece polished and fit for showing, yet there is also the effect of a glimpse into a workshop where tools are about and many matters afoot." The paradoxical sense of the artwork as both performative process and finished object provokes a desire to witness the scene of writing: "On laying the book down the dominant thought is: 'What will this man do next? He's at something, something we want very much to see.'"[116]

Today it's possible to see a lot of what Fitzgerald was at. A hypercanonical text like *Gatsby* offers many material resources for such looking. The drafts, notes, revisions, and correspondence that went into writing *Gatsby* are widely available in critical editions, published facsimiles, and digital repositories. We know a lot more about the composition of this tattoo than we do about the Harjo brand. If Keller's handwriting is meant to be seen and not read, Fitzgerald's manuscripts are distributed as fountains of interpretive renewal. Paradoxically, the availability of all that ephemera can rhetorically reinforce the primacy of the finished text. The novel starts to seem heroically reified, having realized itself against the odds of a host of counterfactual textual possibilities. In other words, if we have here a gestural history of textual composition recorded in unusual depth and range, it's also one in which all those events of inscription, deletion, transcription, and arrangement are difficult to read as such, as part of an improvisatory process playing out across multiple temporal scales. I'm going to close this chapter by trying to vivify those temporalities in the scene of the tattoo's inscription.[117]

At the point in the novel's life when Fitzgerald revises the scene in the Plaza Hotel, the manuscript is a hybrid document irreducible to any single graphic medium. It is a "manuscript" in the sense of a prepublication draft but not exclusively in the sense of a handwritten text.[118] Fitzgerald's early draft of the novel had, at the time he wrote the sentence about the tattoo— or rather "tatoo"—already been converted by a hired assistant to typescript and then by the press to galley proofs. Working through an extensive revision of these galleys, Fitzgerald entered many small changes directly onto the typeset pages, and when a longer insertion proved necessary, he would add whole new sheets of handwritten script. These were subsequently transcribed by a typist, with Fitzgerald then sometimes penciling further changes on the typed pages before sending to Scribner's.

The sentence in question appears at the bottom of one of the full handwritten page insertions (fig. 3.7). Fitzgerald will eventually cut a sentence at the top of the page (continued from the previous), in which Nick describes

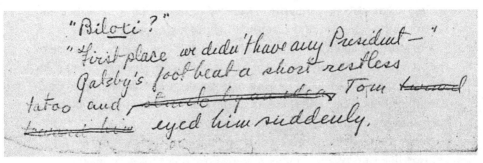

FIGURE 3.7 Gatsby's "tattoo." Partial view of handwritten insertion no. 8 in the revised galleys of *The Great Gatsby*. F. Scott Fitzgerald Papers, Manuscripts Division, Department of Rare Books and Special Collections, Princeton University Library. Image courtesy of Princeton University Library.

how Gatsby and Tom seem to circle each other without moving. Excepting some punctuation changes, everything else on the page will be typeset as is for publication, until the sentence at the bottom about the tattoo. This line is the only one that receives focused attention, whether because it is a climactic moment or because a character's suddenly heightened attention reflexively cues the author's own. Between the moment when Fitzgerald starts writing it and its printing in the first edition, four changes occur to the sentence: Fitzgerald deletes "struck by an idea"; he changes "turned toward him" to "eyed him suddenly"; a comma suddenly appears to divide "short" and "restless"; and, as I discussed at the opening of this chapter, a third *t* appears in "tattoo."

The first two alterations—cutting the "idea," adding "eyed"—are obviously the most provocative in their substance. They alter the representation of Tom's behavior from a two-step procedure (he thinks and then turns), a sequence that dramatizes the classical divide of body and mind, to a moment of embodied cognition.[119] We can infer that these two verbal revisions are made during the sentence's composition, not after later reflection, because there is no terminal punctuation after the elided "turned toward him," at which point the line as first written could have come to a grammatical resting place. The very shape of the elisions suggests a restless momentum: the doubled lines of the two longer strike-throughs (, struck by an idea, and toward him) join in a sharp point at their left end, the pencil moving back against the direction of writing before turning acutely to carry the line forward. Such evidence may support the spirit of Mencken's intuition that Fitzgerald "tore up" the drafts of his manuscript and then "tore [them] up again." But in practical terms, these marks indicate the converse.

The writer did not destroy and re-create from scratch, per a model of improvisation as merely continual spontaneous outburst. He rearranged, edited, and transmuted one narrative event into another, with a relation between these events in the form of an echo.

The point here is less to shoehorn the improvisatory poetics of this process into a category called jazz than to question the distinctions—fugue and fury, composition and improvisation—that organize a story like Mencken's about how such a text comes to achieve its fine surface. There's both motor habit and memory in the finish of this text. It is, in other words—and allowing for some flex to the term—gestural. Like a ritual, like a gift, a text can make a gesture. But writing relates to gesture not only analogically (they can perform similar functions) but also materially (writing requires the body).[120] Gesture is conventionally downplayed, if not eliminated, in a discursive transcript, and it's categorically excluded from the understanding of writing—an understanding that has played an outsized role in how we have conceived of "culture" for over a century—as the graphic reflection of phonemic utterance. This excluded modality is also, however, constitutively necessary for the written transcript, in that it is one name for the practices, hardly disembodied and hardly silent, of the graphic object's making.[121]

An act of both listening and performance, Gatsby's tattoo is not only an object of transcription, a dubious motor habit that reveals its performer's unease, nervousness, failure. The tattoo, with its typewriterlike tapping, is also itself an act of notation, both in that term's musical connotations—the tattoo responds to the music below, as if trying to leave a record of it on the floor—and in Efron's sense of bodily notation as a mode of narrating, in the unfolding of a gesture's form, the underlying shape of a stretch of speech. The narrator of *The Love of the Last Tycoon* claims that her father, a Hollywood producer, has no "more than a drummer's sense of a story," and to read this as anything other than a random category confusion requires recognizing its admission of the possibility of percussion as a mode of storytelling.[122] What kind of story, then, does the tattoo tell? Its staccato form minimally captures an experience of iterative, progressive improvisation. One might say that it reduces such experience to abstraction, except that the tattoo is so bodily and its performance and reception so inseparable from the histories of racialized corporeality. Each strike of the foot may have a similar attack and decay; their seriality may resemble, to some, the rivet gun's mechanical repetition. And its reductive description, reflecting the limits of Tom's attention, can't capture the microtiming, the infinitesimal hesitations, so important to the musicology of swing.[123] But still, this sound does nothing less than choreograph the scene. The "compelling insinuation" of its form—to draw from Zora Neale Hurston's description, in 1934, of the modes of Black dance—turns its auditor's body in time with the changes playing out below.[124]

I mentioned four changes to the sentence at the heart of all this, but I've only discussed three. That leaves the comma between "short" and "restless": "short, restless tattoo." Fitzgerald didn't put it there. Scribner's corrected the absence. Recent scholarly editions have in turn restored the author's commaless version of the line, but with the novel having now entered the public domain, one can expect both versions to circulate widely in the future.[125] As with the *t* added to "tattoo," the addition of the comma, when it was first introduced to the text, probably seemed standard, in accordance with the most current typographic style and habit: the correction of an "accidental" rather than a "substantive," in a foundational distinction of textual criticism.[126] But that isn't a full or final explanation of the change. After all, it would also have been customary to insert a comma between "tattoo" and "and," separating the two independent clauses, and that didn't happen. So what does this silent correction do?

It might score new music. If we accept that a comma indicates a pause, the inclusion of this one adjusts the potential mimesis between the tempo of the sentence and that of the tattoo it reports. It could mean that a reader doesn't rush through the line quite as restlessly as one might imagine the foot to tap.

But as a grammatical as well as a rhythmic marker, the comma also shapes the content of that imagination, our sense of the qualities of the behavior. As the line unfolds, this punctuation visually flags the status of the two adjectives attached to the tattoo as parallel elements in a list of qualities. It opens the angle of distinction between these elements. "Short" and "restless" go well together, of course—neither "short, patient" nor "long, restless" would pair as naturally—but they do differently construe the object. In fact, they register a difference in *how* to construe it. "Short" measures. "Restless" interprets. Imposing a pause in the space between these modes, this punctuation has something in common with the action in question— even as the mechanisms of its insertion, bringing an audiovisual anomaly into alignment, have something in common with the reflexes that make Tom look.

4 No-Tongue's Song

Fieldnotes and Fiction

A big blue *X* covers the page. Among Franz Boas's notes from an expedition in 1883–84 to Cumberland Sound and Baffin Island in what is now Nunavut in the Canadian Arctic there's a copy of his transcription of lyrics composed by one of his hired guides.[1] The text is in black ink, taken down in Inuktitut in the Latin alphabet (rather than the Inuktitut syllabary introduced by missionaries at around the same time). A scattered selection of phrasings, at various points on the page, are translated into German, in the same handwriting. The blue *X* across the face of the script is drawn in what seems to be wax pencil or crayon. The mark was probably meant to keep track of the fact that this text had been retranscribed for publication elsewhere.[2] It registers a move from handwriting to print. But just when this mark was made is hard to say, since variations of the same song-text will be reproduced in at least half a dozen of Boas's own publications.

One of these variations appeared in 1922, in a unique context: Boas's only published work of fiction, titled "An Eskimo Winter." Here the song-text is attributed to a character named No-tongue, though elsewhere, in nonfictional publication contexts, it is consistently attributed to a guide named Utitia'q. (This is the most common spelling, and for that reason the one this chapter will generally use, of a name sometimes given as Utitiaq, Utitiak, Utütiak, or Utityak.) Boas wrote the story, drawing on his notes and previous academic publications about that early expedition, at the request of Elsie Clews Parsons. While serving a term as president of the American Folklore Society, she had called on her network of connections with leading Americanist ethnographers, archaeologists, and linguists and pulled together a volume of ethnographic fiction, titled *American Indian Life: By Several of Its Students*.[3]

According to Parsons, *American Indian Life* grew from the seed of another recent publication of hers. In a 1919 issue of *Scientific Monthly,* she had published a kind of biographical sketch, based on fieldwork in the Southwest, titled "Waiyautitsa of Zuñi, New Mexico."[4] Boas accompanied her on that trip to New Mexico and Laguna Pueblo land. According to the recollections of the novelist Leslie Marmon Silko's grandmother, Parsons finished all their interviewing because "the Laguna language is tonal" and "Boas, as it turns out / was tone deaf."[5] Parsons synthesized from those interviews the narrative of a life. The premise of the experiment in genre: "In our own complex culture biography may be a clarifying form of description. Might it not avail at Zuñi?"—and, implicitly, at other locations as well?[6] With the idea of a volume of fictional "biographies," birth to death (although only a few of the eventual contributions actually followed that format), Parsons secured a deal with B. W. Huebsch—who had recently handled Sherwood Anderson's *Winesburg, Ohio* and is now perhaps best remembered as James Joyce's publisher in the United States—and pressed ahead.[7]

Parsons's aim in editing *American Indian Life* was to direct scientists' professional expertise toward genres that would appeal to a broad public readership. As she writes in the preface, though the project emerges out of professional anthropology, its contents steer away from boring readers with the current debates in the field. "It is a book of pictures" rather than of problems. If, for the reader, "the pictures remain pictures," that's fine; "if they lead him to the problems, good and better."[8] Similarly, A. L. Kroeber's introduction frames the book as "a picture of native American life," a kind of "composite photograph" built of biographical sketches—accurate in many ways except, Kroeber notes, in its paucity of humor, notoriously difficult to translate.[9] Here the "pictorial" operates both negatively—these fictional representations are *not* theoretically declarative—and positively, allowing, as Parsons writes, for a happy medium between the "forbidding monograph" and the "legends of Fenimore Cooper." The rejection of those "legends" leads into a reflection on bias. "The white man's traditions about Indians have been disregarded" by the contributing authors, Parsons writes. At the same time, though, "few, if any of us, succeed, in describing another culture, of ridding ourselves of our own cultural bias or habits of mind. Much of our anthropological work, to quote a letter from Spinden"—referring here to Herbert Spinden, one of the contributors to the volume—"is not so much definitive science as it is a cultural trait of ourselves."[10]

The moves that Parsons makes here may sound familiar. If they anticipate the self-reflexive critiques and literary experiments of anthropological discourse in the late twentieth century, they also echo the argument of "On Alternating Sounds"—as that argument is paraphrased, at least, in the critical commonplaces that, as I discussed in the introduction, emerged after George Stocking's 1965 account of Boas's relativist intervention. But my approach here to the representational politics of the book will have less to do with "cultural" bias (notwithstanding Parsons's own reference to that principle) than with the questions of aurality, typographic materiality, and spatial dislocation that more directly informed that 1889 essay and its reflections on sound-blindness. Primarily concerned with Boas's 1922 story and its prehistories, the chapter will also discuss another entry in *American Indian Life*—a story coauthored by Parsons and a Hampton Institute student named Thomas B. Reed. Placed immediately before Boas's story in the published volume, its textual histories and formal idiosyncrasies reveal the strange pressure that ethnographic fiction places on the implication of authorship.

Tracking these texts in the preconditions of their publication means moving outside a space that is intuitively recognizable as "American literature." But even Boas's transcriptions of Inuit song, on Indigenous land claimed by the Canadian settler state, are carried out in contact with the theoretical and pragmatic horizon of US empire. (It needs to be underscored that the same cannot automatically be said of the music these transcriptions claim to represent.) Boas traveled to Baffin Island three years after control of the region had been transferred from the British Colonial Office to Canada. This was done in large part because British officers became aware, in the 1870s, of several exploratory expeditions and mining enterprises by American operators. The transfer of sovereignty presented itself as a means of limiting the prospects of US control in the Arctic (partly by diminishing the grounds on which the United States might invoke the Monroe Doctrine, its policy of forceful response to European intervention in the hemisphere).[11] In one of Boas's earliest publications about the Cumberland Sound expedition— an 1884 article for the *Journal of the Geographical Society of New York*—he mentions coming into contact with one of the mining operations in question, "a Philadelphia mica company" from which he gathered "valuable ethnographical information from the west shore of the sound."[12] The United States' recent purchase of Alaska, the path to the statehood of which is also inseparable from the economies of extraction, pertains here as well—both to the transatlantic imperial politics of the Canadian Arctic (in that the purchase served as a precedent for British concerns) and also to the second work of ethnographic fiction I'll discuss, the story coauthored by Parsons and Reed. Reed came to the United States from a Deg Hit'an community on the Yukon River in the village of Anvik, in what was, during his youth, first the District of Alaska and then, beginning in 1912, Alaska Territory.

The question of American empire's northern reach thus hums in the background of this chapter. But while the question of settler-colonial space matters a great deal, as I'll suggest, in the processes that eventuate in these stories, I will not here engage the politics of territory as closely as in chapter 1's discussion of allotment in Indian Territory. I will, though, want to follow through here on the idea developed in chapter 1 of speechlessness and circumspection as sites for the refusal of coloniality; on the question in chapter 2 of how the visible features of typographic representation mediate acts of identification; and on the analysis in chapter 3 of a temporality that emerges as the uncanny expression of a suppressed musical sociality. As echoes do, these themes will resonate differently in the space of the texts in discussion here, and this chapter will stay quite close to the textual histories of the idiosyncratic literary objects that find themselves iterated as entries in *American Indian Life*. If in these stories, the arts of fiction are imagined in terms of pictorial showing, the contingencies of their production through the transcription of vocal telling—and the questions of how to produce faithful records of oral performance—play a primary role in the way that they come to sketch Indigenous biography, both at the level of narrative voicing and also in the literally visible features of the text. So while I began this book with the problem of how to pronounce an ink mark (the illustration of Harjo's brand) that is at best dubiously available to utterance, much of what I'll want to consider in concluding are features of print—lineation, punctuation—that are often placed in even more explicit opposition to voice but that are also indissociable from the priority of voice's representation.[13]

In this chapter's position as last, it may have been noticeable that it has a wayward title. It references a sonic genre after the three previous chapter titles in my table of contents had set a pattern of graphic terms. Brand, handwriting, tattoo . . . song. Of course, "tattoo" already began to blur things by naming a sonic event through a word that evokes the visual. I break the pattern more explicitly here because this "song" does something similar, in reverse: the object that I reconstruct as "No-tongue's song" is in fact, in its ontology, textual—even as the music that it claims to represent is not. The blue wax instrument that marks the *X* on Boas's fieldnotes is as much a means of this object's making as a voice or drum. This ontology is tied up with one of the connotations of tonguelessness here: juxtaposed against the idea of the singing voice and printed on paper, it may invoke the ostensible silence of the page. It also, though (and this is the problem toward which the chapter will move), imagines linguistic disability as a kind of spatial experience off tilt—as a disruption of orientation in fiction and other fields.

Drum-Dancing on the Line

John M. Oskison saw too many typos. He reviewed Parsons's book for the *New York Times Book Review*. As might be expected given my earlier discussion of his references to the "culture" concept in other publications, he never uses that term in the piece—despite writing a lengthy review (covering a full page of the paper) of a book in whose preface and introduction that word appears about two dozen times. Oskison opens by noting that "the great novelist is, of course, a scientist" whose "reconstructions of controlling environment and motivating color of life are as sound and penetrating as (for example) the anthropologist's monograph on skull variations among the prehistoric peoples of Western Pennsylvania." In turn, Parsons, as the editor of this new collection, had "very nearly succeeded . . . in convincing us that the real scientist—or at any rate the passionate ethnologist—is a first-rate novelist." The title of Oskison's review, "Real, Not Paleface Fancy, Indian Life," sets up this claim on behalf of the scientists' experiment (however qualified a claim it is: "*nearly* succeeded"). And it also returns to the "fancy" so complexly thematized in what he claimed as his first publication, "A Laboratory Fancy," itself a story about a paleface scientist's fancy. As in the conclusion of that early sketch, with its rude awakening to academic discipline, Oskison's review of *American Indian Life* ends in an abrupt turn to material conditions. The book is very expensive, he writes, but if a more affordable edition ever comes out, "the opportunity may well be grasped to correct certain needless errors of punctuation."[14]

To Oskison's point, one such error does appear at a conspicuous moment: just a few words before the end. Boas's story, "An Eskimo Winter," is given pride of place as the final text in the book, not including the appendices. He concludes it by giving his central character, No-tongue, the last word, in the text of a song rendered as verse. No-tongue has two songs in the story, both of them drawn from Boas's fieldnotes from the 1883–84 Baffin Island expedition. The one in question reads,

> Ayaya, beautiful is the great world when summer is coming at last!
> Ayaya, beautiful is the great world when the caribou begin to come!
> Ayaya, when the little brooks roar in our country.
> Ayaya, I feel sorry for the gulls, for they cannot speak,
> Ayaya, I feel sorry for the ravens, for they cannot speak.
> Ayaya. if I cannot catch birds I quickly get plenty of fish.
> > Ayaya![15]

The typo is there in the penultimate line: "Ayaya. if . . ." While a more self-evident punctuation problem than the dubious comma I discussed at the end in *Gatsby*, this period probably doesn't change much in a reader's understanding. The reason for this has to do with the anaphoric repetition of the untranslated vocable. In performance, "ayaya" would work as a fluid transition between two lyrical segments, so that it would have been equally appropriate to swap the placement of the commas and periods—giving a comma at the end of each line, in other words, and moving the terminal punctuation marks to follow each "ayaya." Doing just this, the exclamation point after the final repetition of "ayaya," isolated in the seventh line, rehabilitates the misplaced period in the line above: if this last cry can not only begin but also end a line of text, surely the one before it could have been imagined, in the real time of its articulation, as potentially doing the same. So maybe the error was not in the period at all but in the lower case of what followed it: "if." The question then becomes, What is this untranslated vocable doing here, in the print contexts of its circulation?

Part of what it does is to indicate the importance of phonemic and vocalic modulation. In *The Central Eskimo* (1888), one of the earlier places where Boas put his Baffin Island transcriptions into print, he writes that, in their performances of such songs, "some Eskimo are very good narrators and know how to express the modulations of the different persons by modulations of the voice. In addition, as a number of tales are really onomatopoetic, an artistic effect is produced."[16] Here one's rank as a narrator depends not on emplotment, characterization, or dialogue—nor "pictorial" representation—but on tone and timbre. And while it is perfectly reasonable that Boas would refer to the performer of a song like the one transcribed here as a "narrator," given that many songs in its genre take the form of stories, this also sits in tension with one of the ways that the texts he transcribes then come subsequently to circulate: that is, as lyric verse and so—given some powerful aesthetic norms in settler literary culture—as expressions of individual feeling rather than as narrative embodiments of "different persons."

Boas's construction of these lyrics as lineated verse, and his inclusion of the untranslated vocable in repetition, involves a highly selective emphasis on certain features of the performance genre in question. Often transcribed as *ayaya, ajaja,* or *ajaaja* or as only two syllables (*aya, aja*)—or as extended into a whole iterative series of the same alternating sounds—the vocable repeated in the preceding lines is a minimal marker of drum-dancing. The Inuktitut term for these songs, often but not always hunting stories, is *pisiq.* It's a genre whose political context changed significantly from the time that Boas transcribed these texts in the winter of 1883–84 to when he published this story in 1922. The first Christian mission on Baffin Island was established in the 1890s by Edmund Peck, missionary and linguist, a decade after Boas's first expedition, and one of the eventual consequences (arriving in the same decade that *American Indian Life* was published) was the banning of Inuit performance genres and spaces—drum-dancing being conventionally performed in the central social space of the *qaggiq*. This ban extended to the drums themselves, instruments invariably present in performance (but never mentioned in the context of the songs in "An Eskimo Winter"). Those spaces have, nevertheless, persisted, and those genres have been sustained and renewed by Inuit people over the past century; during this time, the once-banned tradition has also come to bear a complex relation to Christianity, as registered by the fact that *pisiq* now also carries the sense "hymn."[17]

As a southerner in relation to these forms and practices, I claim no authority in the representation of the genre. My questions about these texts' meanings and effects develop from the outside of things: How does the *qallunaat* (non-Inuit, white) Boas transform these song-texts over several decades, and what do these transformations tell us about the poetics of tone and translation at the print-cultural interface between literature and the social sciences in the United States—as the primary space of these texts' circulation, though not their composition or recording? While I will develop a line of inquiry about some of the expressive effects that Boas may have missed, or chosen not to represent, in the performances that he claimed to record—and while I hope to share here some details about the compositional circumstances of particular songs in ways that may be of interest to drum-dance practitioners—I also want to take at face value at least one element of Parsons's preface: its affirmation of Spinden's reflections on ethnographic representation as "not so much definitive science."

Boas's "Eskimo Winter" is not biographical in the mode that Parsons recommended. It doesn't follow the birth-to-death arc. No-tongue enters as an outsider to a village several paragraphs into it, as winter approaches. The story follows his life only until the weather warms, allowing No-tongue and his family, having experienced a certain amount of friction during their stay, to depart in the direction of another community. "The time of happiness was approaching," the story concludes, "of which No-tongue once sang," followed by the indented lines I quoted earlier—the lines about the beauty of summer's advent, about the pathos of the birds' speechlessness, and about finding something to eat.[18]

When Boas writes "once" here—"of which No-tongue *once* sang"—he creates a curious effect. This "once" is unsituated in time. Placed here at the end of the story (as opposed to the more familiar "once" of a story's opening), the word sounds as though it will cue up some familiar refrain, allowing us to recollect the previous moment when we were told about this song. But that had never happened: these lyrics are new, even though they arrive at the end, or in fact *after* the end, of the plot. Like the looping vocable it contains, the song is given outside any emplotted sequence of cause and effect.[19] Still, if we take seriously the momentary effect of that "once" (that it's a misleading effect doesn't mean it doesn't happen), part of what it does is to call us back to the other song that, earlier in the story, did in fact arrive as a specific event tied into the causal chain of the plot.

In previous and subsequent publications, the song at the end of the story—the one I've already quoted, with the punctuation error—is often given the title "Summer Song," while the other one that No-tongue sings midway through the story is, in its previous print iterations, typically titled "Utitia'q's Song." Neither title, to be clear, appears in *American Indian Life*; they are given in the story as untitled expressions, performed by an individual without audience. It's important to note that although Boas identifies both of these songs as the compositions of a single character, the source texts are in fact created by different people: "Summer Song" is by one Kenningnang and "Utitia'q's Song" by, of course, Utitia'q. This transforms a kinship into a singularity: Utitia'q was Kenningnang's nephew, leading Boas, in earlier nonfictional publications, to connect these two song-texts as the productions of a "family of poets."[20]

Most of the names in "An Eskimo Winter" are given in phonetic approximation of Inuktitut pronunciation, not in English translation. "Ayaya" is conspicuous in its nontranslation; "No-tongue" is its opposite. Boas wasn't the first person in his own orbit to enter this name into the folkloric record. In two linked articles that appeared in 1913 and 1916 in the *Journal of American Folklore* (which Boas edited at the time), George F. Will relayed a Numakaki (Mandan) story of a boy who cuts off his own tongue and gives it to the Sun and Moon.[21] One difference between this figure and the character in Boas's story is that there's no indication that the latter loses or even injures his tongue. While the injury of Will's No-tongue does not prevent him from speaking (in the 1916 entry, he announces himself by name), Boas's character uses his voice in ways that even more conspicuously require a tongue: the articulation of the diphthongal alternations in "ayaya."[22] If the name caught Boas's ear as a reader and editor and then resurfaced as fitting for the character in "An Eskimo Winter," perhaps it was for other reasons having to do with a longer-standing, if inchoate, concern with the relationship between ability and habituation: in the semantic drift of "tongue"—both an organ and a language—the phrase ambiguates an impaired ability for linguistic articulation with a more general condition of languagelessness.[23]

Kenningnang's "Summer Song," republished at the end of "An Eskimo Winter," addresses the latter condition. The text begins with the appreciation of so-called dumb nature: "beautiful is the great world when summer is coming at last," with the inarticulate "roar" of its waters.[24] From this roar, the song moves to a sense of pity for the exclusion from linguistic community that characterizes certain nonhuman life.[25] "I feel sorry for the gulls, for they cannot speak, / Ayaya, I feel sorry for the ravens, for they cannot speak." When "ayaya" goes untranslated, it seems to be because it serves as the index of something culturally particular; but here it also seems to register as the kind of nonsemantic vocalization—an expression of woe, for instance—often understood to articulate human and nonhuman, singer and bird.[26] "Summer Song" celebrates its author's ability to vocalize artfully in implicit contrast to the natural speechlessness of the nonhuman, but its untranslated element softens this contrast.

Both songs in "An Eskimo Winter" express an effusive appreciation of the environmental surround. But "Utitia'q's Song" develops this appreciation with rueful irony.[27] In this way, perhaps, the name "No-tongue" has less to do with a discursive lack than with a specific discursive mode—not saying nothing but saying something in negation. When the central character is faced with a life-threatening situation, the details of which I'll discuss later, he responds with humor:

Aya, I am joyful; this is good!
Aya, there is nothing but ice around me, that is good!
Aya, I am joyful; this is good!
My country is nothing but slush, that is good!
Aya, I am joyful; this is good!
Aya, when indeed, will this end? this is good!
I am tired of watching and waking, this is good![28]

The phrasing and formatting in which Boas reproduces this song differ substantially across other versions. "A Year among the Eskimo" (1887), an article Boas published in the *Journal of the American Geographical Society of New York*, presents a radically different verbal style. "Awaking from my slumbers in the dawn," one line reads in pentamer. Here the text is broken into four stanzas, with "Aya" set to the left at the beginning of each. The last stanza, for example, approximating certain elements of the last two lines as given in "An Eskimo Winter," reads,

Aya: O when I reach the land
       It will be nice!
       When will this roaming end?
       When will I be at home?
       Then it's nice![29]

The inclusion of the lyric "O" fits the Romantic register experimented with here.[30] But then, one might wonder at the fact that *both* this expression and "aya" are included in the line: that is, it might seem as though "O" is present here in part as a translation of "aya," so that their copresence produces a multilingual redundancy. But the two expressions do not, of course, do exactly the same things. Whereas "O" is often understood as an index of lyric subjectivity, a drop into apostrophic affect, *aya* serves a more syntactic function. It affords a site for emotive indication in performance, no doubt, but it also distinguishes and bridges segments of text.

Boas's notation of the song in *The Central Eskimo* uses the musical staff as a means of trying to preserve and to rationalize this same syntactic function—the way, that is, that the series of lines given in a drum-dance song, often but not always developing a sequential plot, loops through this smaller oscillation of vowels. Boas's monograph gives "Utitiaq's Song" (the name is given in this version without the apostrophe) only in a brief snippet of melody and rhythm, notated in the five-line format of Western musical notation with lyrics in the Latin alphabet, untranslated from the Inuktitut running below the staff (fig. 4.1). After an opening two measures giving the conventional vocable—which, as the symbol above the staff indicates, the performer should sing at a slower pace than the allegro marked as the general tempo—the transcription then scores seven measures of a repeating melody, looping back after a second "A—ja," so that the vocable is included within the loop as the song moves forward.

This notation reflects a particular theory of musical meaning that applies dubiously in this context. In *The Central Eskimo*, Boas himself comes close to reckoning with these songs' formal incommensurability with the intervallic conventions of Western notation: "On the whole," he writes in the last paragraph of the monograph proper, "the melodies, even to our musical sense, can be traced to a key note. However, changes often occur."[31] The

VI. UTITIAQ'S SONG.

FIGURE 4.1 "Utitiaq's Song" on the five-line staff. Franz Boas, *The Central Eskimo* (1888), 654.

drum-dance composer Donald Suluk—a well-known figure, sometimes referred to as a prophet, whose songs often incorporated Christian elements—described the priorities of drum-dance performance and reception: "In the Inuit way of listening to songs, you don't really listen to the tune but to what is being said." Boas's notation may have been, in this context, "tone deaf" (per Silko's grandmother) less because of inaccuracies of intervallic representation—less because of a sound-blindness of frequency or key—than because of a persistent theory of melody that emphasizes formal stasis, even in the face of the fact that "changes often occur." But while changes to a melody may be typical in drum-dancing, changes to a text are another question. To avoid insult to a composer or their family, Suluk suggests, the text of a song "has to be sung completely and followed according to how it's composed."[32] This is not to say that song-texts cannot be altered, but typically an *ikiaqtagaq* (an iteration of a *pisiq* in which a performer may incorporate some new lyrics) should nod to its sourcing and to the fact of its alteration.[33]

In subsequent republications of Boas's transcriptions in later collections of verse, it will be no surprise that their textual variations are rarely indicated; nor are the conditions of the songs' sourcing. Although "Utitia'q's Song," as the song-text's title is typically given, seems to carry with it a note of attribution right there in its possessive apostrophe, this does not always stick in the reception history. A recent anthology uses precisely that title while also, just below, tagging the text as "Inuit, Traditional"—a designation that conventionally implies *author unknown*. (Meanwhile, in the same republication, somebody else still gets their due: "Translated by Franz Boas.")[34] Such a slippage involves its own contingencies, but attribution is already problematized in Boas's own iterations. Embedding the songs in the form of private lyric expressions—as selected verbal elements extracted from complex performative wholes—the fictional space of "An Eskimo Winter" compresses the work of two song composers into a single print-cultural subjectivity.

"Little things in print have a long life," Herbert Spinden wrote to Parsons in June 1922, soon after *American Indian Life* was published. Like Oskison, he had caught some typos. This letter was a less happy correspondence than the one that Parsons quotes from Spinden in the book's preface. He had contributed a story to the volume but evidently hadn't yet received a copy himself when he saw the book at a friend's house. Finding his own entry, he noticed that Parsons had added a footnote on its first page, indicating that "at the request of the author, there has been no editing" of the story.[35] As Spinden reminds Parsons in his letter, he had indeed cut some things that the editor asked him to cut. Changes did occur. So (according to Spinden), the footnote not only wasn't quite true but was also embarrassing, making it seem as though some "pretty plain errors" that ended up in the final versions—errors he felt he could have fixed if he'd had the chance to review proofs—were his fault for being stubborn. "Otherwise," he signs off, a little salty, "congratulations!"[36]

If Boas noticed the stray period in the song at the end of "An Eskimo Winter," he recorded no complaint I know of. Having begun to describe the generic problems that attend his inclusion of such songs in this short story, I'll want to return to the more extended composition contexts of No-tongue's other song (that is, Utitia'q's song). But it will be helpful, first, to develop more of a sense of what it means for it to appear in *American Indian Life*. To that end, the next section will focus on another entry that we might take as a kind of practical synecdoche for Parsons's editorial imagination: "Cries-for-salmon, a Ten'a Woman," the chapter that she coauthors with Thomas Reed. I took a moment to mention her footnote to Spinden's entry because its rhetorical complexities—which, at least in Spinden's reception of its meanings, position the author as both the final voice in the construction of the text and also as one who is naïve, obstinate, pridefully unaware in their errors—are deepened and distended when, as in the case of "Cries-for-salmon," the editor is also the coauthor. The section will begin with the conditions of performance, audition, and institution in which the piece was conceived. It will then move into particular narrative forms emergent in these conditions: a first-person voice that slips between folklorist and informant; a plot that slips between recursion and event.

Graphic Talks

On the evening of February 7, 1920, the Hampton Institute hosted its annual celebration of Indian Citizenship Day, commemorating the Dawes allotment legislation of 1887.[37] While Hampton was a predominantly Black institution in its student population, the school also ran an Indian education program from 1877 to 1923. The program's closure was largely a result of the controversies over such integration from outside the institution. The writing was on the wall for the program as early as 1912. Charles Carter—the Oklahoma congressmember and Chickasaw citizen who, as I discussed in chapter 1, recited poetry at the unveiling of Sequoyah in Statuary Hall—argued strongly against federal funding for Hampton. According to Carter, "social equality" with Black students was detrimental to the assimilatory potential of Native students.[38]

While the program was still in operation, the idea of English was central to the policies of integration at the institution. As a condition of attending classes with other nonwhite students, the students in Hampton's Indian education program were prohibited from speaking Native languages and required to demonstrate a certain level of competence in English. The linguistic prohibition did not extend, though, to the context of music. As a result, while the Citizenship Day event was an apt expression of the assimilationist philosophy of the institution (and, counterintuitively, of the critics of its multiracial classrooms), in practice the celebration also afforded forms of song and dance performance that were explicitly banned at similar institutions in the period.[39]

This is not to say that such performance would, in every instance, necessarily be nonassimilationist in the rhetoric of its presentation—simply that, at Hampton, the question was staged in unique ways. Thomas B. Reed took the stage more than once. For much of his childhood, Reed had lived with other Deg Hit'an youth at a residential school in Anvik, Alaska. The school was run by John Chapman, a missionary and occasional anthropologist who published the volume *Ten'a Texts and Tales* in 1914 in a series edited by Boas.[40] ("Ten'a" was an imprecise designation used by Chapman and a small number of other non-Native writers to refer to certain communities along the Yukon River and nearby; "Ingalik," meanwhile, is a term used by some Deg Hit'an people while considered pejorative by others.)[41] The next year, Chapman facilitated Reed's transition to Virginia to work toward a teaching degree at Hampton.[42] Reed entered in the fall of 1915.

Already in that first academic year, he played a prominent role at the 1916 Citizenship Day event. After performing an Athabaskan dance, he delivered a talk on the "customs of Alaskan Indians," with a version of this presentation then published in the *Southern Workman*, accompanied by photographic illustrations.[43] The next year, he left Hampton to serve in the Great War, returning a few years later to finish his degree.

In February 1920—the same month that he published an article titled "Fishing on the Yukon" in the *Workman*, again featuring several photographs—he once more takes the stage for another Hampton Citizenship Day event.[44] This time, he choreographs a performance of "Alaskan dances," with masks that he designed and fabricated. Though this performance is accompanied by a talk by another student, "present[ing] the folk life of Indians living on the upper Yukon," Reed himself was at the time, a local paper reports, already "well known locally for his simple, graphic talks on Indian life and his interpretation of Alaskan dances."[45] The *Workman*, too, after the performance, gives him "great credit" for fabricating the masks and other physical elements, for having choreographed the dance and taught other students to perform it, and generally for "giving the large audience so faithful a reproduction of some of the very interesting customs of his people."[46]

Elsie Clews Parsons might have been part of that audience. She traveled to Hampton that weekend, though her notes and correspondence don't reveal the precise time of her arrival. Her visit involved "a lot of work in very comfortable circumstances," as she wrote from Virginia to her husband, Herbert Parsons, that Tuesday. For a couple of hours each afternoon, she explained, she was making herself available to the Hampton students "to come singly to tell tales." Appropriately for the folkloric collector, she held her office hours in a museum.[47] At the end of the week, a couple of days before her return, Parsons wrote again to Herbert: "talks to students, teachers, recording tales + riddles and getting material from an Alaskan student fill my time."[48] This student was Reed. Whether or not Parsons had reached campus in time for his performance on Saturday, she quickly heard about it, because he talked about it himself while giving Parsons the "material" of his conversation. Some of the "tales + riddles" that Parsons collected at Hampton were recorded with a phonograph. Parsons had mentioned in her letter on Tuesday that, as a woman traveling alone with such a device, she had received some unwanted attention on the boat from Baltimore.[49] But for the recording of her interactions with Reed, she used paper, and these interview notes became the basis for "Cries-for-salmon." From a series of meetings with Reed during that second week of February 1920—and through also the reading and annotation of a number of texts, including some by Chapman, related to Athabaskan lifeways—Parsons put together a picture.

The story's title character, Cries-for-salmon, appears only intermittently. Loosely structured as a biographical sketch, the bulk of the text is made up of digressions on norms of Deg Hit'an courtship, medicine, artisanship, ceremonial performance, and more. I'll focus here less on its story or ethnographic content than on the interplay between its rhetorical structures and its revision history. There are three pertinent moments in the recording and publication of the text. First, there are the meetings with Reed during the week of February 9, 1920. Second, there is an initial publication titled "A Narrative of the Ten'a of Alaska" published in the journal *Anthropos* later the same year; here, one distinctive element is a brief preface in which Parsons never names Reed but does describe the situation in which she interviewed him, explaining that "the resulting narrative was so vivid and so illuminated by the psychological insight that we commonly fail to get in more systematic enquiry that it has seemed well to me to keep the data in approximately the original form rather than to reclassify."[50] Third, there is the lightly revised version of this article republished in *American Indian Life*, minus the article's preface and with Reed and Parsons now named as coauthors.

Their coauthorship is not presented as a symmetrical writing act, even in the third and final of these texts. Its opening line indicates as much: "You ask me to tell you the story of somebody's life at Anvik, my home in Alaska."[51] The brief opening paragraph establishes the "I" of the story as the informant or storyteller and the "you" as the ethnographic auditor. Given that these sentences are only present in *American Indian Life* and not in previous iterations, it would seem that this "I," though voiced as Reed, is composed by Parsons. In fact, here she repurposes language from her own preface to the journal version. There, in the earlier publication, she had written, "I asked him to present his information as if he were telling the story of an Anvik villager from birth to death."[52] In the book, where there is no similar paratext at the top of the story, the content of this sentence is revised and distributed to two points. First, as I've already indicated, the ethnographer's query is integrated into the textual record of the informant's reply. Second, that query is reiterated in the book's appendix, which contains brief notes about the sourcing of each story. Here Parsons indicates that Reed "was asked to present his information as if he were telling the story of an Anvik villager from birth to death."[53] The language is almost identical to the article version, except that the "I" of Parsons's previous "I asked him"—having first shifted into the "you" of Reed's address—now disappears in the passive voice of scientific procedure.

From one publication to the next, Parsons also shifts the formatting of editorial comment. In *Anthropos*, Parsons deployed a number of footnotes to offer editorial interventions and references. In *American Indian Life*, many of the same remarks, shorn of citation, are brought into the main text but set apart from Reed's narrative through the use of parentheses.[54] Usually the fact that these parentheticals are editorial additions is implicit. On one occasion, though, near the end of the text, the shift in implied authorship marked by parenthesis becomes explicit. Describing how a particular Deg Hit'an belief manifests itself in behavior, Reed exhales demonstratively during the interview with Parsons.[55] Marking this moment, Parsons writes, "(A prolonged, gentle expiration, as Reed showed me.)"[56] The first-person voice has attached to Reed throughout the text, from its first three words, "you asked me," all the way up until this moment on the penultimate page. But now, in "Reed showed me," this voice switches to the ethnographic auditor. This isn't a simple reversal, either. If Reed was the *I* and Parsons the *you* of the story's opening framing, here Reed is not the *you* but instead a third person to the exchange. With Parsons having situated herself and Reed as coauthors, she also here claims a special subjectivity, sensitive to shifts in affect, possessed of the capacity to register even gentle expirations.[57]

The question of Parsons's own authority in representing this material is tied up with the status of her informant—one of those "absentee informants," as she puts it in the preface to the *Anthropos* version of the piece, who are not currently resident among the society in question and therefore whose data "should be supplemented by field enquiry."[58] But Reed also dramatizes absence and inquiry in his own testimony. While the primary subject of the text is ostensibly Cries-for-salmon and her (at least in part fictional or hypothetical) biography, the facts of his own life are equally present. The narration refers to a number of episodes related to his service in the war, his attendance at Hampton, his boarding-school experience in Anvik, and his relationship to Deg Hit'an elders. The act of composition seems to afford Reed an occasion to reflect on the affective experience of displacement. One of the few times when Cries-for-salmon is represented with a particularized psychological experience involves an interaction with the narrator himself. Reed does not give all the details. Indeed, he implies that he does not *know* all the details and that this ignorance was itself centrally at issue in the interaction. Cries-for-salmon explains to him that she "would do almost anything" for Reed but that she can't. It would turn out poorly for her, she knows, and she "must live for [her] children." He explains, "Cries-for-salmon spoke this way to me because a while before she had said something to me which I did not understand, and it hurt her. An old man present said, 'You can't expect much of him' (as a Mission boy)."[59]

While here it's unclear whether "(as a Mission boy)" is Reed's explanation or Parsons's, this point is clarified by reference to the *Anthropos* version. In that earlier version of the text, the phrase is clearly marked as an editorial intervention by its placement inside brackets.[60] But Parsons's interjection adds little that we can't already infer from the dialogue. "With all the white man's knowledge, you have no intelligence whatsoever," Cries-for-salmon says to Reed.[61] This isn't the first time Reed situates the conditions of his own knowledge as related both to the experience of assimilatory settler institutions and to the protocols around the sharing of Deg Hit'an knowledge. Early in the text, he mentions his ignorance about a particular custom: "and when I have asked the old men they would answer, 'Who of us knows?' as they often answer when they *do* know but have not enough confidence in you to tell." Later in the story, too, Reed references elders who "talk to us, only on the outside of things."[62]

Indexing the conditions that limit his own authority, Reed also unsettles that of his interviewer. Do his references to the limits of what he knows register his displacement "as a Mission boy," or does his limited confidence in his auditor lead him, too, in speaking with Parsons, to talk on the outside of things? In the article version, Reed indicates just that kind of doubt with respect to his audience at the Citizenship Day performance a few days earlier. Describing a customary practice in handling ceremonial masks, he notes, "I did not explain this to the people here at the school at the dance I arranged for them. They would not have understood and they would only have laughed." The editorial voice of Parsons then adds, in brackets, an explanation of why "the narrator felt justified in making the masks for the school entertainment" anyway. But then in a remarkable break from the rhetoric of the piece's formatting as it appears in this version, all of this— *including* Reed's "I"—occurs in a footnote.[63] At the parallel point in *American Indian Life*, Reed's reference to the dance audience is simply deleted.[64] The entrance of Reed's first-person reference into the space of editorial comment may have seemed too much of a rhetorical exception when Parsons was revising the narrative for book publication.

The moment is also distinctive—and potentially troublesome for the project of Parsons's book—because, quite simply, of the way it uses the word "would" or more precisely the construction "would have." When Reed suggests that, if he had shared certain knowledge, the Hampton audience "would only have laughed," he uses a verb tense that he often does in the parts of the narrative that describe the life of his title character. Occasionally, Cries-for-salmon performs particular actions on particular occasions, and these actions are represented in the singulative past tense; more often, though, Reed describes what a person like Cries-for-salmon *would* do in a given set of circumstances. Imagining Cries-for-salmon's reactions to new developments—birth, death, transgression—his narration often also typically identifies what she *would have* done, as a function of custom, gender, and age. Her character oscillates between a real person familiar to Reed and a construction of ethnographic fiction and between the past of "would" (what this person did as a regular habit) and the probabilities of "would have" (the customary actions of such a person in such a place). Although this pattern participates in the ideological structure of what's often referred to as the "ethnographic present"—a grammar that represents Indigenous life as static and ahistorical, as a space in which changes don't occur—its form, in Reed's articulation, involves a shuttling between the conditional and the imperfect.[65] When he uses a similar grammar to describe his choice not to convey particular information to an audience that "would only have laughed," he not only hints at the potential that he could similarly withhold information from the folkloric collector but also repurposes the grammar of customary probability to describe events that *didn't* happen and that didn't happen not by probability but by choice.

The songs of Reed's performance are in the background here as one among other metonyms of biographical rhythm. One of Parsons's parenthetical interjections identifies another relevant feature of Reed's style. He has used an idiom related to the change of the seasons, describing how Cries-for-salmon learns certain prohibitions about singing in the wrong way at the wrong time, which could have the effect of extending the winter, "perhaps making it run into two winters (a frequent expression of the narrator meaning that the already short summer is further shortened)."[66] Since Reed does not use the expression elsewhere, the parenthetical implies a longer history of exchange. Parsons instructs the reader that she knows Reed's style—she knows what he *would* say—like Reed knows Cries-for-salmon's routine. That likeness is contoured in a specific way by the reference to frequency ("a *frequent* expression") and by the proximity of this reference to a discussion of discouraged musical expression. Frequency can measure behavioral recurrence, whether the habit of social custom or the habit of a narrator's verbal tic, but frequency can also indicate a measure of tone, of musical pitch—the kind of recurrence, below the threshold of perception, sometimes generated in song, graphed in a wave, or recorded on the phonograph that Parsons didn't use for the interview. The narrative's grammar of recursion registers the context of musical performance through which Parsons may have first learned of Reed. While the "picture" may have been Parsons's own trope for the narrative mode of the book, this has competition from the idea of a fictional biography as a representation of biographical temporalities imagined in terms of sound. This imaginary is sometimes explicit. Edward Sapir's entry, for instance, imagines a character whose life "flowed on insistently to the very rhythm of rising and falling wave."[67]

A lot happened in Reed's own life after he left Hampton. In the late 1930s, having come to live on the Tuscarora Reservation in upstate New York, he superintended a widely publicized fair of "Indian antiquities" that involved building a bark house.[68] During World War II, when clothing pins were running low in stores, he started fashioning them by hand and providing them to his neighbors.[69] In 1955, his daughter, Claudia Reed, became New York State Fair Indian Princess.[70] In 1958, his wife, Lucinda Reed—also Hampton class of '22—was part of a coalition resisting Robert Moses's plans to build a New York State Power Authority reservoir on Tuscarora land.[71]

Closer to the book history at hand, it's Sapir who happens to record what may have been Reed's last interaction with Boasian anthropologists. A question about the frequencies of speech provides all the drama in the interaction. The year after *American Indian Life* was published, a year in which Parsons became president of the American Ethnological Society, Reed was working as a photography instructor at a camp in northern Pennsylvania.[72] Sapir, who knew of him due to their status as cocontributors to Parsons's volume, traveled for a visit in order to gather information about Deg Hit'an vocabulary—or "Anvik Dialect," as Sapir wrote on the first page of his notebook for these sessions. He compiled an extensive list of individual words, then phrases, then sentences.[73] The *Southern Workman*, keeping tabs on Reed as a recent alum, reported in July that Reed and Sapir planned to keep working together through the summer.[74] The same month, though, Sapir wrote a letter to Boas mentioning that "Tom Reed (the Anvik Indian) proved disappointing."[75] Reed, he complained, was relatively ignorant of the language, due to his long time in residential schools.[76] As more than one moment in "Cries-for-salmon" suggests, Reed might have been quick to acknowledge the truth of this complaint. But Sapir's interest in what Reed knew, in how Reed talked, was not impartial. It was motivated by his dispute with another settler linguist, Pliny Goddard, about the particularities of tone in the Athabaskan language family. Goddard didn't believe Athabaskan speech to rely on tonal contrasts. Sapir did.[77] Reed's sense of the language, to Sapir's frustration, seemed to align with Goddard's. However, several years after the meeting with Reed, Sapir would himself come to cast doubt on his own position: "Later investigations," he writes in 1927, "may disclose the fact that the absence of tone is one of the distinguishing characteristics of the Pacific group of Athabaskan dialects."[78] In 1923, bending his ear toward the music of Reed's speech—sound-blinded not by his categories of phonemic apperception but by his cartographies of linguistic variation—he just hadn't heard what he thought he would.

Sapir had recently floated a new way of talking about such variation. In a chapter of his book *Language* (1921) titled "Language as a Historical Product: Drift," he writes that individual linguistic quirks of pronunciation and usage are not "the only kind of variability in language," insisting that "language is not merely something that is spread out in space, as it were—a series of reflections in individual minds of one and the same timeless picture. Language moves in a current of its own making. It has a drift."[79] The current of language is, unlike the "timeless picture," dynamic, but it is not random: "only those individual variations embody it or carry it which move in a certain direction, just as only certain wave movements in the bay outline the tide."[80] The absence of significant tonal contrast in Reed's voice didn't constitute a meaningful variation in Sapir's hearing until, in retrospect, he learned to recognize it as moving in concert with a greater "drift." In No-tongue's first song (as I'll suggest in the next section, returning in conclusion to Boas's transcriptions), as it transmutes the composition contexts of "Utitia'q's Song," the same metaphor is narrativized in ways that reflect a particular geographical imaginary.

Mapping the Sound

A few months after Oskison's review of Parsons's book appeared in the *New York Times*, another review appeared in the *Southern Workman*, this one by Emily K. Herron, who served as secretary to two Hampton presidents. While she praises the volume (especially Reed's contribution), she notes that it can be difficult for the reader to orient themselves in space and time. "The student who wishes to know the when and the where of these happenings," she writes, "will have to make a more or less careful study of internal evidence to determine whether the authors are referring to pre-Columbian or to present-day times, and will sometimes have to consult the index and notes to guess at the localities referred to."[81] I'm going to guess at a when and a where. In Cumberland Sound, on the water near a whaling station on Kekerten Island, on Friday, November 2, 1883, between midafternoon and 8 P.M.: this may have been the window of time and space in which somebody composed a song to which Boas, for the rest of his life, wished that he knew how to listen—a *pisiq* he stayed hungry to hear.[82]

Boas publishes a version, or rather versions, of "Utitia'q's Song" in an 1894 article for the *Journal of American Folklore*. In the header of the transcription, a cross-reference indicates that this is the same song whose melody had been notated, as I discussed earlier, on the five-line staff in *The Central Eskimo*; but here, Boas gives more lyrics. He gives them in three different ways (fig. 4.2). One is in Inuktitut using slightly different orthography than in *The Central Eskimo*. A second, rendered in small type between the lines of that "original" in English, presents an ostensibly literalist, phrase-by-phrase translation. A third, formatted as a stand-alone stanza, appears below in more normalized English syntax. For instance, whereas line 4 of the interlineal version above reads, "we have for our land slush," in the version below, Boas instead provides "my country is nothing but slush." This third version is closest to the one that appears as No-tongue's composition in "An Eskimo Winter" (with small differences such as *y* rather than *j* for *aya* in the 1922 text). Note that in the 1894 publication, this text is explicitly designated a "TRANSLATION," as if the interlineal version above it on the page were too clunky to qualify.[83]

Note, too, that the backstory offered here is placed between these versions of the text, facilitating the movement from scientific documentation to humanistic transmission. Whereas Boas's introduction of "Summer Song" asks the reader to remember a prehistory that they were never given ("once . . ."), many publications—both Boas's and others'—have given us the backstory for "Utitia'q's Song." Perhaps something about the way it winks needs context to be legible. But the story, as Boas iterates it across print contexts, doesn't always play out in exactly the same way, and here I'd like to elaborate what's at stake in these departures.

First, the standard account, in composite. In the 1894 piece, Boas writes that Utitia'q, a "young man," composed the piece in response to going "adrift on the ice when sealing," only reaching safety "after a week of hardships and privations."[84] In another article, Boas describes how Utitia'q "drifted on the floe at the mercy of the winds. Heavy snow-falls covered the drifting ice, the swell broke up the floe, and death started at him continually.

VIII. UTITIA'Q'S SONG. (TUNE, *l. c.*, p. 654.)

Aja ; adlēnaipunga ; ima adlenait !
    I am joyful;   that   is joyful!

Aja ;   sikuqdjualimena   adlenait !
    when it makes great ice for me   it is joyful!

Aja ; adlēnaipunga ; ima adlenait !
    I am joyful;   that   is joyful!

Nunagivuktarun tangerangitu, adlenait !
    We have for our land   slush,   it is joyful !

Aja ; adlēnaipunga ; ima adlenait !
    I am joyful;   that   is joyful!

Aja ;   qangaliqia   taba, adlenait !
    When indeed I do not know enough,   it is joyful !

Iqumanguadlunga   iqumalirpunga, adlenait !
    When I get tired of being awake   I begin to be awake,   it is joyful!

This song was composed by a young man named Utitiaq, who went adrift on the ice when sealing, and did not reach the shore until after a week of hardships and privations

TRANSLATION.

Aja, I am joyful; this is good!
Aja, there is nothing but ice around me, that is good!
Aja, I am joyful; this is good!
My country is nothing but slush, that is good !
Aja, I am joyful; this is good!
Aja, when, indeed, will this end ? this is good !
I am tired of watching and waking, this is good!

Franz Boas.

FIGURE 4.2 "Utitia'q's Song" in Inuktitut and English. Franz Boas, "Eskimo Tales and Songs" (1894), 49–50. Courtesy of JSTOR.

Yet he did not despair, nor even lose his temper, but, in mockery of his own misfortune, he composed the following song."[85] In still another, he uses almost the same language, though specifying that it was "for eight days"—a *long* week—that Utitia'q "drifted to and fro at the mercy of the winds."[86]

In 1922, "An Eskimo Winter" converts the language of these composition stories into fiction:

It had grown very cold. An icy slush was forming on the surface of the sea and the waves were rapidly calming down. The breaking up of the floe which seemed imminent through the night was no longer to be feared and immediate danger of drowning had passed. Still it was doubtful how the drift would end. With the changing tide, the current changed again, and the floe drifted away from the shore. The play of tides continued for days. Now the shore seemed near, so that the hopes of No-tongue were raised to a high pitch, and now the shore receded. In these days of anxiety No-tongue never lost courage, but, mocking his own misfortune, he composed this song:

Here, Boas embeds the song-text; then we return to the prose of the story, as the narrative describes No-tongue, "after a week of privations," finally drifting back to shore and trekking to rejoin the community.[87]

Utitia'q was personally familiar to Boas. He was one of the Inuit guides whom the anthropologist—or, at that point in his career, the geographer—hired in late 1883, and Boas's journal refers to him quite often, either as Utitia'q (in Boas's German orthography, often given as Utütiak) or by the nickname Yankee. We know, from Boas, that Utitia'q was deaf in one ear, as a result of a rifle fired too close to his face while hunting seal.[88] In Boas's journal entry from November 2, 1883, he records the following incident: "In the afternoon I climbed the hill with [James] Mutch to look around. There is a very heavy swell from the S[outh] which is breaking up the ice. As far as the entrance to the harbour the ice is all adrift. Yankee had drifted away with the ice and had lost his harpoon so he could not get back. I therefore lent the Eskimos my boat and around 8 they brought him back safely."[89] The scene and the phrasing in this 1883 journal entry—the swell breaking up the ice, the references to multiple forms of *drift*—involve several similarities both to the 1887 composition histories that appear in periodicals and to the context given in the 1922 short story.

The timing of this event in early November also lines up well with some versions of the misadventure that led to "Utitia'q's Song." For instance, although the 1887 version in the *Journal of the American Geographical Society of New York* does not mention any specific date (nor does the word "November" appear), it does appear in a passage just *after* a description of the weather patterns in September and October and just *before* a paragraph about December.[90] In an 1884 article for the same journal—a lengthy account of the expedition, with descriptions of material culture but no song transcriptions—Boas's account of the same month mentions that the Inuit "have to look out for every change of wind, as it happens very often that they go adrift," and he describes his routine of using daylight hours to survey shorelines and make tidal observations, while in the evenings he would carry out "ethnographical studies," as Inuit people told him "about the configuration of the land, about their travels, etc."[91] According to his field-notes, this "etc." included music. Throughout November 1883, Boas was taking down songs with regularity: on November 14, "Ssigna arrived and I transcribed a song"; on November 16, "I heard a new song from Kakodscha"; on November 27, "Kikker was here and gave me a new song that was linked to a story"; on November 29, "Kikker came in the evening to give me some new songs"; so on into December.[92]

Plausibly—though, to be clear, in contradiction with some of Boas's accounts—Utitia'q's song could have been composed in response to the November 2 event and, soon after, its text transmitted to Boas. (Not necessarily *given* to him, though this is the verb he often uses, implying a transfer of ownership that did not apply.) I say "plausibly" because it cannot be positively ruled out that there occurred some other, prior incident, well in the past by the time Boas arrived in Baffin, in which Utitia'q did indeed drift on an ice floe for over a week (rather than for less than a day, as Boas's field-notes indicate about this incident). Perhaps, too, in that case, there would be some explanation for why Boas never chose, in later accounts, to mention the striking fact that there were two such similar incidents that happened to this same person—one that Boas wrote about in his journals, another that he wrote about in later publications—but, for some reason, the two never mentioned in the same breath.[93] If we do trust the journal account over the inconsistent later iterations of the backstory, we might see these as the permutations of fictional revision. This would mean that Utitia'q did not happen to drift back to shore and then walk back on his own, as Boas reported, but was saved, much more quickly than Boas later suggested, by the intervention of others nearby—by people who had, most likely, kept Utitia'q's whereabouts within eyesight the whole time. And whether or not the anthropologist himself got into his boat with the others at this point—it doesn't sound as though he did, from the journal entry—he was materially involved: he lent something.[94]

Relying on the truth of some elements of the report in order to parse the unresolved incongruities between other versions of the story, my inference is speculative. I risk it so as to throw into clearer relief what's at issue in either version of the scene (and in Boas's choice to reiterate this story, out of all the stories he heard, as often as he did). How does it alter the rhetorical effects of this song-text to imagine that its composer was stuck on an ice floe for more than a week, as opposed to less than a day, and that it was fortune rather than community that saved him?[95] Of course, there is a certain dramatic heightening at play in these differences. But that explanation does not seem to fit with the reasonably reliable facts that Boas erases his own witnessing of this scene of emergency (which, too, would have heightened things), while referring to Utitia'q as if he were some songster known primarily by reputation rather than somebody with whom the anthropologist spent every day, in difficult circumstances, for months. By isolating the event from the immediate setting and detaching the song from a scene of collective aid, the framing of the song becomes able to note that Utitia'q's kin and community "had almost given him up for lost."[96] This starts to carry the emergency energy of salvage anthropology.[97] The real danger here, in the violence of this thinking, is that the scientist almost gets to the song too late.

It is important that this is a song that Boas could not have heard and transcribed in the moment of its first singing. More precisely, *nobody* could have done so, other than its composer: that is the condition identified in its content. The decontextualized drift that haunts transcription is the situation of this song's making. The song itself calls this situation joyful. This ironic voice opens up another way to think about the possible revision to the backstory, one based not in the rhetorical forms of the anthropologist's justifications but in the style of the composer. That is, if we know that Utitia'q is a satirist, perhaps it is also the case that he is a hyperbolist; that the exaggerations of the song's backstory are themselves authored by its composer, not its transcriber; and that these revisions, transparently known as such to everyone who was around, then make their way into the record as a silent correction of history.[98]

One of the other things that we know about Utitia'q—or, more precisely, that we know Boas recalled about him, on the basis of a brief anecdote in *Eskimo Story*—is that the guide was both curious about and then quickly disinterested in the mapping project that was one of the major purposes of the expedition. As their companions were making camp one afternoon, Boas writes, he and Utitia'q climbed a hill "to take a number of observations that [Boas] needed in order to complete the map of the [Cumberland] Sound": "While we were up there, Utütiak looked with wonder at the instruments, the use of which, of course, he did not understand."[99] Whether Boas's "of course" is justified (it isn't), Utitia'q, he reports, soon "tired of this." Later, Boas explains that mapping what he misnames as "unexplored land" requires "different kinds of instruments to determine one's location on the earth": "We had a compass to determine the direction in which to travel, and other instruments to observe our position relative to the stars and sun."[100] A mixture of wonder and boredom, the affect of Utitia'q's response to these navigational and surveying instruments correlates with the posture adopted in his song, at least as Boas's publications, on some occasions, represent it:

> Aya: Awaking from my slumbers in the dawn,
> Monotonous fields of ice
> And gloomy lanes of water
> I behold.[101]

But if the affect is similar, the situations make for a pointed contrast. The singer is in a landscape of "fields" that are not "land," a landscape of indeterminate "slush" rather than mappable territory, and even when sitting still, he drifts, without ability or agency "to determine the direction in which to travel," from one "location on the earth" to another.[102]

For Boas, affect was intrinsic to the study of geography. In 1887—earlier in the same year that the idea of sound-blindness comes to his attention—he publishes an article (now cited almost as often as "On Alternating Sounds") titled "The Study of Geography." In it, he distinguishes between two modes of inquiry. One is associated with the "aesthetical disposition" of the physicist, whose systematic thinking "sees only the beautiful order of the world" and is allergic to "confused impressions."[103] The other is the cosmographer, who "holds to the [individual] phenomenon" in question, no matter its confusions.[104] Insofar as geography is beholden to the concrete particularities of "the physiognomy of the earth," it belongs to cosmography; that is, because the material variety of the face of the earth can only coalesce as a representational unity in the context of a subjective response, the work of the geographer "approaches the domain of art."[105] Often the Cumberland Sound expedition is represented as a moment when Boas's early interests in physical sciences moved to the mature phase of his career in humanistic research and the study of "culture."[106] The fact that it predates his discussion of sound-blindness in "On Alternating Sounds"—another discussion of "confused impressions," though of speech rather than of land—thus makes the expedition a good plot point in the narrative of that essay as the crux of a paradigm shift in cultural theory. One effect of this is to position that shift as an almost incidental effect of the encounters he experienced while carrying out geographical research. But the print lives of "Utitia'q's Song" might remind us that the geographical imaginary is more than incidental to such study.

In one of the first major reports to come out of the expedition—*Baffin-Land*, published in Germany in 1885—Boas uses "Anthropogeography" (*Anthropogeographie*) as the header of an extended section on population distribution.[107] Here Boas argues that the Arctic landscape, with its "immense stretches of uniform land," affords an ideal space for anthropogeographical research because it eliminates some of the environmental variables that otherwise muddy our understanding of "simple relationships between land and people."[108] If part of what keeps pulling Boas back to this song, over the decades, is its play of irony and pathos, perhaps another factor is the way that its narrative of drift troubles the idea that this relationship could be simple. His transcriptions decontextualize these lyrics from the performative spaces of Inuit drum-dance—including the *qaggiq* that he attempts to diagram on other loose pages of the same fieldnotes that first record "Utitia'q's Song"—yet the content of that song-text still registers, by unsettling, another urgent context, one always present in the anthropological surround of colonial expansion (if not always named as anthropogeographical): the epistemology of territory.[109] The expanded site of these early transcriptions, Baffin Island, was, even when *American Indian Life* was in preparation, a space of real cartographic doubt for the imperial powers that sought to map it. The ubiquitous publicity of Donald B. MacMillan's 1921 expedition to Baffin Island reminded US newspaper readers that this was uncharted land, that even the shorelines of one of the world's largest islands remained largely unknown (at least to *qallunaat*).[110] The same year, one Canadian government officer, looking back at the 1880 transfer of sovereignty—the vagueness of which continued to fuel disagreements about where exactly the lines of sovereignty had been drawn—reported that "the Imperial Government did not know what they were transferring, and on the other hand the Canadian Government had no idea what they were receiving."[111] The line verges on a thumbnail parody of empire. For Boas, the maps of whose earliest expedition were sometimes cited in this discourse, No-tongue's predicament on the floe might have troped all this trouble over the shoreline.

One of the effects of Boas's naming of the composer of this song-text "No-tongue" is that it brings together, in the de- and recontextualization of translation, two concepts that sit in close proximity in Inuit methods of navigation. Certain forms of snowdrift, *uqalurait*, derive their name from the Inuktitut term for "tongue," due to the tongue-like shape with which they come to a point. Because the wind pushes these drifts into a consistent directional orientation, and because they often harden into semipermanent features of the winter landscape, *uqalurait* serve as navigational markers. "In Winter we used Uqalurait to tell us which direction to go," as the sculptor Mariano Aupilarjuk has said.[112] As climate change affects wind patterns in Nunavut, it has also made the formation of these drifts more variable, affecting their utility for spatial orientation.[113]

There's no indication that Boas, in using the name No-tongue for a character who sings about drifting on the Sound, anticipated the verbal collapse of tongue and drift in the geographical indices of *uqalurait*. Nor was this, as far as the evidence shows, a relevant resonance in Utitia'q's actual drum-dance composition. This translingual resonance is only an effect that is relevant to "Utitia'q's Song" as it becomes verse and then as it is integrated into fiction as No-tongue's song. But I close with this resonance as an effect of the text's historical drift and return. Recently, along its route—a route whose passage through scientific and popular print brought it, in the closing chapters of Parsons's book, into contact with the models of linguistic assimilation and racial difference that made the tones of Thomas B. Reed's voice so hard for some to hear—the song has appeared in a prominent anthology of "American poetry."[114] This seems amiss; even if his nickname was Yankee before his pseudonym became No-tongue, Utitia'q didn't give or even lend his song to America. But it's perhaps right, too, for "Utitia'q's Song"—the object iterated in print rather than the musical work, the object not deleted but inaugurated by the blue *X* across a page of notes—to be called American poetry, as its ironies and affects project themselves in a singer's desire for and alienation from the waveformed line of the land.

Postscript

· ·

Two more stories about sound-blindness:

1. On January 10, 2015, hifi nub posted "an odd question" in the forums of the website Head-Fi, devoted to headphone talk: "Do you guys get sound blindness? As in, you listen to your devices for so long that you adapt to it? = buying better items than what you have already."[1] Other forum users commiserated. "Yeah, I've noticed that," replied BrownBear. "I usually end up taking a break and then trying a different headphone for awhile to kind of readjust my mind."[2] ProtegeManiac offered a curt correction: "Vision = blind; Hearing = deaf" (followed by a "biggrin.gif" to signal good humor).[3] billybob_jcv, too, had reservations about the label. "I don't know if I would call it 'sound blindness'—I think it is natural for you to become accustomed to the headphones you use all the time. This becomes your brain's idea of 'normal.'" And then "upgraditis hits and you start wanting more and/or different."[4] hifi nub's reference to "sound blindness" positions the dulling of aural experience as an effect of habituation at the interface of sensorium and device. billybob_jcv's "upgraditis" diagnoses the same experience as a periodic inflammation of late-capitalist consumerism.

2. Two years later, in a March 2017 thread on Hacker News, rasur reflected ambivalently on cochlear implant technology. "I don't have a CI myself," rasur clarified, "but my 6 year old son does, and I am somewhat concerned that he is-or-might be experiencing partial sound 'blindness' (meaning: sure speech processing is adequate but there are surely some things that are processed away)." The article under discussion, linked at the top of the thread, had to do with developments in hearing-aid design that use deep-learning software to better pick out individual voices in noisy crowds, changing the way that assistive hearing devices equalize the frequencies of speech sounds. "I have a fair amount of experience in music/sound-recording environments and it makes me somewhat sad for him that he's still 'missing out' (although obviously this is outweighed by the fact that he can actually hear and communicate now, but I'm sure you get what I mean)." This is ultimately an incidental question for rasur, though, whose "main interest here is about

using machine learning to assist people who do not know sign-language to understand signers rather than to 'improve' the actual hearing process."[5]

Unlike the two print objects with which this book began—the clothing-store advertisement and the essay on anthropological linguistics—these posts can't be traced back to a common source. Nor is it probable that either of them was informed by any of the prior definitions of sound-blindness I referred to in the introduction (even if the orthographic quirks of the usernames "rasur" and "hifi nub," which differently exploit the phonetic spectrum of the letter "u" in English writing, could have served as good examples for Boas in "On Alternating Sounds").[6] The question that some early twentieth-century theorists of culture might ask of these phrasings would be whether their similarity is an effect of independent invention or of diffusion. The distinction often carried a political charge. As the debate is often (if too schematically) represented, narratives of independent invention—insofar as they implied that all peoples would be likely to have the same ideas at different points along one big human timeline—sometimes turned universalism into a foundation for social-evolutionary racism, while diffusionism emphasized the historical particularities of influence across geographies of human difference.[7]

This book's central questions have had to do with the diffusion and invention of textualities. Where, when, and to what ends have the forms of our textual sociality been elaborated, disciplined, transformed, and refused? These forms matter a great deal in people's everyday conception of their life in common. To orient the study of texts around their own relation to their making *as* texts, then, isn't necessarily to retreat into a sterilized media history; it's to open out onto the consequences of the basic fact of writing as the place where expression is understood to become isolable and reproducible—and often, as a corollary, where sound is imagined to become visual. This corollary is not automatic, natural, or uniformly constructed. Sound, after all, diffuses, in the sense of that term that is connected with refraction, attenuation, and drift.[8] Transcribing that kind of object entails more than making the ephemeral permanent or, in a common metaphor of discursive equity by way of discursive power, amplifying the weak signal; it means a kind of writing that shifts in its modalities of legibility, and it asks for a kind of reading that's less diffusionist as a position than diffusive as a way of moving. So the chapters here have meant to move across histories of visualized sound—of phonetic transparency and sovereignty claims, of visible speech and assimilatory education, of the auditory aesthetics of racialized movement, of mapping music in lines of type—whose political plurality can't easily be stabilized by reference to a culture concept that itself exists in a state of constant flicker. Still, there are continuities here: the same preoccupations with ability, literacy, and medium that tangled in what was, in the late nineteenth century, a brief public fascination with the concept of sound-blindness also touch the way we talk about everything from headphones to family.

In the use of "sound-blindness" to describe experiences of tonality and timbre—and, within those experiences, differences of degree rather than of kind—each of the online instances of the term I've just cited might have seemed a more satisfactory usage to those who, in the late 1880s, felt that the phrase's implicit analogy between color and phoneme made for an awkward fit. The scare quotes that rasur places around the second word in "sound 'blindness'" underscore the metaphoric stretch of an analogy often naturalized. No wonder, since here the trope is asked to cover a lot of ground. This parent's apprehensions involve, directly or indirectly, controversies over assistive hearing technology in Deaf culture, ideas of technological mediation that weigh utility against aesthetic experience, norms of what counts as an "actual" sensory or communicative modality, and concerns about what not only the CI user but also the person who is illiterate in American Sign Language might miss out on. Each of these angles involves contingencies specific to the twenty-first century: new interfaces for sensory transduction; new horizons for, and anxieties about, the virtuality of our communities. These contingencies are outside the scope of this book. It's my hope, though, that having a feel for the depth of their prehistories—for their connection with the oldest and in fact the constitutive political problems of American literature, those that emerge in and as the uneven textualities of bodies and lands—can help us to recognize these futurities and fears less as shocks than as reverberations.

Acknowledgments

Sound-Blind would not be in print without the unflagging support, the critical rigor, and the professional mentorship of my graduate advisor, Dorothy Hale. Thank you, Dori.

I could not have imagined an environment more conducive to the book's completion than Bard College. Thanks to every one of my students, whose own intellectual passions perennially revitalize my work. What I think about sound would be thinner without my Sound Cluster colleagues: Matthew Deady, Laura Kunreuther, Danielle Riou, Whitney Slaten, Maria Sonevytsky, Julianne Swartz, Drew Thompson, and Olga Touloumi. What I know about literary history would be narrower without fellow Americanists Elizabeth Frank, Donna Ford Grover, Peter L'Official, and Matthew Mutter. Gracious readers in more than one writing group have helped me get through difficult stretches of the manuscript; thanks to Celia Bland, Maria Cecire, Lauren Curtis, Lianne Habinek, Erica Kaufman, and David Ungvary. While I don't have space to acknowledge every other wonderful colleague at Bard, I do want to nod to a few more folks who—as mentors, collaborators, or both—have supported my work: Deirdre d'Albertis, Krista Caballero, Cathy Collins, Christian Crouch, Adhaar Desai, Lory Gray, Cole Heinowitz, Peter Klein, Marisa Libbon, Nathan Shockey, Yuka Suzuki, Éric Trudel, and Marina van Zuylen. Thank you to each Stevenson librarian who handled one of the interlibrary loans that made the research possible.

Thank you also to archivists Brian Carpenter of the American Philosophical Society Library, Justin Gardiner of the Helen Keller Archive at the American Foundation for the Blind, and Gina Rappaport of the National Anthropological Archives at the Smithsonian Institution.

Formative occasions in the project's development included a seminar led by Cindi Katz at the Futures of American Studies Institute at Dartmouth and a workshop at the First Book Institute hosted by Penn State University's Center for American Literary Studies, codirected by Sean X. Goudie and Priscilla Wald. A session led by the latter together with institute faculty Grant Wythoff helped me to reimagine the manuscript, as did the feedback and comradery of coparticipants Matthew Bolton, Abby Goode, Jessica Hurley, Joo Ok Kim, Jarvis McInnis, Sunny Yang, and Meina Yates-Richard. I'm grateful to the organizers and audiences of conference sessions at which I've presented pieces of the research, including panels chaired by Rita Felski (Modern Language Association, 2014), Loretta G. Woodard (American Literature Association, 2016), Gavin Jones (Modern Language Association, 2018), Lavelle Porter (American Studies Association, 2018), and Sara Kaplan (American Studies Association, 2021).

Many other teachers, scholars, and friends have influenced the project in sometimes less formalized but no less generative contexts and conversations over the years, from grad-school days to yesterday; thanks to Elizabeth Abel, Duff Allen, Aaron Bady, Ashley Barnes, Etienne Benson, Stephen Best, Mitchell Breitwieser, Benjamin Cannon, Juliana Chow, Daniel Clinton, Jean Day, Marcy Dinius, Jeffrey Doker, Maude Emerson, Christopher Fan, Zachary Gordon, Blake Hausman, Javier Huerta, Monica Huerta, Nicholas Junkerman, Naomi Kohen, Anjuli Raza Kolb, Benjamin Lempert, Manya Lempert, Michael Lucey, Cody Marrs, Gillian Osborne, Samuel Otter, Megan Pugh, Scott Saul, Matthew Seidel, Katherine Snyder, and—a mentor who offered crucial guidance as the project came into shape and therefore last in this list only alphabetically—Bryan Wagner.

At the University of North Carolina Press, it's been my great fortune to have the editorial insight and counsel of Lucas Church. Many thanks also to Thomas Bedenbaugh, Iris Levesque, and everyone else whose meticulous work helped bring this text to print. The manuscript was greatly improved by the feedback of three reviewers: Julie Beth Napolin (whose own writing about literary sound has deeply influenced my work) and two anonymous readers whose care in responding to the argument, both in the details and in the larger arc, puts me in their great debt.

Several paragraphs of chapter 1 appeared in the editorial introduction to "'A Laboratory Fancy' by John M. Oskison," *PMLA* 137, no.1 (January 2022) and are republished with permission of Cambridge University Press. An earlier version of chapter 3 appeared as "Gatsby's Tattoo: Gesture, Tic, and Description" in *Criticism* 46, no. 4 (Fall 2014) and is republished with permission of Wayne State University Press.

Thanks to my family: my parents, my siblings, my nieces and nephew and cousins and aunts and all the other extended (and proximate!) kinfolk. We are so lucky to have you all in our corner. I shift to "we" to include two people: Alexis Lowry, whose brilliance and love have made every page of what I've written here both possible and better (*thank you*), and Louis, my other favorite new person to read books with.

Notes

Introduction

1. See Bucholtz, "Politics of Transcription," for an influential piece on sociolinguistic transcription. For an important earlier study in a similar vein (if less explicitly invested in the political than in the pedagogical and psychological), see Ochs, "Transcription as Theory." On the selectivity of both aural and automatic musical transcription, see Winkler, "Writing Ghost Notes." For a recent literary-critical engagement with "the politics of transcription" in just those terms (I'll soon cite other studies where the idea pertains less explicitly), see Edwards, *Epistrophies*, 65.

2. Boone and Mignolo's *Writing without Words* remains a touchstone in the critical challenge to colonial ontologies of textuality. See also Garcia, *Signs of the Americas*.

3. U T K Clothing House, "Sound Blindness" (advertisement), *Minneapolis Journal*, January 10, 1888.

4. Boas, "On Alternating Sounds," 52. Borrowing the term from Fechnerian psychophysics, Boas refers to a "differential threshold" ("On Alternating Sounds," 49) — the point at which some difference between sensory information (the weight of two objects, for instance) becomes "just noticeable" to a human subject. Fechner describes the counterintuitive logic of this threshold: "A stimulus or stimulus difference can be increased up to a certain point without being felt; above that point it is felt and its growth is noticed. How can something that does not reach consciousness when it is weak begin to affect the mind when it is strengthened?" (*Elements of Psychophysics*, 205). Stocking develops the connection between "On Alternating Sounds" and Fechner in "Polarity and Plurality," 55. On Fechnerian measurement and contemporaneous ideas of racialized sensation, see Fretwell, *Sensory Experiments*, with reference to Boas on 259.

5. My formulation of these senses of "culture" adopts Stocking's claim that in the early 1880s Boas "still thought of culture in a preanthropological sense, not as *embodying* custom and tradition, but rather as standing in *opposition* to them" ("From Physics to Ethnology," 150). If "preanthropological" implies a clear definitional chronology, see Williams on the staggered adjustments in the term's usage ("Culture," in *Keywords*, 76–82). On the difference between Stocking and Williams on this point, see Handler, "Raymond Williams, George Stocking." My account here is also indebted to B. Evans, *Before Cultures*; see esp. 4–7.

6. Darnell, *Invisible Genealogies*, 40; Silverstein, "From Inductivism to Structuralism." Harvey similarly writes that the linguistic insight of Boas's 1889 essay "became one of the bases for that anthropologist's broader insistence upon cultural relativity" (*Native Tongues*, 142).

7. Gaskill, *Chromographia*, 32; B. Evans, "Introduction," 436. Wagner, too, writes of the same text that "Boas redescribes the intractability of primitive culture as the noise endemic to the encounter between cultures, establishing in the process the modern concept of human diversity" (*Disturbing the Peace*, 88). Wagner's larger project here—attending to how ideas of Black voice and music mediate histories of, and responses to, legal exclusion, while working on questions of sound via histories of print—influences my attention to the discursive and material histories that inform, and are sometimes occluded by, discourse about "culture."

8. Hochman, *Savage Preservation*, 91.

9. Stocking, "From Physics to Ethnology," 160.

10. Wead, "Study of Primitive Music," 75; Miller, "Strobophotographic Analysis," 49; Jakobson, "Franz Boas' Approach," 191. Incidentally, Jakobson's well-known 1954 study of aphasic disorders in their relation to linguistic principles of selection/metaphor and combination/metonymy—"Two Aspects"—uses as an opening example the question of phonetically "alternating sounds," though not described with that phrase: the utterance of "pig" as opposed to "fig" in *Alice's Adventures in Wonderland* (241).

11. Lowie's 1937 chapter on Boas's work cites from a number of his mentor's early essays without mentioning "On Alternating Sounds" (*History*, 128–55); nor does it appear in Herskovits's book-length 1953 appreciation (*Franz Boas*). While I agree with Reichel (in a recent application of Boas's essay to the poetic experiments of his students) that "scholars of sound and literature" should "consider 'On Alternating Sounds' for profitable use in current debates," I'm here arguing against the ancillary point that the 1889 text, "in its contemporaneous reception, was frequently understood as providing strong grounds for the use of new sound reproduction technologies as ethnographic tools" (*Writing Anthropologists*, 84).

12. Stocking, "From Physics to Ethnology," 159. It may be relevant to Stocking's diction that the term "foreshadowing" recurs frequently in Herskovits's *Franz Boas*, a book that Stocking knew well; Herskovits uses the term in a claim that Stocking singles out for critique (Herskovits, *Franz Boas*, 9; Stocking, "From Physics to Ethnology," 136–37).

13. Sundquist, *To Wake the Nations*, 5, 6. Sundquist quotes Stocking in a discursive note (659n48).

14. "One could say that Literary Sound Studies specialize in sounds as signs. But audible sounds, too, qualify as signs" (Mieszkowski, *Resonant Alterities*, 23). Ong argues that "our complacency in thinking of words as signs" stems from a tendency, especially predominant in typographic societies, "to reduce all sensation and indeed all human experience to visual analogues" (*Orality and Literacy*, 74).

15. B. Evans, *Before Cultures*. When "culture" did feature in late nineteenth-century discourse about sound-blindness, it was, as Evans's work cues us to notice, not necessarily in the modern anthropological sense; in an 1888 *Phrenological Journal* article titled "Sound Blindness," the term indicates cultivation or training: "unless the person is *deaf*, by which is properly meant some imperfection in the auditing apparatus, culture will improve his perception of tone difference" (114). On "side-shadowing," see Morson, *Narrative and Freedom*.

16. Simpson, "Why White People."

17. Mitchell and Snyder, *Narrative Prosthesis*. Relevant here as well is the authors' conception of disability as "that which provides writers with a means of moving between the micro and macro levels of textual meaning," a movement they describe as "the materiality of metaphor" (57). See also Schor, "Blindness as Metaphor." Ruth Benedict's "Anthropology and the Abnormal" (1934) is often cited as (and is) an important early entry in the anthropology of disability; there she argues that conceptions of the normal and good in human behavior are just as contingent as the range of phonetic articulations. Part of what I'm suggesting here is that "On Alternating Sounds," referring to the pluralities of physical ability as a way into understanding linguistic difference, has more in common with an argument like Benedict's than is commonly recognized; to whatever extent, then, that the field retains a sense of Boas's essay as foundational, his argument's predication on ideas of impairment deserves more consideration.

18. Lane, *Mask of Benevolence*, 43.

19. U T K Clothing House, "Deaf or Blind" (advertisement), *Minneapolis Tribune*, January 12, 1888.

20. "Reader's Notes," 79.

21. LeConte, "Sound-Blindness," 312.

22. Boas, "On Alternating Sounds," 47. Rossi writes that the term's implicit "analogy with color blindness situated phonetic confusion within the familiar body of work on color perception and culture" (*Republic of Color*, 134). On contemporaneous discourse about the distribution of color-blindness across racial groups, see Gaskill, *Chromographia*, 26–28.

23. Wiltse, "Sound-Blindness," 99. In the same republication, Wiltse adds an epigraph: "He cared for their heads as he did for their hearts, demanding that whatever entered them should be plain and clear as the silent moon in the sky.— Pestalozzi" (99). The next sentence of the source text, which Wiltse does not quote, is telling: "To insure this, he taught them to see and hear with accuracy, and cultivated their powers of attention" (Pestalozzi, *Leonard and Gertrude*, 157).

24. On deafness as a "critical modality," see L. Davis, *Enforcing Normalcy*, 100.

25. See Levin, "Tones," on the technological and intellectual history of the waveform. For an exhortation that we recognize sound as a phenomenological medium (like light), not as a category of objects, and that "the ears, just like the eyes, are organs of observation, not instruments of playback," see Ingold, "Four Objections," 137. In a foundational text of sound studies, Schafer critiques the development of acoustics into "the science of sightreading" (*Tuning of the World*, 128).

26. "The transcript turns oral sources into visual ones," writes Portelli, "which inevitably implies changes and interpretations" (*Death of Luigi Trastulli*, 47). Portelli places such revisions in the loss column: textual distortions to be remediated through oral history. This book takes them as primary objects: interventions to be understood through print history.

27. Oliveros, "Some Sound Observations," 103. For a related point on the way that dynamics of narrative voicing are mediated in the visual qualities of textual representation, see D. Hale, *Social Formalism*, paraphrasing Bakhtinian studies of

the novel: "the written form of reported discourse makes visible the speaker's necessary relation to a social other different from himself while preserving the autonomous discourse of both quoted and quoting speaker" (151). See also Rancière on the construction of "the sayable and the visible" as the interface of aesthetic genre and political regime (*Politics of Aesthetics*, 15).

28. Although my method is often close to the practice of "thick description" that Geertz influentially identified as a crucial methodological overlap between literary-critical and ethnographic writing, the project here differs in at least one key premise: Geertz's underlying conception of culture as a kind of text. His work takes culture as an "acted document" and ethnography as "trying to read (in the sense of 'construct a reading of') a manuscript—foreign, faded, full of ellipses, incoherencies, suspicious emendations, and tendentious commentaries, but written not in conventionalized graphs of sound but in transient examples of shaped behavior" ("Thick Description," 10). If, though, one understands text-making as practice—as itself a transient example of shaped behavior—this weakens the analogical leverage of defining culture as an "acted document." All documents are acted. Thus, my interest in processes of "transcription" aligns more closely with something like the model of "entextualization" and "(co)textualization" proposed by Silverstein and Urban as a way to encompass the contingency of text-making. This model understands textuality—that is, the idea that some discursive events can be segmented off from the world—not as a static fact of language or print media but as a "metadiscursive construct" that is useful for particular social ends ("Natural History of Discourse," 2). The various *ways* in which ideas of textuality become useful (and the relation between those uses and the practical circumstances of text-making) then become the key question, together with the historical contingencies of how "things refuse integration into signifying systems" (Gallagher, "Raymond Williams," 88).

29. Some related experiments include Kane on the acousmatic effects of the literary text (*Sound Unseen*), Napolin on the acoustical unconscious of modernist narrative (*Fact of Resonance*), M. Smith on the soundscape of American sectionalism (*Listening to Nineteenth-Century America*), and G. Stewart on the phonotext (*Reading Voices*). My approach to textual history also has affinities with what is sometimes termed "genetic criticism" (see Hay, "Genetic Criticism").

30. On "hearing across media," see Edwards, *Epistrophies*, 253–67. On print and sound in African American cultural production, see (in addition to works cited elsewhere in this introduction) Dinius, "Look!!"; Noland, *Voices of Negritude*; A. Reed, *Soundworks*, and Vogel, *Stolen Time*. On the "detail," see Schor, *Reading in Detail*; and Vazquez, *Listening in Detail*. On "weak" or "partial" methodologies, see J. Chow, *Nineteenth-Century American Literature*; Dimock, *Weak Planet*; Saint-Amour, "Weak Theory"; and Sedgwick, "Paranoid Reading," 133–36. Both the question of print materiality and that of weak versus strong theory, not to mention the context of theories of culture around the turn of the twentieth century, bring my study into conversation with Michaels's *Our America* and *Shape of the Signifier*. The former book, concerned in part with the nativist and white-supremacist overtones of the category "American," elaborates how "culturalist" discourse reproduces racialist logic and depoliticizes economic relationships. The latter argues that in-

terpretation grounded in "cultures," seeming to afford respect to the differences of individual responses to aesthetic phenomena, actually reduces those responses in ways that (a) approximate racial essentialisms and (b) neutralize disagreement and stymie class-based organization. For Michaels, these effects are mirrored in post-structuralists' evacuation of intention and their affinity for the meaningless mark. These claims—and the historical narratives through which Michaels develops them—inform *Sound-Blind* in several key respects; indeed, one way to frame my interest in textual history is as a way of attending to situated intentionalities. Yet the way I treat such situatedness also aligns with Wang's critique that, in *Shape of the Signifier*, Michaels's "distinction between meaning and the nonmeaning of materiality, or sensation, does not allow for the possibility of materiality as the sensation of meaning" nor of "a politics to sensation that ineluctably informs the politics of meaning" ("Against Theory beside Romanticism," 4, 27); and at the level of method, where Michaels is explicitly interested in what people "ought to" believe out of (strong) theoretical consistency, I prioritize here the processes through which people "actually" come to write what they write (*Shape of the Signifier*, 14). This doesn't entail a straightforward positivism. Some speculation is necessary in studying what Sedgwick calls the "dynamic and historically contingent ways that strong theoretical constructs interact with weak ones in the ecology of knowing" ("Paranoid Reading," 145).

31. Scott, *Domination*, 5.

32. Scott, *Domination*, 6.

33. Livermore, *My Story of the War*, 261. I cite the edition that Raboteau does (*Slave Religion*, 312–13, 372n39), but the text is republished several times in the period. Scott himself notes that *Domination* "is not a close, textural, contingent, and historically grounded analysis" (x) but a structural one, making it misguided to present the contingencies of requotation as if their correction would alter Scott's account on its terms. But given Scott's use of "transcript" as "a complete record" that "would also include nonspeech acts such as gestures and expressions" (*Domination*, 2n1), it would seem to make sense to enfold the fact, for instance, that Raboteau's transcription erases Livermore's explicit representations of Aggy's gestures. Of course, I don't fantasize that I will capture the full range of relevant contexts of the material I cite either. What I'm trying to get at, though, is a difference in orientation: in *Domination*, the transcript is primarily a figure *for* politics; in *Sound-Blind*, a transcript is primarily a site *of* politics. This approach is, in fact, more congruent with some aspects of Scott's later work, as in his account of the rejection and recuperation of literacy as practices of resistance to settler states in *Art of Not Being Governed* (220–37). Yet there, too, when referring directly to a "transcript of . . . words spoken," Scott positions texts as exempt from worldliness: whereas "oral culture exists and is sustained only through each unique performance at a particular time and place," the "written record, in radical contrast, can persist more or less invisibly for a millennium and suddenly be dug up and consulted as an authority" (230). In one sense, this persistence is precisely what allows us to compare different entextualizations of Aggy's prophesy. But the drift of those versions also suggests that the contrast that Scott describes is not so radical, in that both the writing and the

excavation(s) of the record also constitute contextually responsive performances. Conversely, the argument that historical revision meets less "friction" in oral traditions because "what is in fact quite novel can pass itself off as the voice of tradition without much fear of contradiction" (234) is only true to a point: novelties can be marked and disputed by those who themselves have iterated the tradition.

34. On the varieties of linguistic politics that informed the circulation of dialect poetry, see Jones, *Strange Talk*; and Nurhussein, *Rhetorics of Literacy*.

35. This formulation is indebted to Abu-Lughod's articulation of "narrative ethnographies of the particular" ("Writing against Culture," 153). Also relevant here, in a different theoretical register, is Silverstein's analysis of "micro-social and macro-social frames of analysis" as dialectically related in performance ("Indexical Order," 193). In literary studies, my approach aligns with Pratt's argument that nineteenth-century American literature "pluralized time," rather than reinforcing a temporally homogeneous nationalist/imperialist print culture (*Archives of American Time*, 5).

36. Robinson constructs the phrase—which gathers a spectrum of auralities touched by settler-colonial epistemology, in "an admittedly uncomfortable pairing of Indigenous and settler orientations"—"from two Halq'eméylem words: shxwelítemelh (the adjective for settler or white person's methods/things)," which is derived from a term meaning "starving person," and "xwélalà:m (the word for listening)" (*Hungry Listening*, 2). I have not read the section of Robinson's book written exclusively for Indigenous readers, and my paraphrase may reflect this partial reading. While agreeing with Robinson (and others) on the importance of critical positionality in the study of aurality, I also appreciate Ingold's argument that, because sound circulates, "attentive listening . . . entails the opposite of emplacement"; it requires movement ("Four Objections," 139). My interest in, say, the U T K Clothing House is in some small part due to the fact that I grew up a couple of miles south of its Nicollet Avenue location, while the method I bring to bear on histories of print citation is a cousin to the questions of phonographic history that led me, as a young person, up and down the same street—named, as I didn't then know, after the nineteenth-century geographer J. N. Nicollet—to the dollar bins of the record shops that dotted it in the 1990s: Wide Angle, Roadrunner, Let It Be. See Weheliye's conception of sampling-based historiography via Du Bois (*Phonographies*, 73–105).

37. Peirce, *Collected Papers*, 2:172.

38. Peirce, *Collected Papers*, 2:171.

39. Silverstein's work on indexical order has been important to the more recent usage of the term. "Every discourse event manifests, by degrees, authoritative, warranted, or heretofore uncountenanced or even contested entextualizations," he writes. "The flow of value thus comes to be mappable as a felt effect or adjunct of interlocutors' strategic positionalities—presupposed or entailed—in such complex macrosocial space and of people's stasis in and/or movement through its ever-changing configurations" ("'Cultural' Concepts," 623).

40. "Nonsymbolic representational modalities"—iconicity and indexicality—"pervade the living world," writes Kohn, "and have underexplored properties that are quite distinct from those that make human language special" (*How Forests Think*, 8).

41. Although *Sound-Blind*'s method does not fully align with a postcritical stance articulated by Felski and others, I'd agree with Felski's critique of the "boxes" of literary-historical periodization and her call for a model of historicity whose "interconnections are . . . woven out of threads crisscrossing through time" ("Context Stinks!," 578).

42. Brinton, "Language of Palaeolithic Man," 8. See also H. Hale, "On Some Doubtful or Intermediate Articulations." Hochman, building on Stocking, positions J. W. Powell's *Introduction to the Study of Indian Languages* as the principal text that Boas is implicitly engaging (*Savage Preservation*, 88, 214n51). Giving "On Alternating Sounds" as an example of Boas's tendency to avoid directly naming contemporary interlocutors, Swyers writes that "reading Boas . . . is like reading half of a telephone conversation" ("Rediscovering Papa Franz," 227).

43. "Mental Science."

44. Wiltse, "Experimental"; on the clipping, see 702. Ross characterizes Wiltse's work with Hall (founding editor of the *American Journal of Psychology*) as "the first study in America of hearing defects" (*G. Stanley Hall*, 294). It's possible that Hall and Boas discussed Wiltse's article in person soon after its publication and before the writing of "On Alternating Sounds," since they met each other by chance on a train in early September 1888 (Ross, *G. Stanley Hall*, 196), and their subsequent correspondence suggests that they probably discussed Fechner (Franz Boas to G. Stanley Hall, October 1888, Franz Boas Papers).

45. Stocking, "From Physics to Ethnology," 159.

46. Bauman and Briggs interpret Boas's sense of ethnographic authority in a way that is relevant to this claim: "The question is not that Boas was wrong about culture. It is rather that he told anthropologists that they are the only ones who are right" (*Voices of Modernity*, 297). My point about "purification" echoes Latour's well-known account of modernity and the laboratory (*We Have Never Been Modern*, especially 10–12).

47. Tarver, "Sound-Blindness," 475, 476.

48. Kingsford, *Soprano*, 135; "Field Meeting," 69; Hamilton, *Aesthetic Movement*, 98.

49. Tarver, "Sound-Blindness," 475; Sayce, *Introduction*, 311. (Here Sayce paraphrases Max Müller.) Tarver and Sayce both belonged to the Society for the Promotion of Hellenic Studies in the early 1880s ("List of Members," xxxi–xxxii).

50. Sayce, *Introduction*, 311.

51. Sayce, *Introduction*, 312. For an instance of his argument about the Parent-Aryan language, see Sayce, "Address," 172. On Sayce's place in late nineteenth-century debates about English ethnicity, see Cook, "Making of the English," 633–39. Mackert includes Sayce's volume among the potential objects of Boas's critique in "On Alternating Sounds" ("Franz Boas' Theory," 365). For a more explicit contemporaneous critique of Sayce, see Whitney, "On Inconsistency," 106–11.

52. "The break or interruption," write Deleuze and Guattari, "presupposes or defines what it cuts into as an ideal continuity" (*Anti-Oedipus*, 5).

53. Particularly relevant interlocutors here are Brown on allotment and Cherokee nationhood (*Stoking the Fire*); Hochman on alphabetics and salvage anthropology

(*Savage Preservation*); and Ochoa Gautier on the aftereffects of colonial linguistics in late nineteenth-century Colombia: "a faith-based politics of listening to indigenous languages . . . implies the reinscription of the politics of conversion as what guided the juridical sphere in indigenous affairs" (*Aurality*, 162).

54. Du Bois, "Helen Keller," in Porter, *Double Blossoms*, 64. See Fretwell on this document in the context of a compelling account of how Keller and Du Bois each theorize the affective, intersubjective site of the skin (*Sensory Experiments*, 248).

55. This chapter is consistently engaged with what Stoever calls the "sonic color line," where the taxonomic marking of "the auditory unseen" compensates for the visual ambiguities of race (*Sonic Color Line*, 36).

56. Previous studies of Parsons's volume include Darnell's account of its role in discipline formation (*Invisible Genealogies*, 210–30) and Elliott's interpretation of Boas's story as mediating models of culture, individuation, and literary realism (*Culture Concept*, 29–34).

57. "Especially in a colonial context," Werkmeister writes, literature "can no longer be regarded as a neutral medium" ("Postcolonial Media Studies," 253).

58. Dimock argues that shifts in analytical scale will necessarily destabilize a national category like "American literature" (*Through Other Continents*, 3–6). See also Weinstein's critical engagement with Dimock's argument (*Time, Tense*, 9–12). In an analysis of (New) American Studies' inter- and transnationalization, Wiegman argues that disavowals of the field's nationalist frame serve, in US universities, as institutionally legitimizing gestures of noncomplicity (*Object Lessons*, 197–238).

Chapter 1

1. John M. Oskison, "The Problem of Old Harjo," *Southern Workman*, April 1907, 237, 241. Subsequent quotations from this source are cited parenthetically in the text.

2. Kaplan identifies these political histories' intersections in regionalist writing ("Nation, Region, Empire"); Brodhead describes the genre in relation to postbellum rights discourse (*Cultures of Letters*, 119).

3. Barthes, "Reality Effect," 141.

4. Oskison, *Brothers Three*, 45. For another approach to the problem of representing cattle brands in fiction, possibly familiar to Oskison, see Andy Adams's collection *Cattle Brands* (1906). Its front matter includes a full table illustrating the brands mentioned in the stories alongside their verbal equivalents (vii). Elsewhere Adams describes how brand types differently lend themselves to theft: whereas "character brands" are known by name and therefore not easily altered by thieves, "there is scarcely a letter in the alphabet that a cattle thief can't change" (*Wells Brothers*, 53). Oskison's *Black Jack Davy* includes dialogue about "alterin' brands" (25), while *Brothers Three* refers approvingly to Adams's gritty cowboy realism (335).

5. Melville, *Moby-Dick*, 89.

6. Why did Oskison place this story in the *Southern Workman*, not the New York publications to which he more frequently contributed? He had published the essay

"Outlook for the Indian" (1903) in the magazine, but perhaps a more immediate factor is that he and its editor, Hampton principal H. B. Frissell, both spoke at the 1906 Mohonk Conference ("Mohonk Conference," *Indian Leader*, November 9, 1906). Oskison mentions his own *Southern Workman* subscription in 1912 (Society of American Indians, *Report of the Executive Council*, 97).

7. W. E. B. Du Bois, "Strivings of the Negro People," *Atlantic Monthly*, August 1897, 194. On Du Bois and Harjo's "problem," see Manzanas, "Ethnicity, *Mestizaje*, and Writing," 29.

8. Hawthorne, *Scarlet Letter*, 26.

9. This number is cited in Larré, introduction to *Tales of the Old Indian Territory*, 9.

10. Oskison recalled the impact of "now-limited free range" in his autobiography manuscript: by 1896, "the longhorns had disappeared" ("Tale of the Old I.T.," 97). On livestock in Oskison's *Brothers Three*, see Hudson, "Domesticated Species."

11. Oskison, *Singing Bird*, 77. Subsequent quotations from this source are cited parenthetically in the text.

12. In *Red on Red*, Womack argues for the importance of using specifically Creek frameworks to interpret Creek texts. I cite Womack's argument neither because Oskison's story is straightforwardly within a Creek literary tradition (written by a Cherokee author, it centers on the perspective of a non-Native character) nor because my reading satisfies Womack's call; it doesn't. I do hope to show, though, that our understanding of Oskison's story transforms when we recognize its mediation of specific Creek political histories.

13. "The fence, which was called *Cheth*, (haith) represented a much stronger aspirate than our H. . . . The picture of the fence represented two fence posts, with three boards joining them" (Skinner, *Story*, 97).

14. William R. Harper, "'The American Cadmus': What a Cherokee Citizen Says of This Great Man," *Fort Gibson Post*, May 12, 1904. In the Cherokee lexicon, the same word, ᏍᏕᏈᎣ (galeyadv), refers both to printing and to branding (Cherokee-English Dictionary Online Database, s.v. "galeyadv," http://cherokeedictionary .net). This is alternately given, in another article published in the *Fort Gibson Post* just the day before the piece interviewing Camell, as "De-Gah-La Tah-Naah" ("Sequoyah, Inventor of the Cherokee Alphabet," *Fort Gibson Post*, May 11, 1904).

15. Oskison, *Brothers Three*, 327.

16. Oskison, "Tale of the Old I.T.," 94, 95. Though not completely accurate, these anecdotes contain some biographical truth. The piece appears a month before Oskison's name appears in the masthead of the magazine, confirming his later chronology. Oliver Jenkins ran the marine laboratory at Stanford and taught Oskison's physiology class in fall 1896.

17. Oskison, "Laboratory Fancy," 110.

18. Oskison, "Laboratory Fancy," 111. On interactions between settler scientists and Indigenous peoples, see Whyte, "Sciences of Consent."

19. Oskison, "Laboratory Fancy," 110.

20. On the death drive and narrative conclusion, see P. Brooks, *Reading for the Plot*.

21. John M. Oskison, "Heard at Random," *Sequoia*, November 13, 1896, 109, 110.

22. E.g., "Heard at Random: A Few Stray Shots Amalgamated in the Pan," *Butte Miner*, January 7, 1895. In *Brothers Three*, Oskison summarizes the contents of one such column of "Interesting Items" in a local paper (103). In a 1938 radio interview, Oskison noted that newspapers are particularly valuable "both for the historian and for the novelist," giving an intricate picture of "what people wore, what they ate, what their common slang expressions were, details of social affairs, how they got places." Pressed by the journalism student interviewing him, he acknowledged that newspapers hardly tell the whole story ("Finding Literary Material from State Newspaper Files," *Sooner State Press*, November 12, 1938).

23. Oskison, "Heard at Random," 110.

24. Oskison, "Laboratory Fancy," 111.

25. Oskison, "Laboratory Fancy," 110.

26. Levin describes nineteenth-century developments in acoustic technology as transitioning from muteness to microscopy: in the graphic soundwaves of the phonoautograph, sound "becomes *mute*," whereas the sonic reproductions of the phonograph, as "the first fully functional acoustic read/write apparatus," came "at the price of the virtual invisibility of the traces involved" ("Tones," 40).

27. After Fewkes wrote about the technology, "no ethnographer tackling fieldwork could take the notebook-and-pencil method of recording for granted" (Brady, *Spiral Way*, 2).

28. Mabel L. Miller, "Burial Customs and Ideas among the Indians of the Sacramento Valley," *Sequoia*, March 15, 1895, 288.

29. We already knew that it wasn't; he published "A Trip to Yosemite Valley: Graphic Picture of Grand Scenery Drawn by a Vinita Boy" in the *Indian Chieftain* on August 8, 1895. Conceivably, though, in recounting his career in fiction, he might have excluded a travel story, whereas these two *Sequoia* pieces share both venue and, roughly, genre.

30. Bernice Cosulich, "The Literary Lantern," *Arizona Daily Star*, December 8, 1935; Hildegarde Hawthorne, "Different Tale Told by This Western Book: 'Brothers Three' Lacks in Melodrama but Depicts Oklahoma Life," *Oakland Tribune*, September 15, 1935. Oskison's first marriage, to Florence Day Oskison, ended after his infidelity while in service in Europe during the Great War. Hawthorne—also in France during the war—began her writing career earlier than Oskison, with early work including ghost stories; she later wrote travel pieces, historical narratives, and novels, including *Lone Rider* (1933), sometimes falsely attributed to Oskison.

31. "The lunatic, the lover and the poet," says Theseus, "are of imagination all compact" (Shakespeare, *Midsummer Night's Dream*, 5.1.7–8).

32. This is unsurprising given Oskison's work in the 1900s and 1910s in financial journalism, a period of his life on which, by the time he wrote this novel in the early 1930s, he had cause to reflect anew; the recency of the 1929 crash may make further sense of his memory of the laboratory fancy's title as "Two on a Slide," which both evokes an idiom related to slide-rule calculation—two on the stock, two on the slide—and hints at a decline.

33. Native American Cultural Center, Stanford University, "History Timelines."

34. "Quads," *Daily Palo Alto*, September 29, 1899.

35. On "fantasies of identification" as techniques for marking, classifying, and governing the unstable corporealities of national subjects, see Samuels, *Fantasies of Identification*, 2–3.

36. Oskison, "Tale of the Old I.T.," 105.

37. Oskison, "Tale of the Old I.T.," 123.

38. John M. Oskison, "'The Quality of Mercy': A Story of the Indian Territory," *The Century*, June 1904, 178.

39. Tylor, *Primitive Culture*, 1:1.

40. Arnold, *Culture and Anarchy*, viii. There's a proto-Gramscian hint of "culture" as a means of hegemonic pacification here; for a discussion of "urban and rural-type intellectuals" relevant to the character contrast in "Quality of Mercy," see Gramsci, *Selections from the Prison Notebooks*, 14–15.

41. The three were "charged with finding a symbol long used by all tribes" and "chose an ancient bird figure discovered in a Peoria, Illinois, mound which they called the Thunder Bird" (Grover, "Society of American Indians," 40). For Oskison's committee assignments, see Society of American Indians, *Report of the Executive Council*, 67, 160.

42. Society of American Indians, *Report of the Executive Council*, 7.

43. Hazel Hertzberg argues that in the rhetoric of the society, "cultural evolutionary theory . . . reflected what was hoped to be the forward pragmatic thinking of the time" (quoted in Lopenzina, "Good Indian," 737). Larré suggests that the reference to social evolution in the society's mission statement may reflect a model of cultural hybridity (introduction to *Tales of the Old Indian Territory*, 18). His more general framing of Oskison's political imagination (evading anachronistic definitions of assimilationism) is compelling, but this claim looks unlikely given Parker's intellectual formation. Because "cultural relativism did not easily lend itself to applied Indian reform," writes J. Porter, "there was little purchase for Parker in the idea" (*To Be Indian*, 32).

44. Kroeber, "Superorganic," 163. On the relevance of Kroeber's article to discourses of local color, see Braddock, *Thomas Eakins*.

45. This was not an uncomplicated persona for Rogers; in a March 14, 1900, letter to Betty Blake, he writes, "I know it would be a slam on your Society career to have it known that you even knew an ignorant Indian Cowboy" (*Papers*, 191). In 1893, Rogers and Oskison, along with two other friends, traveled to Chicago to attend the Columbian Exposition. In Oskison's recollection, one can hear a strain of anti-elitism that echoes the satiric deflation of Churchfield's sense of "culture" over cattle: "To us . . . a wonderful silver-decorated saddle and bridle . . . was far more important than the Rembrandts and Corots" ("Tale of the Old I.T.," 86).

46. See the contrasting perspectives on Oskison's politics offered within the front matter of *The Singing Bird*, edited by Timothy B. Powell and Melinda Smith Mullikin. Powell reads Oskison's novel as provoking a movement from "the despair of allotment to the hope of tribal sovereignty" (introduction to *Singing Bird*, xliii), while Weaver takes it as fundamentally assimilationist (foreword to *Singing Bird*, xii). Cox reads Oskison as supporting US expansionism into Mexico ("Learn to Talk

Yaqui"), while Brown argues that Oskison is invested in Cherokee governance (*Stoking the Fire*). Justice, who coordinates Cherokee literary history in terms of the principles of Chickamauga resistance or Beloved diplomacy, argues that Oskison largely sticks to a Beloved path but is also, in his essays, "inconsistent" (*Our Fire Survives*, 112).

47. Oskison, *Brothers Three*, 315.

48. Fewkes, *Preliminary Report*, 26. Fewkes argues that "changes in pottery symbols are not due to evolution of the modern from the ancient, but reflect the advent of new clans" (28).

49. John M. Oskison, "The Road to Betatakin: Part I," *Outing*, July 1914, 394.

50. I borrow from Clifford: "culture is a deeply compromised idea I cannot yet do without" (*Predicament of Culture*, 10).

51. Oskison, "Road to Betatakin," 394.

52. Garland, *Crumbling Idols*, 59, 57, 64.

53. Tylor, *Primitive Culture* 1:1.

54. "Bachelor of Law," *Weekly Chieftain*, June 9, 1898.

55. Some Indian Territory papers, such as the Choctaw Nation *Branding Iron*— "Devoted to Indian and Stock News," per its motto—did include over a full page of brand ads.

56. "Now that schools have opened [incipit]," *Indian Chieftain*, September 2, 1897, 2.

57. "The Sequoyah Club," *Daily Chieftain*, April 4, 1904, 4.

58. This implicit inheritance reverses the terms of—while perhaps serving similar ends as—Rasmussen's description of how claims for "settler indigeneity" in the United States required casting "Native people . . . as the symbolic ancestors of the settler nation," with pictographic representation imagined as the bridge between preliteracy and written language (*Queequeg's Coffin*, 46).

59. "The First Indian Writer," *Daily Chieftain*, January 17, 1905.

60. Justice likewise notes that "*Sequoia*" was "a fitting name for the first site of a Cherokee student's work" (*Our Fire Survives*, 112).

61. Oskison, "Tale of the Old I.T.," 67.

62. Oskison, "Finding Literary Material," 3. The *Advocate* was the only paper printing in Cherokee at the time, per *Dauchy and Company's Newspaper Catalogue* (644). On nineteenth-century Cherokee newspapers, see the Oklahoma state guide that Oskison coedited with Angie Debo (*Oklahoma*, 74–79). On Cherokee print history more generally, see Murphy and Murphy, *Let My People Know*; and Coward, *Newspaper Indian*.

63. In the early 1930s, Oskison wrote a biography of Ross (*Unconquerable*), rejected by the University of Oklahoma Press partly on the grounds that it took too many speculative liberties; it remained unpublished until 2022 (see Rhea, *Field of Their Own*, 160–61; and Larré, introduction to *Unconquerable*, xii–xxii). In the biography, Oskison describes pro-Removal agents' association of missionaries with printers as threats to federal control because of their support for Cherokee literacy (*Unconquerable*, 66). As Powell points out, the missionaries, although more self-evidently fictional characters than Ross, Sequoyah, or Boudinot, are not

pulled from thin air either; there are strong resemblances between, for instance, the character of Dan and the historical Daniel Butrick (introduction to *Singing Bird*, xxxvi). Such research may help us better date Oskison's composition of *The Singing Bird*, which has thus far remained unknown. Powell has suggested that the idea may have germinated when Oskison wrote a short story by the same title in 1925 and then been completed very shortly before his death (introduction to *Singing Bird*, xxii). But a pair of press interviews from 1938 and 1939 suggest that he turned to this work in earnest during that winter and completed at least a first draft by that summer. Residing primarily in New York in 1938, he had gone to Tulsa to visit the archives then known, after the oil industrialist, as the Frank Phillips Collection (Oskison, "Finding Literary Material"). He next went to the family ranch in early 1939 to write a novel drawing on these materials ("Author Returns for Novel on Oklahoma," *Stillwater Daily Press*, January 8, 1939). The novel reproduces the texture of this archival work, with documents, correspondence, and inventories of property represented at length. By the summer of 1939, it was reported that he had finished a novel titled *Beloved Woman* ("Oskison Is in Charge of Final Session," *Oklahoma Daily*, July 1, 1939). It seems likely that this refers to the manuscript that would eventually be titled *The Singing Bird*. A Cherokee honorific described within the novel (53), the "Beloved Woman" is specifically contrasted with the "singing bird."

64. See Crain, *Story of A*, 175 (citing Kesserling, *Hawthorne's Reading*); and more generally see Crain on the relationship between alphabetization and domestic ideology. In Davy's 1772 account, Hawthorne would have learned that scholars were unsure "who this Cadmus was, at what time he lived, or whether any *particular person* is to be understood by this name" (*Conjectural Observations*, 63).

65. Hawthorne, *Grandfather's Chair*, 55–71; Hawthorne, *Scarlet Letter*, 118.

66. Hawthorne, *Tanglewood Tales*, 84.

67. Hawthorne, *Scarlet Letter*, 65.

68. "The Cherokee Alphabet," *American Magazine of Useful and Entertaining Knowledge*, January 1836, 194.

69. Nathaniel Hawthorne, "Sketches from Memory," *New-England Magazine*, November 1835, 326; Nathaniel Hawthorne, "Life of Eliot," *American Magazine of Useful and Entertaining Knowledge*, August 1936, 495–96.

70. Samuel Knapp, "See-quah-yah: The Cherokee Philosopher," *Cherokee Phoenix, and the Indians' Advocate*, July 29, 1829.

71. Knapp, *Lectures on American Literature*, 22.

72. Knapp, *Lectures on American Literature*, 37. The same issue of the *Phoenix* that printed the Knapp excerpt included a note by editor Elias Boudinot—executed by "conservative" (anti-Removal) Cherokees in 1839 for coming to advocate acceptance of Andrew Jackson's plan—appending its own comments about the syllabary's quick acquisition by Cherokees and clarifying that the equipment used to print it in the paper was "not procured by the general government, but at the public expense of the Cherokee nation" ("In reference to the complimentary notice of Se-you-yah on our first page [incipit]," *Cherokee Phoenix, and the Indians' Advocate*, July 29, 1829).

73. Knapp, *Lectures on American Literature*, 26.

74. Knapp, *Lectures on American Literature*, 29.

75. Knapp, *Lectures on American Literature*, 25. Compare Wolfe on the Australian context: "Settler society subsequently sought to recuperate Indigeneity in order to express its difference" from England ("Settler Colonialism," 389).

76. The excerpts are, as in the *Phoenix*, framed by commentary from Boudinot, affirming that Knapp's facts are "derived from Sequoyah himself, through the interpretation of intelligent Cherokees" (Boudinot, "Invention of a New Alphabet," 174).

77. "English Orthography."

78. On this aspect of the syllabary and nineteenth-century philology, see Harvey, *Native Tongues*, 124–33.

79. "Self-Taught Men," 166.

80. John M. Oskison, "The Passing of the Old Indian," *Munsey's Magazine*, April 1914, 535; Oskison, *Singing Bird*, 75, 115.

81. Traveller Bird, *Tell Them They Lie*, 115.

82. Traveller Bird, *Tell Them They Lie*, 12.

83. While *Singing Bird* does not offer the same explanation that Traveller Bird does, Oskison does make choices that resonate with that account, representing Sequoyah's final journey as a search not just for a community of Cherokees in Mexico (as most histories of Sequoyah agree) but for lost symbols (Powell, introduction to *Singing Bird*, xxxi–xxxv, xxxvii–xxxix; on the Traveller Bird controversy, see xlvin34). Other responses to Traveller Bird's account include Lepore's dismissal of it as "spurious" (*A Is for American*, 210n4) and Fogelson's argument that historians should reckon with alternate sources of historical knowledge ("On the Varieties"); accounts both of the nineteenth-century sources and the recent debates are available in Kalter, "'America's Histories' Revisited"; and Giemza, "Strange Case." Rasmussen writes that Sequoyah's experiments with "picture-script" may have been influenced by "older pictographic conventions indigenous to the area" (*Queequeg's Coffin*, 123).

84. Traveller Bird, *Tell Them They Lie*, 144.

85. For Spillers, the category of the bastard, distinguishing impostor from heir, reinforces patriarchal transmission in ways inseparable from racial taxonomy ("Mama's Baby, Papa's Maybe," 65).

86. On the syllabary in the Cherokee public sphere in the 1830s and beyond, see Round, *Removable Type*, 123–49.

87. Hoxie became a teenage art star after making a bust of Lincoln in 1864. One of her admirers was Elias Cornelius Boudinot, son of the famous *Phoenix* editor. When Vinita was founded, Boudinot named it after Hoxie.

88. *Statue of Sequoyah*, 29. Clark's reference to "the philosophy of this alphabet" makes for a close parallel in phrasing (and a contrast in argument) with one of the probable objects of Boas's critique in "On Alternating Sounds"; in the same 1888 talk that I quoted in the introduction, Brinton remarks that "the theory of our alphabet"—that is, the Latin alphabet as used in English—is consistency ("Language of Palaeolithic Man," 8). Yet one of the other texts in the background of "On Alter-

nating Sounds," J. W. Powell's *Introduction to the Study*, makes a point closer to Clark's: "the English language, in many respects the most highly developed of all the tongues spoken by civilized people, is . . . absurdly burdened with a barbaric orthography" (3).

89. On philological attitudes toward syllabaries, see Hochman, *Savage Preservation*, 18.

90. *Statue of Sequoyah*, 9.

91. *Statue of Sequoyah*, 6.

92. *Statue of Sequoyah*, 33.

93. *Statue of Sequoyah*, 17.

94. Sterne, *Audible Past*, 15.

95. *Statue of Sequoyah*, 38.

96. *Statue of Sequoyah*, 38, 39.

97. *Statue of Sequoyah*, 38.

98. If Oskison did not cross paths with Piburn around this time, it is possible that he did later while writing his biography of John Ross, the final chapter of which describes his visit to Ross's descendants in Tahlequah (Oskison, *Unconquerable*, 199).

99. Frances Rosser, "She Is 'Face' of Sequoyah's Famed Statue," *Daily Oklahoman*, October 6, 1957. More accurately, she's the top half of the face. Zolnay used her likeness from the upper lip up. The chin was modeled on Treasury registrar Houston B. Teehee, also an enrolled member of Cherokee Nation.

100. Anne Ross Piburn was probably not directly descended from Sequoyah, but the relation is suggested in at least two publications soon after she modeled for Zolnay. One piece about her Red Cross service during the war—like Hildegarde Hawthorne, she was in France—notes that "it was Anne Ross who posed for Zolnay's statue of Chief Sequoya, her great uncle" (Betty Adler, "The Princess Who Listened," *LaCrosse Tribune and Leader-Press*, August 27, 1919). Another piece describes her as Sequoyah's "lineal descendant" ("Anne Ross, Indian Princess, Reader and Singer of Note and Now with the American Red Cross in France," *Themis of Zeta Tau Alpha*, November 1918–May 1919, 321). However, this latter piece includes other informational errors, and Piburn is not quoted directly in either piece as confirming the relation. Nor does she mention him as kin in articles about her modeling for the statue. Her archives (in what is now the Western History Collections at the University of Oklahoma, though called the Frank Philipps Archive when Oskison studied there in the late 1930s) include an extensive personal genealogy in which—although Sequoyah's name appears in historical notes jotted alongside lists and trees of family members—he does not seem to be identified as her ancestor (Genealogy, folder 2, box 1, Anne Ross Piburn Collection).

101. "An Indian Princess and Uncle Sam's 'Scrap of Paper,'" *St. Louis Post-Dispatch*, April 2, 1916.

102. *Statue of Sequoyah*, 39.

103. According to Holden's 1920 obituary, giving his age as eighty, the Irish American "sage of Fort Gibson" moved to Indian Territory around 1890, was devoted to Indian affairs, possessed a "unique" character exemplified in the fact that he was

a Lincoln-voting Republican who later befriended Robert E. Lee and Jefferson Davis, and "inclined his hand often to poetry usually setting the type as he composed the verse" ("J. S. Holden Is Dead at Fort Gibson," *Muskogee Times-Democrat*, February 9, 1920).

104. Holden's own newspaper represented the unveiling as the successful end of a long, continuous campaign to enshrine the inventor's fame: "A poem on Sequoyah, by J. S. Holden, was read. . . . And we feel happy in this the termination of our efforts of 25 years" ("Sequoyah Statue Unveiling," *Fort Gibson New Era*, June 21, 1917). Holden's plan to attend the unveiling was reported in advance in "Nation Will Honor Memory of Sequoyah in Washington by Unveiling of a Statue," *Muscogee Times-Democrat*, June 4, 1917.

105. *Statue of Sequoyah*, 39. "Cadmus of his race" (line 1) is a common formulation; Mooney uses the phrase in his 1900 volume *Myths of the Cherokees* (in *History*, 108); see also his account of Sequoyah at 108–10 and 219–20n40. On Mooney's inaccurate prediction of the syllabary's imminent obsolescence and on more recent Cherokee attitudes toward the syllabary, see Bender, *Signs of Cherokee Culture*, 40–41.

106. "The American Cadmus," *Fort Gibson Post*, March 16, 1899.

107. "The State of Sequoyah," *Fort Gibson Post*, September 29, 1904.

108. "Nation Will Honor Memory of Sequoyah." Holden's poem was recited at the Sequoyah Constitutional Convention in 1905. Per Malcomson, in a telling indication of the fraught historical overtones of resistance to federalization, it was sung on that occasion to the tune of Dixie (*One Drop of Blood*, 104).

109. Exactly when Holden first put the third version, with "no place," into print is difficult to say. An extant clipping from the *Fort Gibson New Era* announces the inclusion of the poem in Oklahoma's third-grade school reader and prints the version with "no place" ("Clipping Referring J. S. Holden / Unknown," folder 1356, John Ross Papers, http://collections.gilcrease.org/object/3027206). Given its reference to a budgetary appropriation for the statue, this document dates from somewhere between 1910 and 1917, probably well before the unveiling ceremony. Not having located a copy of the school reader, I can't corroborate which version was circulated to students. The *New Era* clipping is a weak source on this point because it was probably written by Holden himself, who edited the *New Era* after the *Post*; even if a prior version of the poem had been printed in the readers, he might have used—or composed—a different version when typesetting this news item.

110. "The El Reno Democrat suggests [incipit]," *Daily Oklahoman*, September 2, 1905. The *Oklahoman* editors were critical of the movement, arguing on the same page that its real aim was preserving a status quo for "fat cats" ("What's the Use?," *Daily Oklahoman*, September 2, 1905). The *McAlester Capital*, meanwhile, which often antagonized Holden for his fixation on Sequoyah's legacy, put forward Thomas Jefferson as a possible namesake, in recognition of his management of the Louisiana Purchase and on the argument that "Sequoyah" offered only a sentimental gesture to the "dying race," while "Jefferson" would more likely be ratified ("Sequoyah as a Name," *McAlester Capital*, August 31, 1905).

111. *Chitto* is Creek for "snake," with *Harjo* translating approximately to "crazy brave," as per the title of poet Joy Harjo's memoir, *Crazy Brave*.

112. See Samuels's argument "that the originary function of blood quantum in American jurisprudence was to associate Indian blood with disability" and therefore that policies from land allotment to language bans constituted "a deliberate attempt to 'rehabilitate' the Indian person into the normative white citizen defined by his able-mindedness" (*Fantasies of Identification*, 168). On allotment and race, see Chang, *Color of the Land*.

113. "J. J. Beavers, Aided by Alex Posey, Interpreter, and D. C. Skaggs, Stenographer and Notary," *Muskogee Times-Democrat*, October 4, 1904. When Posey and Skaggs interview Harjo, Beaver is not mentioned as their colleague.

114. Posey, *Poems*, 32.

115. The article's author wonders "whether these stories are the real thing or whether Posey and Skaggs just 'trumped them up'" ("Experience of the Clerks: Alex Posey and D. C. Skaggs of Muskogee Talk," *Oklahoma State Capital*, February 11, 1905).

116. "We shudder to think" [incipit], *South McAlester News*, October 22, 1905.

117. Littlefield, *Alex Posey*, 243.

118. Posey, "On the Capture and Imprisonment of Crazy Snake, January, 1900," in *Poems*, 88. In May 1904, there were reports of Posey coauthoring a play, *The Stolen Empire* (whether it was ever realized is unclear), whose subject—the "broken treaties, violated contracts and final dissolution" of Indian Territory—sounds unconvinced of statehood as progress ("The Stolen Empire," *South McAlester Capital*, May 26, 1904).

119. "Old Crazy Snake Is Full of Talk," *Muskogee Times-Democrat*, October 17, 1905. On Posey's notes from this meeting, see Posey, *Lost Creeks*, 1.

120. Vazquez, in a chapter on the bandleader Perez Prado, quotes Watson Wylie on "ugh" as language converted to sheer respiratory force by "removing the vowels and the consonants from the word before exhaling" (*Listening in Detail*, 151). In the context of the story about Posey and Harjo, the monosyllable takes a stereotype of Native speech (Graham, "From 'Ugh' to Babble," 735) and applies it to a (Native) colonial administrator.

121. In this aversion to depicting violence, it's been argued, Oskison and other Native American realist writers avoided reinforcing a narrative of Indian Territory lawlessness often cited by statehood advocates (Piatote, *Domestic Subjects*, 45; Littlefield and Parins, "Short Fiction Writers," 36).

122. I paraphrase Rose: "People got in the way just by staying at home" (*Hidden Histories*, 46).

123. Du Bois, "Strivings," 197.

124. "Old Crazy Snake Is Full of Talk."

125. Asad describes conversions as "narratives by which people apprehend and describe a radical change in the significance of their lives" ("Comments on Conversion," 266). In the same issue of the *Chieftain* with the article "The First Indian Writer" appear two reprinted paragraphs by Henry Roe Cloud, in which the language

of "solution" is connected with conversion: "There is only one sure and radical solution to the Indian question, that is through this missionary association"
("Henry C. Cloud, an Educated Winnebago, Declares His Race Is Capable of Improve-
ment," *Daily Chieftain*, January 17, 1905). The initial here is "C." rather than "R."
because he had not yet changed his middle name to "Roe," as he did in an expression of kinship with the missionaries who adopted him in his early twenties. Cloud
would later be Oskison's colleague in the Society for American Indians.

126. Oskison, *Brothers Three*, 338, 368; John M. Oskison, "The Biologist's Quest,"
Overland Monthly, July 1901, 56; Oskison, *Singing Bird*, 163.

127. "Humanity's Mute Appeal," *St. Louis Globe-Democrat*, July 9, 1888. The phrase
"mute appeal" appears in the transcript five times. The sermons that Oskison mentions were by T. DeWitt Talmage ("Tale of the Old I.T.," 71). The concept of the "appeal" also suggests a particular narrative structure: an effort to reverse something
ostensibly settled—such as the effort that led, in *McGirt v. Oklahoma*, to the Su-
preme Court's 2020 restoration of Creek Nation jurisdiction, a ruling whose consequences remain, as of this writing, too early to fully judge.

128. On the question of vocal redemption and the way that "dumbness cannot be
tolerated in writing," see L. Davis, *Enforcing Normalcy*, 123. See also R. Chow on a
pattern of Western scholarly "image-identification" in which the silence of the
"native . . . becomes the occasion for *our* speech" ("Where Have All the Natives
Gone?," 130).

129. "How can Old Harjo bear a likeness to the patriarch Abraham, the father of
nations," asks Piatote, "while Harjo's family is represented without children?"
(*Domestic Subjects*, 47). This "absence of Indian children" carries "sobering implications," and so "it is curious that Oskison ends the analogy there" (190n72). I suggest that he doesn't end it, exactly, but complicates its sobering effect with the
implied possibility of intermarriage. In describing the final question of Oskison's
story as open to reply, I'd extend, at an oblique angle, Piatote's argument that this
sentence fragment presents "indigenous politics (writ small as a polygamous marriage) as the unanswerable question that will continue to haunt the nation" (44).
On narrative temporalities in connection with reproductive biopolitics, see Rifkin's
Temporal Sovereignty.

130. On this fantasy, see Tuck and Yang, "Decolonization," 13–17. Of all the possible resolutions here, intermarriage is quietly urged by the story's multiple references to Mormonism and, implicitly, white polygamy, particularly controversial at
the time given the recent process of Utahan statehood. On the paradoxical imagination of the white/Native family as a means of white racial purity, see Michaels,
Our America, 50–52.

131. The fact that Evans's crisis hardly involves these characters correlates with
Spivak's argument that the "native female" (as a discursive figure) "is excluded
from any share" in the imperial project, within which "childbearing and soul making" constitute parallel tracks of feminist individualism ("Three Women's Texts,"
244). Childbearing hovers around the language used to introduce the Harjo brand:
"two . . . mares *bore*" it (Oskison, "Problem of Old Harjo," 237, my emphasis).

132. On quotation marks as presenting in microcosm a general function of language—bracketing experience as interpretable—see S. Stewart, *On Longing*, 19.

133. Per one nineteenth-century French grammar, "strictly speaking, h is no letter" (Chambaud, *Grammar of the French Tongue*, 58). See also Heller-Roazen, *Echolalias*, 33–44. Hakluyt, cited in Melville's *Moby-Dick* as "Hackluyt," condemns the occasional exclusion of the *H* in "whale" (xv).

134. On the interplay of recognition and refusal in Indigenous politics, see Simpson, *Mohawk Interruptus*.

135. Traveller Bird, *Tell Them They Lie*, 14.

136. Lauter, *Heath Anthology*, 510; Allen, *Voice of the Turtle*, 138; Nagel, *Anthology of the American Short Story*, 494; A. Davis, *Hearing the Call*, 139; Nagel and Quirk, *Portable American Realism Reader*, 533.

137. "The term 'fidelity' (first applied to sound in 1878) indicates both a faith in media and a belief that media can hold faith," writes Sterne—"faith" because "identity between original and copy is impossible" (*Audible Past*, 221–22).

Chapter 2

1. Helen Keller, "A Chat about the Hand," *The Century*, January 1905, 455. The previous page of this 1905 essay features a layout with elements similar to *My Religion*'s frontispiece: a photograph of Keller (a flower held in one hand, the other on an open book) above her reproduced signature (454). My commentary on this frontispiece may evoke the opening paragraphs of Clifford's "On Ethnographic Authority" (see *Predicament of Culture*, 21–26), an essay that informs my work even as it takes vision and voice as commensurable figures for textual rhetoric in ways that this chapter aims to complicate.

2. Keller, *My Religion*, ii.

3. "Helen Keller's Autograph Reaches This City," *Waco Morning News*, May 16, 1915. On Poe's experiments with the "co-presence of handwriting and print," see McGill, *American Literature*, 141–217, quotation at 177. On the singularity and iterability of the mark of the author's name, see Derrida, *Limited Inc*, 32–34. Printing has particular historical meanings in the educational context that I'll discuss, as a "profession for which the deaf were prepared in residential schools" (L. Davis, *Enforcing Normalcy*, 181n66). Keller did not live in such a school, but she took vocal lessons at one that, in 1897, hosted "an exhibition of typesetting and printing. The children set up and print the lesson cards, school notices, etc., and some have learned the business so well that on leaving the school they were able to take positions as compositors" ("Exhibition at the Horace Mann School," *Boston Evening Transcript*, May 22, 1897).

4. On the body's spiritualization in Keller's autobiographies, see Werner, "Helen Keller," 7. "A photograph," writes Peirce, "not only . . . has an appearance, but, owing to its optical connexion with the object, is evidence that that appearance corresponds to a reality" (*Collected Papers*, 4:359). Mitchell and Snyder note that in contrast to other identity categories, "disabled people's marginalization has

occurred in the midst of a perpetual circulation of their images" (*Narrative Prosthesis*, 6).

5. Fretwell's reading of Keller on touch leads to a relational model where finger-spelling features as "a way of being both subject and object" (*Sensory Experiments*, 240). Werner's account of Keller's early fingerspelling practice notes that some-times the same subject/object collapse requires no external observer: "When the right hand spells into the left it is a way of being self and other at the same time" ("Helen Keller," 5).

6. Anna M. Sullivan and Helen Keller, "Helen Keller's Visit to the World's Fair," *St. Nicholas*, December 1893, 177. On the importance of *St. Nicholas* in representa-tions of Keller's early education, see Klages, *Woeful Afflictions*, 178–86.

7. Keller and Boas corresponded at least once late in life. The exchange suggests political affinities but little personal familiarity. Keller requests a contribution to a fund for Spanish refugees from Vichy France; Boas sends a donation. See Hellen Keller to Franz Boas, November 12, 1940, and Boas to Keller, November 18, 1940, Franz Boas Papers.

8. Peirce and Jastrow, "On Small Differences," 73; the article concludes with a discussion of outcomes in which subjects' ability to correctly distinguish between the intensity of two stimuli exceeded their confidence in these judgments, on the basis of which Peirce and Jastrow recommend further study of (gendered) intu-ition and telepathy (83).

9. Boas, "On Alternating Sounds," 49.

10. I quote Jastrow's text for the fair's official catalogue, reprinted in US World's Columbian Commission, Committee on Awards, *Report of the Committee on Awards*, 384. See also "Experimental Psychology at the Fair," *Chicago Tribune*, November 5, 1893.

11. On Keller's "performance" at Jastrow's laboratory, see Cressman, "Helen Keller," 120; Bank, "Representing History," 593n9; and Fretwell, *Sensory Experi-ments*, 232.

12. Jastrow conducted three trials on Keller using the "pain-tester" designed by James McKeen Cattell (Jastrow, "Psychological Notes," 359). For Sullivan, the scene may have echoed a prior experience: in her youth, she had met Laura Bridg-man and disapproved of her treatment as an experimental subject (Herrmann, *Helen Keller*, 35).

13. Sullivan and Keller, "Helen Keller's Visit to the World's Fair," 177.

14. Jastrow, "Psychological Notes," 361.

15. T. Kroeber, *Ishi in Two Worlds*, 238.

16. Brueggemann locates the crucial (and fallacious) articulation of audism in nineteenth-century European and English thinkers for whom "*language is human; speech is language; therefore, deaf people are inhuman, and deafness is a problem*" (*Lend Me Your Ear*, 11). On audism as colonialist, see Lane's *Mask of Benevolence*. Lane's book created controversy. "By equating the very real problems faced by deaf people with the suffering of colonized people," Moores writes, "Lane trivializes the latter and distorts the former" ("*Mask of Benevolence*," 4). My own argument aims not to equate these social realities but to mark their proximities, treating the analo-

gies often constructed between them as a tissue of discursive history rather than as a positive hermeneutic. This approach shares an orientation with Carmody, "Rehabilitating Analogy." On the question of analogy in discourse about race and disability, see also Bell, "Introducing White Disability Studies"; and Schweik, "Disability Politics," 222.

17. My thinking about this reproduction is informed by the dialogue between Moten and Hartman on the question of quoting the scene of Hester's scream in Douglass's 1845 *Narrative*; see Hartman, *Scenes of Subjection*, 3–4; and Moten, *In the Break*, 1–7.

18. See "About Book-Writers," *Buffalo Express*, January 2, 1904. The same piece is printed in many other newspapers and at least one trade periodical: "Evidently news of Helen Keller [incipit]," *Book News*, February 1904, 690. John Albert Macy mentions a relevant fact: "For one course alone—English Literature of the Nineteenth Century—Mr. Wade ordered for Miss Keller books which fill a large case and which took a dozen people months to transcribe" ("Helen Keller at Radcliffe College," *Youth's Companion*, June 2, 1904, 338). (As early as February 1899, Keller thanks Wade for procuring books for her; see Keller, *Story of My Life*, 251). Keller studied Romantic-era literature with William Henry Neilson and later recalled his strong influence on her reading ("My Recollections of Boston," xix). Neilson was the only Radcliffe faculty member who "took the time to master the manual finger language so he could communicate directly with her" (Herrmann, *Helen Keller*, 125).

19. Wordsworth, *Prelude*, 256.

20. "About Book-Writers."

21. Noting that one of the primary novelties of the printing revolution was the blank form of customs, census, and tax documents, Stallybrass remarks that "the work of the nation-state is done through a printed form that elicits writing by hand" ("Printing," 112). On blank forms and job printing, see also Gitelman, *Paper Knowledge*, 21–52.

22. Hawthorne, *Scarlet Letter*, 23.

23. "Helen Keller's Signature," *Birmingham News*, January 5, 1905.

24. "Helen Keller," 160–61.

25. "The manual communication that textual production required confused all categories of selfhood," including authorship (Fretwell, *Sensory Experiments*, 245). This confusion has taken an ugly turn recently: conspiracy theories about the possibility of Keller's literacy have circulated widely on the social media app TikTok.

26. Helen Keller, "Helen Keller's Own Story of Her Life: Written Entirely by the Wonderful Girl Herself," *Ladies' Home Journal*, April 1902, 7.

27. Kleege considers a related dynamic of ableist pathos; during a tour of Keller's childhood home, a guide indicated a lovely carpet made for Keller and then reminded the visitors, "Too bad Helen Keller never saw it"—though of course, as Kleege remarks, Keller could have known its loveliness from touching it, imagining it, and having it described to her (*Blind Rage*, 2).

28. "Correspondence with Dorothy McRonald wishing to analyze Helen's handwriting," item 25, folder 3, box 120, Helen Keller Archive. The *Readers' Digest* story

that McRonald mentions is probably a 1950 excerpt from Ishbel Ross's *Journey into Light*: "Miss Keller's handwriting today is square, artistic and always legible" (Ishbel Ross, "The Extraordinary Story of Helen Keller," *Readers' Digest*, July 1950, 165).

29. Bunker, *What Handwriting Tells You*, 177, 179, 180.

30. "Correspondence with Dorothy McRonald." The response from Davidson (same item number) is dated December 8, 1952.

31. Over the first half of the twentieth century, "the discourse of the extraordinary body as medical specimen finally eclipsed the traditional freak show spectacle" (Garland-Thomson, *Extraordinary Bodies*, 75).

32. Dickens, *American Notes*, 49.

33. Lamson, *Life and Education*, 364.

34. Lamson, *Life and Education*, 159.

35. This was a predecessor of mass-produced raised-line or embossed paper.

36. The timing of the visit, not clear from the *St. Nicholas* article, is revealed by an earlier report in the daily press ("With the Abbot Girls," *Boston Evening Transcript*, May 21, 1891).

37. Adeline G. Perry, "A Visit from Helen Keller," *St. Nicholas*, June 1892, 576.

38. On type as the "blind spot" of the writing act, see Kittler, *Discourse Networks*, 195. Fretwell argues that because type "produces a text that erases embodied difference," the facsimiles of Keller's handwriting and her Braille manuscript are "necessary for reincorporating the author's body into her story" (*Sensory Experiments*, 244, 245).

39. Perry, "Visit from Helen Keller," 577.

40. "Scraps," *The Oldhallian*, March 1885, 72–73.

41. Perry, "Visit from Helen Keller," 574.

42. Here I paraphrase L. Davis's conception of the "deafened moment" (*Enforcing Normalcy*, 100). Like the chapter title that Davis uses there, "Deafness and Insight," my section heading here plays on Paul de Man's *Blindness and Insight*; Davis considers the latter text (particularly the essay "The Rhetoric of Blindness") through the lens of disability at 101–6.

43. See Sterne, *Audible Past*, 31–36.

44. Perry, "Visit from Helen Keller," 57.

45. Tarde, *Laws of Imitation*, 67.

46. Parsons's translation was a big professional step for an early-career academic; Tarde's work, theorizing imitation as the engine of social relation, was regarded as a signal study by Boasians interested in transcultural diffusion as the source of invention. Tarde's text "profoundly impressed" Boas (Lowie, *History of Ethnological Theory*, 106) and "definitely influenced" him (A. Kroeber, "Place of Boas," 154).

47. Tarde, *Lois de l'imitation*, 72.

48. Kinsey, *Report of the Proceedings*, 36. On Bell and Gallaudet's disagreements, see Winefield, *Never the Twain*; on the Milan Congress, see 35–42. The ban was finally lifted at the 2010 International Congress on the Education of the Deaf.

49. Wiltse, "Experimental," 705.

50. In 1884, Elizabeth Porter Gould reported that Fuller employed eight teaching assistants trained in phonetics, which was "a necessity, since only the system of

articulation . . . was used in the school" ("The Horace Mann School for the Deaf," *Boston Evening Transcript*, June 25, 1884).

51. Keller, *Story of My Life*, 60.

52. "Brain Bursts Its Bonds: Deaf, Dumb and Blind Girl Learns to Articulate," *Boston Globe*, May 17, 1890.

53. This phrasing is used in Morell, *Sacred Annals*, 182.

54. See Gitelman on "local and contrastive logics for media" (*Paper Knowledge*, 9). See Padden and Gunsauls on contemporary fingerspelling practice, which has become, for many users, "a signifier of contrastive meaning through the exploitation of the structural properties that set it apart from signs" ("How the Alphabet," 15). See, too, on modality shifts and typographic contrasts, Peters, *Deaf American Literature*, 122–24.

55. On the prevalence of speech as "a chance of evolution," see L. Davis, *Enforcing Normalcy*, 118.

56. Gibson, *Miracle Worker*, 92.

57. The "seven-year-old" reference is consistent across coverage; see, e.g., "Statue of Helen Keller Unveiled," *Montgomery Advertiser*, October 8, 2009.

58. This is not to say that the well-pump scene was never marked as important in earlier accounts of Keller's education. It was cited by the Penn psychologist Lightner Witmer in an article about the linguistic training of an ape named Peter ("Monkey with a Mind," *New York Times*, January 30, 1910)—the primate who may have inspired Kafka's "Report to an Academy" (Radick, *Simian Tongue*, 442n19).

59. Quoted in Fuller, "How Helen Keller Learned to Speak," 29.

60. On Keller and Sullivan's stage act as both catering to and tempering audience expectations for freakshows, see Crutchfield, "Play[ing] Her Part Correctly." On Keller's musical study, see Accinno, "Extraordinary Voices."

61. "Former Deaf Mute Delivers Speech," *Buffalo Commercial*, August 17, 1912.

62. "Helen Keller as Speaker," *Boston Evening Transcript*, August 17, 1912.

63. Hellen Keller, "What the Blind Can Do," *Youth's Companion*, January 4, 1906, 3.

64. On critical discourse about the "supercrip" trope, including discourse that does not automatically position it as regressive, see Schalk, "Reevaluating the Supercrip."

65. Keller, *Story of My Life*, 316.

66. Keller, *Story of My Life*, 23.

67. Keller, *Story of My Life*, 7, 58.

68. Keller, *Story of My Life*, 315.

69. Gibson, *Miracle Worker*, 92.

70. Just because such a performance choice may not have seemed practical to Gibson does not mean that it would be *actually* impractical in all contexts. Kleege imagines Keller (addressed as "you") and Sullivan using the manual alphabet on the vaudeville circuit: "you cup your hand loosely around hers, loose enough so the audience can still see her gestures" (*Blind Rage*, 133).

71. Grant Allen, "The Beginnings of Speech," *Longman's Magazine*, May 1894, 59.

72. Allen, "Beginnings of Speech," 63.

73. Noting that "Keller must first surrender her own form of language" (the dozens of gestures she used before Sullivan's arrival) before adopting the manual alphabet, Klages argues that Gibson's play foregrounds "the inescapability of embodiment while it works to erase or transcend the specifics of that embodiment" (*Woeful Afflictions*, 206, 210). On the "dream" in phonetic science (and Oralist pedagogy) of an alphabetic system grounded in the indexical and iconic representations of spectrography, see Mills, "Deaf Jam," 40.

74. "Patty's an 'Animal' for 'Miracle' Role," *Minneapolis Star*, February 7, 1957.

75. Keller, *Story of My Life*, 323.

76. Klages argues that Gibson's play, emphasizing the difficulty of "taming" Keller, aims for (but misses) a nonsentimentalist representation of disability (*Woeful Afflictions*, 197–211).

77. On the narrative tradition in which "violent loss of self-control results in the exclusion of the disabled person from human community," see Longmore, *Why I Burned My Book*, 135. On nineteenth-century associations of disability, "a free-floating signifier for evil and woe," with villainy, see Garland-Thomson, *Extraordinary Bodies*, 84.

78. See Lippit's account (indebted to Derrida) of the cry as "a signal burdened with the antidiscursive force of animality and madness" (*Electric Animal*, 43). My reference to "displacement" echoes a 1908 article by Jean Sherwood Rankin recommending Keller's education as a universal model for elementary language instruction: "she was . . . a savage little animal . . . but with the gift of language, gentleness displaced violence" ("Helen Keller," 85).

79. See Doane, "Voice in the Cinema," 33.

80. "Helen Keller's Picture Soon to Be Shown," *Los Angeles Evening Express*, June 18, 1919.

81. "Miss Keller's Own Work," *New York Times*, August 24, 1919.

82. "Film script for movie revolving around the life of Helen Keller," item 2, folder 1, box 90, Helen Keller Archive.

83. Henry McMahon, "The Art of the Movies," *New York Times*, June 6, 1915. Eaton is quoted in the same article.

84. "The Picture's the Thing," *New York Times*, August 10, 1919.

85. "Screen: Spoken Titles," *New York Times*, October 29, 1922.

86. John Dutton Wright, "Speech and Speech-Reading for the Deaf," *The Century*, January 1897, 343. A passionate Oralist, Wright falsely asserts that soon after working with Fuller, Keller "abandoned finger spelling as a means of expression, and has ever since used speech alone" (343).

87. "Art exists," per Shklovsky, "to make the stone *stony*" ("Art as Technique," 12).

88. On degrees of simultaneity in signing, see Sandler, "Phonological Organization." Keller writes that the linearity of the manual alphabet is not dominant in user experience: "I do not feel each letter any more than you see each letter separately when you read. . . . The mere spelling, is, of course, no more a conscious act than it is in writing" (*Story of My Life*, 62).

89. The titles were a special site of collaboration and contention since preproduction. Keller and Sullivan approved of the project based on Miller's synopsis, but when in March 1919 they received the script to be used for production, they wrote to him that they would not permit the film to go ahead in its current form (Helen Keller Film Corporation to Francis T. Miller, March 30, 1919, item 13, folder 2, box 90, Helen Keller Archive). A compromise was, however, reached, and the next month Sullivan sent Miller a revised list of titles (Anne S. Macy to Francis T. Miller, April 16, 1919, item 17, folder 2, box 90, Helen Keller Archive).

90. "Film script by Francis T. Miller, for movie 'Deliverance' about Helen Keller," item 1, folder 1, box 90, Helen Keller Archive, pp. 33–34.

91. Keller, *Story of My Life*, 10, 11.

92. On the larger arc of Nadja's character, see Salerno, "Helen Keller."

93. Keller, *Story of My Life*, 12.

94. See Hitz, "Helen Keller," 311, fig. 14. Hitz introduced Keller to Swedenborg's work. The same letter is transcribed as the first sample of Keller's letters in *Story of My Life*, 145; John Albert Macy writes in his introduction to these letters that those up to 1892 have been "printed intact, for it is legitimate to be interested in the degree of skill the child showed in writing" (144).

95. Monroe, *Fourth Reader*, iii.

96. Fretwell argues that in *Story of My Life*, the narrative of friendship with Washington "reproduces the postbellum racial order" in a reconciliation romance that excludes "black children . . . from autobiography's progress narrative," while facilitating Keller's implicitly "queer marriage" with the white teacher Sullivan (*Sensory Experiments*, 249–50). *Deliverance* reconfigures this dynamic, the Washington story overlapping with (rather than, as in the memoir, preceding) Sullivan's pedagogy as the fictional Nadja newly triangulates each relationship.

97. Hughes, "Helen Keller," in Porter, *Double Blossoms*, 95.

98. On this theme's variations in Keller's memoirs and elsewhere, see Paterson, *Seeing with the Hands*, 184–206.

99. Roulston, "To Helen Keller," in Porter, *Double Blossoms*, 87.

100. Spingarn, "The Great Jokesmith," in Porter, *Double Blossoms*, 16.

101. A few moments that suggest Porter's profile: in 1910, she appears on the cover of *Progressive Woman*, captioned, "Socialist Actress, in the Folds of the Suffrage Flag" (March 1910); in 1923, she appears on the cover of *The Liberator* in a stenciled illustration by Frank Walts (August 1923); in the late 1930s, she is close with the Schuyler family, caring for Philippa Schuyler in the summer of 1938 (see Talalay, *Composition in Black and White*, 86). The same year, she publishes a children's book titled *Mr. Beep, Mrs. Beep, and Beep Jr.: A Story That's All True*.

102. "Stage Hands Quit; 3 More Shows Hit; Film Strike, Too?," *New York Herald*, August 17, 1919.

103. Actors' Equity had planned to meet at the Astor Theatre, but that site was instead taken over by an antistrike group led by Louis Mann and George Cohan, with Cohan (who had previously managed the Astor) promising to fund the "counter revolution" with $100,000 of his own money. Sullivan was with Keller at the

Lexington, vocally interpreting her speech for the crowd. "'Loyal' Actors Mobilize to Smash Equity," *New York Herald*, August 23, 1919.

104. "A review of Helen Keller's 'My Religion' by Edna Porter (1929)," item 13, box 227, series 2, Helen Keller Archives. Keller's preference for direct action, including strikes, over electoral politics factored into her move in the 1910s from the US Socialist Party to the IWW (Fletcher and Davis, introduction to *Heller Keller*, 6).

105. Quoted in "Presentation to Dr. Keller," *Magazine for the Scottish Deaf*, August–September 1932, 140–44.

106. These additions are mostly texts but also include a drawing, "Helen's Hands," by Zhenya Gay.

107. "Poems to Helen Keller Appear in Book Form," *Brooklyn Daily Eagle*, November 10, 1931.

108. On poetry as "abnormal," see Davidson, "Disability Poetics."

109. Aptheker, *Writings*, 164.

110. Du Bois, "Helen Keller," in Porter, *Double Blossoms*, 64.

111. This book is held by the Helen Keller Archive; thanks to the archivist Justin A. Gardiner for sharing the inscription with me. Keller's own recollections do not resolve the discrepancies. She writes about James's visit in *Midstream* without mentioning Du Bois or other students and without a date (316). When she does mention him in a 1957 letter, her version of the event is just as brief and vague as (and perhaps, too, influenced by) his own in *Double Blossoms*: "I felt Mr. DuBois's kindly interest in me, and the dynamic quality of his personality" (Helen Keller to Van Wyck Brooks, January 28, 1957, Helen Keller Archives). Andrews dates the meeting in 1892 ("Toward a Synaesthetics of Soul," 173), as do Fretwell (*Sensory Experiments*, 248) and, writing in a fictional-historical mode, Cohen (*Chance Meeting*, 66). All align with Richardson, whose biography of James puts the meeting in May 1892 but—whereas most accounts treat the encounter as if James, Du Bois, and Keller were the only ones present—also says that there were sixteen graduate students present, presumably Du Bois and fifteen others. Richardson's work is deeply researched but, on this point, difficult to verify; the only source cited in direct relation to the anecdote is Keller's *Midstream* (see Richardson, *William James*, 321, 564n8), which, again, does not include the relevant details. Richardson describes Keller as twelve years old at the meeting, though her twelfth birthday was not until the next month (321)—not a telling discrepancy in itself, except when added to the surrounding murk. Eugene Taylor's placement of the meeting "in the early 1890's" seems exactly right ("William James and Helen Keller," item 4, folder 6, box 222, Helen Keller Archive, p. 2).

112. Helen Keller, "From a Friend," *The Crisis*, April 1916, 305.

113. Quoted in Nielsen, *Radical Lives*, 39.

114. "Helen Keller Indicates Her Attitude Anent the Advertisement in Local Paper of Recent Date," *Selma Times*, April 8, 1916. As Nielsen notes, Keller's distinction between "social" and "legal" equality is unclear (*Radical Lives*, 39).

115. "Sassing Back," *The Crisis*, July 1916, 133; "'Justice' Raps Miss Keller's Defamers," *Selma Times*, April 8, 1916.

116. The historiography of this episode has knotted together Du Bois's recollections in *Double Blossoms* with a part of the story that Keller later mentioned to Van Wyck Brooks. In a notebook entry dated January 1945 (subsequently published in his book *Helen Keller*), Brooks uses Du Bois's reference to Keller being "blind to colour differences" to frame an aspect of the 1916 episode that Du Bois does not explicitly mention. In Selma, a "Negro-baiter" asked Keller in public if she had indeed made the donation (yes, she answered) and whether she believed in "marriage between whites and Negroes" ("No more than they do," she answered; V. Brooks, *Helen Keller*, 138). In the republication of Du Bois's *Double Blossoms* paragraph that's usually cited (Aptheker, *Writings*), Brooks's story is the only source cited as context. This implies that Du Bois's reference to her refusal to retract was related to Keller's face-to-face exchange with the racist. But I'm aware of no evidence that that story (told to Brooks by Keller) about the conversation ever reached Du Bois. The simpler explanation of his reference to retraction has to do with how things played out in *The Crisis* and the newspapers. It was a story about steadfastness in print, not face-to-face.

117. "Dr. Keller Replies to Her Questioners." *Magazine for the Scottish Deaf,* August–September 1932, 146.

118. W. E. B. Du Bois, "Helen Keller" drafts, ca. June 8, 1927, W. E. B. Du Bois Papers. There are two versions of this document in the archive, both bearing the same citation.

119. See Obasogie's critique of this logic in *Blinded by Sight.*

120. Edna Porter to W. E. B. Du Bois, May 9, 1927, W. E. B. Du Bois Papers.

121. W. E. B. Du Bois to Edna Porter, June 8, 1927, W. E. B. Du Bois Papers.

122. Edna Porter to W. E. B. Du Bois, June 12, 1927, W. E. B. Du Bois Papers.

123. Edna Porter to W. E. B. Du Bois, December 27, 1927, W. E. B. Du Bois Papers.

124. W. E. B. Du Bois to Edna Porter, December 29, 1927, W. E. B. Du Bois Papers.

125. Edna Porter to W. E. B. Du Bois, May 4, 1928, W. E. B. Du Bois Papers.

126. Edna Porter to W. E. B. Du Bois, July 2, 1928, W. E. B. Du Bois Papers.

127. W. E. B. Du Bois, "Criteria of Negro Art," *The Crisis*, October 1926, 294.

128. Edna Porter to W. E. B. Du Bois, May 9, 1927, W. E. B. Du Bois Papers.

129. Du Bois, "Criteria of Negro Art," 296.

130. Du Bois, "Helen Keller" drafts.

131. Keller, *World I Live In*, 48. Anticipating some skepticism about her description of the cries of wild animals, Keller clarifies "that *with my own hand* I have felt all these sounds" (48). On techniques of aural inference and vibratory sonic experience, see Friedner and Helmreich, "Sound Studies Meets Deaf Studies," 75–78.

132. This reference to "understand[ing] without sound" also invokes the metaphor of the plate-glass vacuum that became, Stoever explains, a key metaphor of racialized experience for Du Bois—one connected with his interest first in the "color blind" affordances of radio and then in the possibilities of radio production by and for Black listening communities (*Sonic Color Line*, 259–62). Part of my aim is to ask what happens to Du Bois's metaphor (in Stoever's analysis) of the

white-supremacist observer/auditor as "blind *and* deaf to the realities of black life" (261) when these categories of disability are understood as embedded—and constructed as medically literal—in histories of education.

133. Keller, "From a Friend," 305.

134. Bérubé discusses the wider prehistories of such figuration, considering American autobiography through the paradigm of the slave narrative as a claim to the "capacity for . . . self-authorship" ("Autobiography," 341).

135. Comeau ("Friendship") puts the date of this meeting in 1892, but, without direct documentation otherwise, circumstantial evidence makes 1891 seem probable; see Keller, *Story of My Life*, 135–36; Perry, "Visit from Helen Keller," 576; and "Letter from Oliver Wendell Holmes to Helen Keller about language and speech. August 1, 1890," item 1, folder 12, box 60, Helen Keller Archive.

136. Whittier, "Howard at Atlanta," in *Anti-Slavery Poems*, 265; Du Bois, *Souls of Black Folk*, 75.

137. Whittier, "Laus Deo," in *Anti-Slavery Poems*, 256.

138. Keller, *Story of My Life*, 136.

139. Comeau makes the same inference about this statue as "probably a small replica" of Ball's work ("Friendship").

140. Keller, "My Recollections of Boston," xvii.

141. Keller, *Story of My Life*, 136.

Chapter 3

1. Fitzgerald, *Great Gatsby: Galleys*, 127.

2. My comparison here is indebted to Auerbach's account of the Homeric scene (*Mimesis*, 1).

3. The typescript returned to the press also reads "tatoo," so the correction was not made by the typist Fitzgerald hired in Rome (Fitzgerald, *Great Gatsby: Galleys*, 131).

4. On the last stages of publication, see West, introduction to *Trimalchio*, especially xiv–xviii.

5. Referring to "punctuation, which the natives call tattow," Forster often refers to tattoos as "punctures" (*Voyage round the World*, 390).

6. See *Oxford English Dictionary*, 2nd ed. (Oxford: Oxford University Press, 1989), s.v. "tattoo, n.¹" and "tattoo, n.²," OED Online.

7. Dickens, *Bleak House*, 264. Fitzgerald called *Bleak House* Dickens's "finest" work (Kuehl, "Scott Fitzgerald's Reading," 66).

8. Dickens, *Bleak House*, 387. Dissipation is also the subtext of a "tattoo" in Mayfield's description of Fitzgerald in 1925: "His hands were stained with nicotine, and he was constantly drumming a tattoo" (*Exiles from Paradise*, 113).

9. On modernist surfaces (including tattoos) and racialized performance, see Cheng, "Skins, Tattoos, and Susceptibility."

10. See L. Davis on gesture and disability in *Great Expectations* (*Enforcing Normalcy*, 123–24).

11. This point seconds (and differently contextualizes) Crary's work on "observation" as irreducible to the history of technology or visual culture (*Techniques of the Observer*, 8).

12. L. Davis, *Enforcing Normalcy*, 123.

13. "Musical motion is, first and foremost, audible human motion," writes Iyer ("Exploding the Narrative," 397); on Black soundwork as "*primarily* textual," where "text" does not mean "writing in the narrow sense, but an open-ended will to systematicity, structured by relations of power and capital, that draws and redraws the horizon within which sound techniques, gestures, dispositions, and so on take meaning," see A. Reed, *Soundworks*, 23–24. I coordinate these terms slightly differently, asking how even writing's "narrow sense" gets variously imagined through such relations.

14. On Fitzgerald's contact with social theory, see Berman, "Fitzgerald and the Idea of Society." A well-known scene of *Gatsby* that I'll address caricatures the racist theories of a figure whom Boas likewise critiqued (Lothrop Stoddard). Fitzgerald's writing also reiterates racialist and anti-Black commonplaces that the culturalist paradigm shift of the Boasians was meant, for all its limitations, to combat—as when Nick Carraway, crossing the Queensboro Bridge, laughs at the "haughty rivalry" of Black people in another car (Fitzgerald, *Great Gatsby* [1953], 69). I cite several editions of this novel, but where unspecified, page citations refer to the Scribner's 1953 edition, cited parenthetically in the text and abbreviated hereinafter as *Gatsby*. *Gatsby* scholars may wonder about this choice. Although it is far from a perfect edition—and where relevant, my argument identifies variations—it stands as my default because it is late enough to incorporate some of Fitzgerald's last revisions but early enough and produced in sufficient quantity (a "Student Edition") to have circulated widely during the midcentury Fitzgerald Revival.

15. Noland writes that gestures can "reveal the submission of shared human anatomy to a set of bodily practices specific to one culture" while also exceeding that specificity (*Agency and Embodiment*, 2). The paradox of gesture as revealing linguistic excess *and* lack is crucial to Derrida's reading of Rousseau in *Of Grammatology*; see 235.

16. The processes of diaspora "move the glacial force of the habitus into the quickened beat of improvisation" (Appadurai, *Modernity at Large*, 6).

17. Gilles de la Tourette, *Études cliniques*, 14–15. The translation of the title is mine. The study was supervised by Jean-Martin Charcot.

18. Gilles de la Tourette, *Études cliniques*, 2.

19. Gilles de la Tourette, *Études cliniques*, 1.

20. Gilles de la Tourette, "Étude sur une affection nerveuse." The translation of the title is mine. On this research, see Kushner, *Cursing Brain?* Agamben discusses the two studies I cite here, calling the walking study the first time that "one of the most common human gestures [had] been analyzed according to strictly scientific methods" ("Notes on Gesture," 135), while detecting in the study of nervous tics an omen of mechanization's effects (137).

21. "The Length of a Step," *Scientific American*, December 18, 1886, 390; "Notes and News," 631.

22. "Charcot's Remedy for Nervousness," *Kansas Democrat*, November 9, 1892; "Science of Sounding Skulls: Tap Your Head and Know Your Brain the Latest Fad," *Boston Globe*, May 20, 1899.

23. "Scientific Brevities," *Chicago Tribune*, January 23, 1887.

24. Mauss, "Techniques of the Body," 72.

25. Sapir, *Language*, 2.

26. F. Scott Fitzgerald to Annabel Fitzgerald, ca. 1915, in *Correspondence*, 18.

27. W. James, "Laws of Habit," 65. We are "mere bundles of habit," James writes, "stereotyped creatures" (66). While James anticipates the objection that his account forecloses new habits—these "*can* be launched," he insists, "on condition of there being new stimuli and new excitements" (77)—the view of humans as "copiers of our past selves" (66) would still seem troublesome for the young person trying to keep pace with convention. This essay appeared in James's *Talks to Teachers*, one of Anne Sullivan's favorite books (Herrmann, *Helen Keller*, 238).

28. F. Scott Fitzgerald to Annabel Fitzgerald, 16, 17.

29. F. Scott Fitzgerald to Annabel Fitzgerald, 15.

30. Fitzgerald, "Bernice Bobs Her Hair," 38.

31. F. Scott Fitzgerald to Annabel Fitzgerald, 16.

32. F. Scott Fitzgerald to Annabel Fitzgerald, 16.

33. Fitzgerald, *Great Gatsby: Facsimile*, 129 (emphasis added).

34. Firth, "Postures," 89. William James, too, wrote that the primacy of habit is best appreciated by a military veteran ("Laws of Habit," *Popular Science Monthly*, February 1887, 446). (James revised the essay; the soldier appears here but not in the 1907 version cited earlier, while the line about "stereotyped creatures" appears in that version but not this earlier one.) When Dick Diver and his friends are observing the behavior of restaurant patrons in *Tender Is the Night*, with Diver claiming to be the only self-controlled American, they take note of the West Point training of a "well-known general": "His hands hanging naturally at his sides, the general waited to be seated. Once his arms swung suddenly back like a jumper's and Dick said, 'Ah!' supposing he had lost control, but the general recovered" (110).

35. F. Scott Fitzgerald to Annabel Fitzgerald, 16, 18.

36. Puckett describes the etiquette manual's "necessary resistance to closure" (*Bad Form*, 20).

37. Bailey, "Navaho Motor Habits," 210.

38. Bailey, "Navaho Motor Habits," 216.

39. Fitzgerald, "Bernice Bobs Her Hair," 27, 31.

40. Fitzgerald, "Bernice Bobs Her Hair," 45, 47.

41. Margolies writes that here "Fitzgerald reverts back to . . . ethnic stereotyping" ("Maturing," 79). While Fitzgerald is no stranger to such reversion, the invocation of scalping here ironizes such stereotyping.

42. Fitzgerald, "Bernice Bobs Her Hair," 43.

43. Fitzgerald, "Bernice Bobs Her Hair," 46.

44. Woolf, *Mr. Bennett and Mrs. Brown*, 4.

45. Vaught, *Practical Character Reader*, 3, 5.

46. Boas, *Primitive Art*, 146.

47. The same year saw the publication of perhaps the period's best-known study of adolescent development, M. Mead's *Coming of Age in Samoa*; Boas supplies a foreword that opens with a discussion of "development," but at the scale of cultures (foreword to *Coming of Age in Samoa*, xiv).

48. Boas, *Anthropology and Modern Life*, 146.

49. Boas, "On Alternating Sounds," 48.

50. Boas, *Anthropology and Modern Life*, 145.

51. Stocking argues that in the 1920s Boas had begun to move from the diachronic to the synchronic, shifting from the study of the diffusion and toward the patterns internal to a culture, in ways Ruth Benedict's work will extend (*Ethnographer's Magic*, 137).

52. Boas, *Anthropology and Modern Life*, 144.

53. Frank Thone, "Do You Talk with Your Hands?," *Science News Letter*, September 5, 1936, 154.

54. Thone, "Do You Talk with Your Hands?," 154.

55. The quality of unconsciousness, diminishing the supposed interference of native informants' own theories about their practices, is one reason that Boasians privileged spoken language. "The unconsciousness of linguistic processes helps us to gain a clearer understanding of the [other] ethnological phenomena" (Boas, *Handbook*, 67).

56. This was not always the project that Efron intended to do for Boas. In 1933, Efron asks Boas for help in obtaining a scholarship to stay in the country and research "physiognomic mimetism," hypothesizing that cultural environments influence physiognomy (David Efron to Franz Boas, June 26, 1933, Franz Boas Papers). Boas agreed, but soon the topic—an old one for Boas; see "Changes in the Bodily Form" (1912)—shifted to motor habit.

57. Efron, *Gesture and Environment*, 136–37. Subsequent quotations from this source are cited parenthetically in the text. For recent discussions of Efron's study (republished in 1971 as *Gesture, Race, and Culture*), see Sklar, "Remembering Kinesthesia," 98–100; and Ruby, *Picturing Culture*, 62.

58. Boas, foreword to *Gesture and Environment*, ii.

59. David Efron, "A Bibliography of Gesture and Posture," box 1, David Efron Gesture Research. For Mauss, see 1; Pope, 25; Keller, 57.

60. "United States Educator Declares He Has Documentary Evidence of German-Italian Propaganda Activities in Latin-America," *Corpus Christi Times*, November 28, 1938; "Anti-Dictatorship Conference Told of Fascist-Nazi Penetration of South American Countries," *St. Louis Post-Dispatch*, December 11, 1938.

61. "Argentine Educator Threatened," *The State*, December 12, 1938.

62. According to her memoirs, in 1937 Paloma Efron studied at Columbia in the "Departmento de Música Primitiva" with "Claudio Hertzog"—possibly a misrecollection of George Herzog, who was then establishing the Archives of Folk and Primitive Music. Her(t)zog recommended that she study Black folklore at Tuskegee, where she spent another year (Horvarth, *Memorias*, 34).

63. A note affixed to the back of the print indicates that the Italian delegate is speaking.

64. Franz Boas to Stuyvesant Van Veen, April 13, 1939, Franz Boas Papers. Boas had always been pushing things along: when Van Veen was called for jury duty in the fall of 1934, Boas exhorted him to beg off by explaining the study's urgency to the court (Franz Boas to Stuyvesant Van Veen, October 31, 1934, Franz Boas Papers). Around the same time, Van Veen was also busy working on paintings and illustrations for a lengthy article on burlesque for *Fortune* magazine. Only the illustrations are attributed to him, not the text (authored anonymously), but there are overlaps with the Efron study: "The burlesque show of 1935 is an entertainment almost as stylized as the Chinese theatre where all movement has been conventionalized" ("The Business of Burlesque, A.D. 1935," *Fortune*, February 1935, 67).

65. Mostly the study was conducted in New York City, but upstate locations were also used, largely for technical reasons. In the city, ambient conditions often necessitated filming indoors. Initial recordings came out underexposed. So research shifted to Catskills summer camps and the Saratoga tracks (Efron, *Gesture and Environment*, 107).

66. Boas paraphrases this element of the study in 1938: "The Jew has very few symbolic gestures. The movements rather follow his lines of thought" (*Mind of Primitive Man*, 125).

67. My attention to the difference between thread and dotted line is guided by Ingold, *Lines*, esp. 74–75.

68. Boas, "Dance and Music," 18.

69. Van Veen drew for comics under multiple pen names, including Jack Camden.

70. "The posture of groups of unassimilated immigrants has a local color," Boas writes in a 1938 description of the study, with this local color then washing out among their "Americanized descendants," who "adopt [Americans'] erect posture" (*Mind of Primitive Man*, 124).

71. Thone, "Do You Talk with Your Hands?" 154. The relation of these terms was at issue in an early correspondence between Edna Porter and W. E. B. Du Bois, three years before the exchange I detailed in chapter 2. In a 1924 *Crisis* column, Du Bois sardonically responded to public outcry over the miscegenation plot of a new Eugene O'Neill play (he does not name the production, but the theme and timing indicate *All God's Chillun Have Wings*, starring Paul Robeson and Mary Blair): "Suppose the boy a Jew and the girl American—'Good!' says the world." Porter writes to him asking for a clarification of this line, implying in her question that his opposition of "Jew" and "American" had been antisemitic. While "the use of the word 'American' was not happy," Du Bois explains, he meant "Americans outside of certain prescribed races." W. E. B. Du Bois, "The American Scene," *The Crisis*, May 1924, 7; Edna Porter to W. E. B. Du Bois, May 5, 1924, W. E. B. Du Bois Papers; W. E. B. Du Bois to Edna Porter, June 20, 1924, W. E. B. Du Bois Papers. On the "American" and the "Jew," see Michaels, *Our America*, especially 7–9.

72. I leave "the designer of the diptych" anonymous because, although Boas sends Thone the drawings (see Franz Boas to Frank Thone, May 1, 1936, Franz Boas Papers), it is unclear who captions and lays out the images as printed.

73. While anonymous in publication, the subject of this sketch is identified in the typewritten draft of a caption, affixed to the drawing in Van Veen's hand, as Nathan Straus Jr.—the Macy's scion, print and radio journalist, and housing reformer ("Americanized Jew," folder: Illustrations [1 of 6], box 1, David Efron Gesture Research).

74. Rogoff, "Is the Jew White?," 195. The reference in the caption to the figure as German is particularly telling in light of Rogoff's argument elsewhere that Boas exemplified "that segment of late 19th-century German Jewry who had . . . abandoned the struggle to integrate Jewish identity with German nationality and had opted . . . to assimilate themselves out of existence" ("Types Distinct," 546). Stocking offers a different angle: "Boas had felt [antisemitism's] impact personally—his face bore scars from several duels he had fought with students who had made antisemitic remarks" ("From Physics to Ethnology," 149–50). On Boas's "deracinated" self-presentation, see also Elliott, *Culture Concept*, 28.

75. With World War II, "the idea of the Jew as other-than-white" in the United States is reconfigured by the association with Nazism; in the mainstream, Jewish identity becomes more tightly associated with whiteness, even as the white-supremacist confluence of antisemitism and anti-Blackness persists (Rogoff, "Is the Jew White?," 230). Glenn argues that "Efron ended up amplifying rather than downplaying the issue of whether Jews looked Jewish" ("Funny," 70).

76. I'm indebted to Abel's work on the racial imaginary of the shadow ("Shadows") and her study of photographic representations of Jim Crow signs (*Signs of the Times*). Those signs' assumption of race as biologically intrinsic is contradicted by their materiality and discursivity, revealing racial categories as contingent, graphic constructions—a contradiction Abel frames through the transition from scientific racism to Boasian cultural theory (*Signs of the Times*, 14). On the effects of the observer's shadow in anthropological representations of bodily movement, see Reckson, *Realist Ecstasy*, 121–22; see also Reckson's argument that "the body in ecstasy" unsettles both "Jim Crow regimes of racial legibility and . . . realism's fantasies of intelligibility" (3).

77. See Frankenberg, "Mirage," on whiteness as unmarked.

78. On the mask as a figure for figuration and for the face of the racialized colonial subject, see Fanon, *Black Skin, White Masks*. His engagement with Sartre involves an account of Jewish and Black experience that differs from the history of Jewishness in the American ethnological imagination I cited earlier. Responding to Sartre's argument that in response to antisemitism the behavior of the Jewish person is "overdetermined from within" (quoted in *Black Skin, White Masks*, 115), Fanon writes that the Black person is "overdetermined from without," "dissected under white eyes" (116). For Fanon, "the Jew," as white, can remain "unknown in his Jewishness" except as "his behavior" draws attention (115). For an extension of Fanon's central conceit in a reading of *Gatsby*, see Goldsmith, "White Skin, White Mask."

79. Max Perkins to F. Scott Fitzgerald, November 20, 1924, quoted in Bruccoli, *Some Sort of Epic Grandeur*, 208.

80. Fitzgerald, *Great Gatsby: Galleys*, 141, 141, 140. Later, Fitzgerald deletes the lines about Nick's mimetic frustration and, in a direct reversal, makes this into a moment of descriptive accuracy: Gatsby's expression "looked . . . as if he had 'killed a man.' For a moment the set of his face *could be described* in just that fantastic way" (*Gatsby*, 135; my emphasis). On Fitzgerald's larger structural revisions of this scene, see Dewalt, "Tom's Investigation."

81. Thompson's *Tragic Black Buck* influentially argued that Gatsby racially passes. For further studies of Fitzgerald's racial imagination, see (in addition to scholarship cited elsewhere in these notes) Schreier, "Desire's Second Act"; and Slater, "Ethnicity."

82. Fitzgerald, *Love of the Last Tycoon*, 96. A third rhythmic "tattoo" occurs in *Tender Is the Night*: after Diver strikes a police officer, "fists and boots beat on him in a savage tattoo" (244). Fitzgerald refers to an ink tattoo, also in a law-enforcement context, in the farcical play *The Vegetable* (120–21).

83. Breitwieser positions this scene as a late revelation for Fitzgerald (*National Melancholy*, 277). Nowlin develops a complementary reading (*Fitzgerald's Racial Angles*, 148) while arguing that "Fitzgerald could not conceive of Stahr as a model of assimilation without conjuring up his unassimilable shadow" (147).

84. *Oxford English Dictionary*, s.v. "tattoo, v.²"

85. The story includes several moments that will echo in *Gatsby*: a party at a mansion, witnessed from outside; the family name Katsby; Amanthis Powell telling Jim Powell that he's "better than all of them put together" (Fitzgerald, "Dice, Brassknuckles & Guitar," 252).

86. Fitzgerald, "Dice, Brassknuckles & Guitar," 246, 248.

87. Fitzgerald, "Dice, Brassknuckles & Guitar," 241. N. Evans reads Jim's "involuntarily tapping foot" in terms of a 1920s "trope of anxiety about the rebellious 'blackness' that always already resides within the white self" (*Writing Jazz*, 186; on "Dice" more generally, see 181–90).

88. On percussive call-and-response, see Mowitt: "the sense of each beat becomes the beating it stirs" (*Percussion*, 3).

89. Fitzgerald, "Echoes of the Jazz Age," in *Crack-Up*, 19.

90. Here I refer to Ryle—in a 1968 essay, "Thinking of Thoughts," whose influence was heightened by Geertz's recapitulation in "Thick Description"—on gesture and twitch. The former, writes Ryle, has "very complex success-versus-failure conditions"; a motion intended to signal can be misconstrued or ignored. But a twitch, "neither a failure nor a success," "may be a symptom but it is not a signal." In Ryle's paradigmatic example, "two boys fairly swiftly contract the eyelids of their right eyes." For one, it's involuntary; the other "is winking conspiratorially." To capture the "unphotographable difference" that sets the gesture apart from the tic, the visible data won't suffice. One needs a "thick description" (480). For contrasting applications of Ryle's thought experiment in a literary-critical context, see Greenblatt, "Touch of the Real"; and Love, "Close but Not Deep."

91. Franz Boas, "This Nordic Nonsense," *The Forum*, October 1925, 502.

92. Stoddard, *Rising Tide of Color*, 287. On Nordicism and *Gatsby*, see Decker, "Gatsby's Pristine Dream." The Johnson-Reed Immigration Act intensified immi-

gration restrictions put in place with the Chinese Exclusion Act of 1882, passed largely in response to anti-immigration agitation in California. See Ngai, *Impossible Subjects*, 21–55. Stoddard's writing was directly invoked in debates about the Johnson-Reed Act; see John Carlyle's syndicated column arguing that "Stoddard would undoubtedly be in favor of the Johnson bill" ("It Is Up to the Few," *Buffalo Evening Times*, May 29, 1924).

93. Gesture and interruption have been tightly linked in critical theory. See Benjamin's brief reflection in "What Is Epic Theater?" on the way that theater makes gestures "quotable" through a logic of interruption fundamental to all quotation (in *Illuminations*, 151).

94. On such a fate, see Geertz, "Thick Description," 6.

95. Many critics have read in Tom's "hesitation" about Daisy a racial doubt, but, Korenman notes, he is also responding to Daisy's contempt ("Only Her Hairdresser," 574n8).

96. Beard, *American Nervousness*, 13. See also Lutz, *American Nervousness, 1903*.

97. I punctuate "Yea—ea—ea" as it appears in the 1953 and most other print editions of the novel, but Fitzgerald's manuscript indicates shorter dashes or hyphens. In turn, some of Fitzgerald's own handwritten em dashes (generally those that indicate an interruption in dialogue) are converted, in the typeset novel, to double em dashes, though they're not so long in the manuscript. These marks not being immediately relevant to my argument, I've retained the typical print punctuation.

98. For a contemporaneous (1926) note on the apparent disappearance of the word "yes" from spoken English and its replacement with many "mutilated" forms including, for example, "ye-ah" and "ye-yuss," see the linguist Louise Pound, "Popular Variants of "Yes.'" In *American Language*, Mencken cites Pound's study (353) alongside St. John Ervine's complaints—widely quoted in American newspapers in late 1928—about "yeah" as giving the impression that the speaker "had started out to say *yes*, but had suddenly contracted a violent pain in his stomach" (quoted on 354).

99. The sense of "personality" offered here—gestural, serially iterated—resonates with a pragmatist sense of identity as continually remade. On gestures as "the material out of which selves are constructed," see G. Mead, "Social Consciousness," 404—a text cited in Efron's research notes ("A Bibliography of Gestures and Postures," folder: Bibliography of Gestures and Postures, box 1, David Efron Gesture Research, p. 111).

100. Black feminist theory has offered crucial orientations to the ways in which the very concepts of flesh, human, and animated life (versus inanimate matter) have been constructed as expressions of racialization. See Jackson, *Becoming Human*; Weheliye, *Habeas Viscus*; Wynter, *On Being Human*; and Spillers, "Mama's Baby, Papa's Maybe," esp. 67. Yusoff argues that Blackness emerges as a "contact point of geographical proximity with the earth . . . constructed specifically as a node of extraction of properties and personhood" yet also "repurposed . . . into a praxis for remaking other selves" (*Billion Black Anthropocenes*, xii). Inspirational to Yusoff, as she writes, are the speculative novels of N. K. Jemisin's *Broken Earth* trilogy, in which some people "sess" tectonic activity, a sensory capacity bearing a

caste stigma. These connections are not only relevant to *Gatsby* because of Nick's metaphor of seismic sensitivity; the surplus value created through geological extraction is the condition of Gatsby's self-making, his patron Dan Cody having derived his wealth from copper mines.

101. On heat, air, and narrative reverberation in Faulkner, see Napolin, *Fact of Resonance*, 223.

102. See Ochoa Gautier on "untamed vocality": expressions that resist forms of orthographic and grammatical discipline premised on "an ontology of the voice as a failed writing" (*Aurality*, 205).

103. Fitzgerald, *Great Gatsby: Facsimile*, 193.

104. The same term is associated with jazz at the first party at Gatsby's: "By midnight the hilarity had increased. A celebrated tenor had sung in Italian and a notorious contralto had sung in jazz" (*Gatsby*, 47).

105. "The sound that dance itself produces," Connor writes, "is, in every other case than tap dance, the sound of accident or excess" ("Two-Step," 219). I'd quibble with "every" but am convinced by Connor's claim that tap, in the era of early film, effects the same kind of "acoustic captioning" that one finds with the introduction of sound to moving pictures, as if to say, "this is dance you're seeing here . . . just as the creaking door says, look here at this door you can see opening" (219); and at the same time, in its potential association "with the more spasmodic kinds of click involved in the Touretter's tic," tap disrupts the assumption of aesthetic control (226).

106. "What if the nervous tic," Moten has recently asked, "were one among other interpretations of a given choreography of racial difference?" (*Black and Blur*, 299n43). On the "black mirror" (one way of figuring what the tattoo is to Tom) as "the key to a world of symptoms," see Lott, *Black Mirror*, 9.

107. As Breitwieser writes of Melville's *Typee*, this disquietude is the flip side of tattooing's customary marking of communal belonging ("False Sympathy," 412).

108. Parry, *Tattoo*, 14; Fitzgerald, "Echoes of the Jazz Age," 16.

109. Parry, *Tattoo*, 46, 45.

110. When Fitzgerald published *Tender Is the Night*, Ernest Hemingway wrote him a critical letter in which he associates the visual with subjective observation and the aural with a capacity for receptivity: "A long time ago you stopped listening except to the answers to your own questions. . . . You see well enough. But you stop listening" (Hemingway to Fitzgerald, May 28, 1934, in *Selected Letters*, 407). Hemingway used similar terms in recalling his first impressions of Fitzgerald: "since I was embarrassed by what he said . . . I kept on looking at him closely and noticed instead of listening" (*Moveable Feast*, 149–50).

111. Keller's reflections on jazz superimpose racist commonplaces of African primitivism and the kind of imagery of the "Phantom" with which she characterized her own prelinguistic state: jazz evokes "primal emotions" and "shadow memories, . . . gigantic creatures, . . . sons and daughters of the jungle, . . . the cry of dumb souls not yet able to speak" (*Midstream*, 287).

112. Mencken, quoted in "Jazz Music and Morals," *Salt Lake Tribune*, February 17, 1925. For an example of reporting on the case of Ellingson and her "Jazzmaniac" friends, see Annie Laurie, "Dorothy Like Stricken Thing as Jazz Mask Gives

Way to Reality," *San Francisco Examiner* March 24, 1925. On 1920s reactionary critiques of jazz aesthetics' extension into literature, dance, and the visual arts, see Donald, "Jazz Modernism"; Golston, *Rhythm and Race*; and Johnson, "Disease Is Unrhythmical."

113. H. L. Mencken, "Mencken Reviews Scott Fitzgerald's Latest Novel, 'The Great Gatsby,'" *Montgomery Advertiser*, May 3, 1925. It isn't clear from this passage how Mencken understands the historical importance of improvisation to the fugue tradition. Elsewhere, Mencken describes the fugue as an "un-American" mode (Mencken, *Book of Prefaces*, 187) whose elevated forms are lost on American writers (*Prejudices*, 190).

114. In this regard, Fitzgerald at least passively entertained what G. Lewis terms the "Eurological" theory of improvisatory aesthetics: a "notion of spontaneity that excludes history or memory" ("Improvised Music after 1950," 231). Breitwieser—in an argument that influences my method, attending to Fitzgerald's deletion from the manuscript of a lengthy passage describing the performance of "Vladimir Tostoff's Jazz History of the World" at Gatsby's house—argues that the aesthetics of improvisation were, for the author and his narrator, compelling in their innovation but unsettling in that their uncanny temporalities threatened to interrupt the narrative line of Anglo-American national belonging (*National Melancholy*, 268).

115. Fitzgerald, "Captured Shadow," 418, 419.

116. Hildegarde Hawthorne, "Latest Works of Fiction," *New York Times Book Review*, October 29, 1922. Given the importance that Fitzgerald scholars have attributed to Mencken's review of *Gatsby*, its similarities to Hawthorne's earlier assessment of *Tales* merit attention. Along with the common references to the "finished" nature of Fitzgerald's craft (and the common thesis about social triviality and gorgeous writing), the blunt grammar of Hawthorne's "it exists" also echoes closely in Mencken's review: "The Long Island he sets before us is no fanciful Alsatia; it actually exists" ("Mencken Reviews Scott Fitzgerald's Latest Novel"). Mencken was aware of Hawthorne, having referred to her among other literary "authorities" in an essay published several years earlier (*Book of Prefaces*, 55). His own review of *Tales* dismissed Fitzgerald's collection in a few sentences (West, "Mencken's Review," 3).

117. My approach is informed by musicological interventions including Abbate's description of a performance-centered critical project of "going back for a moment to a certain fork in the road and seeing what was abandoned" ("Music," 506) and Lewis's description of an Afrological theory of improvisation as "temporally multi-laminar" ("Improvised Music after 1950," 108).

118. On the way that typescripts become "manuscripts" through their use as working documents internal to organizations, see Gitelman, *Paper Knowledge*, 69–70.

119. Ryle makes a relevant point: when somebody winks on purpose, this intentionality expands the action's meanings but does not itself constitute a separate action ("Thinking of Thoughts," 481). On suddenness and reification, see Daston: "the all-at-once-ness of habitual perception . . . stamps its ontologies with the imprimatur of the really real" ("On Scientific Observation," 107).

120. Ingold would put a finer point on "writing," arguing that print broke the "intimate link between manual gesture and graphic inscription" (*Lines*, 26). Modernity takes us from "the *trace of a gesture* [to] an assembly of *point-to-point connectors*" (92–93), from texts composed of lines that go for walks (to paraphrase, as Ingold does, the artist Paul Klee) to texts composed of dotted lines, or—we could add—the segmented illustrations of Efron and Van Veen's film analysis. "If handwriting is like walking," writes Ingold, "then the line of print (joining evenly spaced letters) is like the record of gait analysis (joining equidistant plots)" (93).

121. Although I take from the figure of the tattoo a reminder that even print on paper is not *quite* flat—it's slightly bumpy—I second Hayles's argument in "Print Is Flat, Code Is Deep" that "'texts' must always be embodied to exist in the world" and that "the materiality of those embodiments interacts dynamically with linguistic, rhetorical, and literary practices to create the effects we call literature" (69–70).

122. Fitzgerald, *Love of the Last Tycoon*, 28. On improvisatory nonverbal storytelling, see Iyer, "Exploding the Narrative." On drumming and narrative, see Napolin, "Elliptical Sound," 120–24.

123. On microrhythmic variation, see Benadon, "Gridless Beats."

124. Hurston, "Characteristics of Negro Expression," 26. "The spectator is held so rapt," Hurston writes, because "he is participating in the performance himself," forced "to finish the action the performer suggests" (26–27). Hurston published this essay near the end of her time working with Boas, as she had begun to do as a Barnard anthropology student.

125. See Fitzgerald, *Great Gatsby* (1992), 135.

126. Greg, "Rationale," 21.

Chapter 4

1. Franz Boas, "Eskimo ethnographic notes from Baffinland," item 26, Franz Boas Papers, p. 53.

2. Thanks to Brian Carpenter, curator of Indigenous materials at the American Philosophical Library, for consulting on this question (personal communication, August 30, 2022).

3. Darnell posits that Boas chose to write about Baffin Island for *American Indian Life* despite the fact that "most of his own fieldwork was done on the Northwest Coast" because "alternative contributors were easily available for the Northwest Coast" (*Invisible Genealogies*, 221). This does not preclude the possibility that Boas had a positive interest in returning to this material (as is supported by the fact that he viewed this fieldwork experience as lending itself to nonacademic writing projects like the posthumously published *Eskimo Story*).

4. Elsie C. Parsons, "Waiyautitsa of Zuñi, New Mexico," *Scientific Monthly*, November 1919, 443–57. "It was this biography," she writes in a footnote to the revised 1922 version, that "suggested . . . the comprehensive biographic plan of the book" (Parsons, "Waiyautitsa of Zuñi, New Mexico" [*American Indian Life*], 158n1).

5. Silko, *Storyteller*, 246.

6. Parsons, "Waiyautitsa of Zuñi, New Mexico" (*American Indian Life*), 158.

7. Darnell describes some of the practical details of Parsons's approach to recruitment, including a regular "lunch group" with other Boasians based in the New York City area (*Invisible Genealogies*, 227). When Huebsch sent her a letter about a couple of stray items of business on February 21, 1920, he tagged on a handwritten postscript asking how her "round-up of the anthropologists" was proceeding (B. W. Huebsch to Elsie Clews Parsons, February 21, 1920, Elsie Clews Parsons Papers).

8. Parsons, preface to *American Indian Life*, 2, 3.

9. Kroeber, introduction to *American Indian Life*, 13, 14.

10. Parsons, preface to *American Indian Life*, 1, 2.

11. "By quietly transferring Britain's rights in this region to Canada," writes G. Smith, British imperial officers felt "they would be in a better position to forestall or defeat any attempt by the United States, whether based upon the Monroe Doctrine or not, to assert American sovereignty there" ("Transfer of Arctic Territories," 69).

12. Boas, "Journey in Cumberland Sound," 245.

13. On the unpronounceability of punctuation, see Ong, *Orality and Literacy*, 147; and Nurhussein, *Rhetorics of Literacy*—particularly her reading of a stray exclamation point in Langston Hughes's "Cat and the Saxophone (2 A.M.)" (181–82).

14. John M. Oskison, "Real, Not Paleface Fancy, Indian Life," *New York Times Book Review and Magazine*, June 18, 1922. Oskison's reference to novelistic representations of "controlling environment and motivating color of life" suggests the persistent influence of Hamlin Garland's writing on local color.

15. Boas, "Eskimo Winter," 378.

16. Boas, *Central Eskimo*, 241.

17. K. Martin, *Stories*, 66. My references to terms of Inuit song are indebted to this and several other sources, including Bennett and Rowley, *Uqalurait*; Conlon, "Drum-Dance Songs"; and Qaggiavuut, "Pisiq Song Book." The orthography of Inuktitut terms in the Latin alphabet varies; the plural of *pisiq* is often given as *pisiit* (while the editors of *Uqalurait* instead give the terms as *pihiq/pisiit*).

18. Boas, "Eskimo Winter," 378.

19. Elliott more generally connects this idea of recursion to the sense of culture's conformist pressure as a kind of routine against which the individual might break out; and here the "picture," with its stasis, exists in opposition to the diachrony of plot. "The image of No-tongue and his wife leaving the regular rhythms of their own culture to depart upon a journey" situates "No-tongue in a deliberately liminal symbolic space in which he stands, momentarily, outside culture" (*Culture Concept*, 32–33).

20. Boas, "Poetry and Music" (*Science*), 384. On the problem of considering drum-dance songs as "poems," see Martin, *Stories*—arguing, for example, that for figures like Knud Rasmussen, "poetry" accorded a certain level of respect for Inuit art but, at the same time, both decontextualized works from their performative contexts and (more importantly, Martin argues) did not facilitate South-North exchanges based in ideas of reciprocity (66–68).

21. Will, "No-Tongue," 334. Will credits the story to James Holding Eagle—who, in turn, "learned it from his mother, Scattered-Corn Woman" (331).

22. Will, "Story," 402. Thanks to David Cophenhafer for this note on the vocable's articulation.

23. Elliott suggests that the choice of this character's name implies Boas's awareness that "culture, like any explanatory model of such scope, could be used to silence figures such as No-tongue as well as to give them voice" (*Culture Concept*, 34).

24. In early November 1884, Boas seems to have described or recited this text at a meeting of the German Social Science Association in New York, given a reporter's summation of Boas's lecture on the "Esquimaux": "Much of the poetry refers to returning Summer and rushing waters, the sound of which, after the painful silence of a hard Winter, is gratefully welcome to the ears"—though evidently much of Boas's speech, delivered rapidly in a cavernous hall, "escaped the ears of many in the audience" ("Customs of the Esquimaux," *New York Times*, November 6, 1884).

25. See Sider on Boas's interpretation—or, probably, misinterpretation—of the meaning of speechlessness in an Inuit text that Boas described (falsely, Sider suggests) as a riddle (*Skin for Skin*, 92–94).

26. In an essay on the relationship of vocable to semantic text and syntax in Lakota song (and on retaining these relationships in translation), Powers notes that in English-language college instruction, untranslated vocables "have a dramatic effect" possibly due to their sounding "distinctly 'Indian' to an audience that usually knows little about American Indian culture" ("Translating the Untranslatable," 308). Some poetry anthologies including Boas's transcription have attempted to mark the exceptional status of the untranslated word by putting it in italics (R. Lewis, *I Breathe a New Song*, 113) or eliminating it altogether (Swann, *Native American Songs and Poems*, 24).

27. It is telling of this ironic mode that the text has recently been anthologized both as a "poem of gratitude" for nature and as a poem about insomnia. Fragos, *Poems of Gratitude*, 52; Spaar, *Acquainted with the Night*, 115.

28. Boas, "Eskimo Winter," 368.

29. Boas, "Year among the Eskimo," 385.

30. In almost identical versions republished in other periodicals the same year as this one—also the same year that Boas started working at *Science* and that the journal published its first story about sound-blindness—either he or someone else on staff adds an *h* at the same point: "Oh." See Boas, "Poetry and Music" (*Science*), 384; and Franz Boas, "Poetry and Music of Some North American Tribes," *Swiss Cross*, November 1887, 147. This isn't the only version of the vocable element that Boas tested out, in working across languages; in the earliest handwritten copy of the text—the one with the blue *X* across it, where the vocable mostly appears as "Aja"—Boas's German translation reads at one point "a, das ist gut, gut" ("Eskimo ethnographic notes from Baffinland," 53).

31. Boas, *Central Eskimo*, 652. Such "deviations of, e.g., Indian music" from the Western scale are the theme of the ethnomusicologist Wead's 1900 essay extending

Boas's argument in "On Alternating Sounds" in the direction of musical notation. On the one hand, Wead argues, the problem of apparent tonal inconsistencies in non-Western musical performances might be resolved through a more sensitive system of notating semitones or microtones, which "deviations" are sometimes "as significant of history and relationship as the silent letters in many English words"; on the other hand, Wead cautions, precision of tune may not be valued in universal terms ("Study of Primitive Music," 79).

32. Donald Suluk, quoted in Conlon, "Drum-Dance Songs," 14. On Suluk's influence on the tradition, see Blakney, "Connections to the Land," 1–4. Beverley Cavanagh notes that "the songs are logogenic, or closely derived from speech patterns" (quoted in Conlon, "Drum-Dance Songs," 16).

33. See Martin's discussion, drawing on Peter Irniq, David Serkoak, and others, of Inuit norms of musical adaptation—norms that generally permit new words in borrowed tunes but with acknowledgment required and with the fact of a family (or other close) relationship sometimes playing a factor (*Stories*, 80). Samuel Lockwood's *Animal Memoirs* (1888) provides a surprising example of explicit alteration in the immediate wake of Boas's early publications of the texts, not only quoting and commenting on them but also, "for the sake of feeling its tender pathos and homely fun," trying out an alternate translation of Utitia'q's song: "Well, isn't here a go? / Alone upon the floe!"—and so on (79). When the composer Gordon Williamson in 2006 creates a score for both "Summer Song" and "Utitiaq's Song," he does not offer any specific context for the former—which is unsurprising given that most of Boas's publications don't offer it—but does write that "the Utitiaq text is based on the story of an Inuit man who became stranded on an ice floe while sealing, and found himself adrift in the ocean for a week" ("Two Inuit Folks Songs," i).

34. Fragos, *Poems of Gratitude*, 52.

35. Spinden, "Understudy of Tezcatlipoca," 237n1.

36. Herbert Spinden to Elsie Clews Parsons, June 20, 1922, Elsie Clews Parsons Papers.

37. After the 1924 passage of the Indian Citizenship Act—often framed as a realization of the intent of the earlier legislation—the date of this federally recognized holiday would be shifted to June 2.

38. Lindsey, *Indians at Hampton Institute*, 253.

39. My summary of these policies derives from Shipley ("Musical Education"), who also develops a fascinating account of the Hampton instructor Natalie Curtis's work in musical education, transcription, and recording.

40. When Chapman received an honorary doctorate of divinity from Middlebury the year after this publication, he was credited as a "student of the souls of God's children of a vanishing race, whose patient years have been spent in Christlike ministry in the lonely ice-clad north" ("Middlebury Pays Academic Honors to Leading Men," *Burlington Daily News*, June 23, 1915, 3). See VanStone for a history of Anvik schools, including Chapman's, with reference to Reed, identified anonymously as "Parsons' informant" (*Ingalik Contact Ecology*, 201–3, 210).

41. On "Ten'a," see De Laguna, *Travels among the Dena*, 32–33.

42. When Chapman spoke at Hampton in January 1923, the *Southern Workman* noted that he "was responsible for sending to Hampton Thomas B. Reed, a recent Indian student" ("Hampton Incidents, Visitors," *Southern Workman*, March 1923, 148).

43. The text opens by referring to "the Indians in that part of the country" as a "backward sort of people" and closes with a wink: "I could tell you more of these superstitious beliefs, but I am afraid the Creat [*sic*] Crow, who is the father of all the Indians in my tribe, will get mad at me and cause my death!" (Thomas B. Reed, "Alaskan Indians," *Southern Workman*, December 1916, 671, 676). The tone of the talk is potentially estranging for more than one audience. Reed is, on the one hand, dismissing the ostensibly backward superstitions of Anvik in a way that caters to the rhetorical context of the assimilatory institution; but he is also sardonically indicating an authority that derives from Deg Hit'an knowledge and that presumes the auditors' ignorance and desire.

44. Thomas B. Reed, "Fishing on the Yukon," *Southern Workman*, February 1920, 70–74.

45. "Indian Students Celebrated Day: Hampton Institute Scene of Interesting and Impressive Exercises," *Daily Press*, February 8, 1920, 16.

46. "Indian Citizenship Day," *Southern Workman*, March 1920, 138–39.

47. Elsie Clews Parsons to Herbert Parsons, February 10, 1920, Elsie Clews Parsons Papers. Parsons had first visited Hampton in the fall of 1919 (Deacon, *Elsie Clews Parsons*, 283).

48. Elsie Clews Parsons to Herbert Parsons, February 13, 1920, Elsie Clews Parsons Papers. On the other publication outlets for material that Parsons gathered at Hampton, see Zumwalt, *Wealth and Rebellion*, 187. On the Tuesday evening of the visit, Parsons gave a talk titled "The Value of Folk Tales," encouraging the Hampton students to submit texts to the *Journal of American Folklore* ("The Value of Folk Tales," Elsie Clews Parsons Papers). Deacon, quoting from Zumwalt's citation of the text in *Wealth and Rebellion*, dates "The Value of Folk Tales" as March 10, 1920 (*Elsie Clews Parsons*, 462n8), but Parsons's correspondence places the talk in February. Parsons's script for the talk is written for the most part in sentence fragments cuing herself to extemporize, but we can infer a bit more of the content from a summary of the event in the *Workman*. Where Parsons's script indicates, for instance, some bare-bones cues to tell stories—"First, about the Cape Verde Isls stories. People: Portuguese—African. Tales: European and African. Tell 2 stories" ("Value of Folk Tales," 2)—the magazine informs us that "she began with an account of tales she collected in 1917–1918 from Portuguese Negroes from the Cape Verde Islands living in New England, and told one of the tales consisting of a version of the Treasury of King Rhampsinitus, first recorded by Herodotus, of a version of Tar Baby, and of a tale probably derived from the Arabs" ("Importance of Folk Tales," *Southern Workman*, March 1920, 138).

49. She casts this attention as a regional pattern and offers it as a reason she had decided not to go farther south this trip. "A woman travelling alone with a phonograph seems to be all the encouragement needed. They seem so hard up for a woman, + totally indiscriminating." Elsie Clews Parsons to Herbert Parsons, February 10, 1920, Elsie Clews Parsons Papers.

50. Parsons, "Narrative," 51.

51. Reed and Parsons, "Cries-for-salmon," 337.

52. Parsons, "Narrative," 51.

53. Parsons, appendix to *American Indian Life*, 413.

54. Sometimes Parsons will parenthetically add the English translation of a Deg Hit'an word: "kadjim (the men's house)" (Reed and Parsons, "Cries-for-salmon," 337). We can infer that this is not simply a transcription of Reed's own vocal glossing of the word, since the same gloss didn't appear in the article. Similarly, in some cases, Parsons uses parentheses in the book version to add information that compensates for the lack of orienting cues that had been available in the article (through the framing preface) and in the original interview (through the fact of being there): where Reed refers in the article to "the students here," in the book version Parsons specifies the spatial deixis: "the students here (at Hampton Institute)" (Parsons, "Narrative," 57; Reed and Parsons, "Cries-for-salmon," 344).

55. While the content of this belief is of course available in the text, I leave it unspecified here as neither immediately relevant to the discussion here nor mine to relay.

56. Reed and Parsons, "Cries-for-salmon," 360; Parsons, "Narrative," 71.

57. As Clifford paraphrases the rhetorical structure of ethnographic authority, "You are there . . . because I was there" (*Predicament of Culture*, 22). More generally, Clifford's classic account of polyvocal ethnographic experiments that incorporate "the scratching of other pens" pertains closely to what I develop in this reading (26). But I would also signal a different aim in the reading I'm developing. Paraphrasing the position of recent challenges to convention, Clifford wonders rhetorically how a "cross cultural encounter shot through with power relations and personal cross purposes" could be taken "as an adequate version of a more-or-less discrete 'other world' composed by an individual author?" (25). Part of what I'm suggesting about Parsons's project in "Cries-for-salmon" is that its designation of coauthorship and the direct discourse of the informant serves not to represent but to hide the conditions of the encounter and the process of its retroactive construction.

58. Parsons, "Narrative," 51.

59. Reed and Parsons, "Cries-for-salmon," 359. Darnell writes that "Reed and Parsons constructed a secondhand story told by a young man who did not know many things about his traditional culture because he had spent four years in boarding school; the irony of this forced assimilation was not noted in their recording of what was still remembered" (*Invisible Genealogies*, 224). It's true that the text may not carry the empirical authority that Parsons imagined when she began speaking with Reed, but it's my sense that Reed's narrative does address this irony.

60. Parsons, "Narrative," 70.

61. Reed and Parsons, "Cries-for-salmon," 359.

62. Reed and Parsons, "Cries-for-salmon," 337, 345.

63. Parsons, "Narrative," 66n1.

64. Reed and Parsons, "Cries-for-salmon," 354.

65. See Fabian, *Time and the Other*, on the ethnographic present.

66. Reed and Parsons, "Cries-for-salmon," 341.

67. Sapir, "Sayach'apis," 308.

68. "Tribe Exhibit Shows Life in Ancient Time," *Star-Gazette,* August 1, 1938.

69. "Tries to Help His Wife, Gets Too Much Business," *Binghamton Press,* February 15, 1945.

70. "N.Y. State Fair Caravan to Visit TC," *Binghamton Press,* August 12, 1955.

71. Lucinda Reed's class year is recorded in Brudvig, "Hampton." On the conflict with Moses, see "Tuscaroras Win Time in Fight to Keep State from Taking over Land," *Democrat and Chronicle,* July 11, 1958.

72. In a 1924 update about graduates, mentioning that Reed had held this position for several years, the *Workman* also reminds its readers that he had a reputation "at Hampton for his unusually good work in photography" ("Indian Notes," *Southern Workman,* July 1924, 329). Camp Red Cloud had a dark room (Sargent, *Handbook,* 356).

73. "Anvik notebook" (1923), item na.7, American Council of Learned Societies Committee on Native American Languages collection.

74. "Radios from the Front," *Southern Workman,* Graduates' Number, July 1923: 363–64, 364.

75. Edward Sapir to Franz Boas, July 2, 1923, Franz Boas Papers.

76. It's relevant here that the school at Anvik, run by Chapman, was unusual in including some instruction in a Native language: "Emphasis was on instruction in the English language but with frequent translation exercises of Ingalik words into English and English into Ingalik" (VanStone, *Ingalik Contact Ecology,* 158).

77. See Murray, "Creation of Linguistic Structure."

78. Edward Sapir, "A Summary Report of E. Sapir's Field Work among the HUPA, Summer of 1927," Franz Boas Papers, p. 2.

79. Sapir, *Language,* 160.

80. Sapir, *Language,* 165. Sapir's metaphor has obvious resonance with poststructuralist theory, as in Derrida's claims for the "essential drift" of "writing as an iterative structure" (*Limited Inc.,* 9). Derridean différance, though, doesn't readily fit Sapir's investment in variations that "move in a *certain* direction."

81. Emily K. Herron, "*American Indian Life,*" *Southern Workman,* October 1922, 490. Herron describes Reed, "an Indian educated at Hampton," as "peculiarly well prepared by personal experience to depict with the utmost fidelity the daily life and habits, both physical and mental, of the American Indian" (489).

82. The concept of "hungry listening" is, as I noted in the introduction, Robinson's in *Hungry Listening.*

83. For a relevant account of the effects of phrase-by-phrase versus free translation—proposing that the Boasian commitment to faithful reproduction produced lines of "'awkward' English" that "*might . . . have been exploited for literary rather than strictly literal effect*"—see Krupat, "On the Translation," 12.

84. Boas, "Eskimo Tales and Songs," 50.

85. Boas, "Poetry and Music" (*Science*), 384. "*Pihiit* also served to keep people's minds occupied to divert them from cares or worries and to keep them from being anxious due to burdens of the mind," according to Mikitok Bruce (quoted in Bennett and Rowley, *Uqalurait,* 108).

86. Boas, "Year among the Eskimo," 384.

87. Boas, "Eskimo Winter," 367, 368.

88. Boas, *Eskimo Story*, 23. The detail is (probably incidentally) relevant to the situation of translation. As Dorais explains, Inuktitut offers a distinctive connection between translation and the affordances of hearing loss: "The translator (Inuktitut tusaaji, 'listener') must often act as if she or he is hard of hearing (tusilaartuq), constrained to seemingly misinterpreting the immediate meaning or pronunciation of what is said (or written) in the source language, in order to make it more or less understandable to speakers of a widely different form of speech" ("*Tusaaji Tusilaartuq*," 32). *Tusilaartuq* also has a secondary meaning relevant to Dorais's argument: "disobedient" (Schneider, *Ulirnaisigutiit*, s.v. "tusillaartuq," 427).

89. Boas, *Franz Boas among the Inuit*, 132. Mutch's aid was crucial to Boas's work in Cumberland Sound. A Scottish whaler who spent many years in the region, he spoke both Inuktitut and English much more competently than Boas did and, in the years after the 1883–84 expedition, often sent Boas ethnographic material for subsequent publications. See Harper, "Collaboration."

90. Boas, "Year among the Eskimo," 384, 385.

91. Boas, "Journey in Cumberland Sound," 253.

92. Boas, *Franz Boas among the Inuit*, 139, 144.

93. Boas does come *close* to doing so in one unfinished manuscript, "Arctic Expedition—Reminiscence written for children," a recollection of his Baffin Island experiences that was not published during his lifetime but was passed down through generations of his family and finally saw print in 2007 as *Eskimo Story (Written for My Children)*. Here Boas describes Utitia'q's eight-day drift as having occurred "a few years" prior to his voyage, while *also* describing a similar event that befell other members of their party while he was there in the fall of 1883. But the details of this second story are inconsistent with the report in his journal. There, the 1883 event only involved Utitia'q; in *Eskimo Story*, it involves an anonymous group of multiple people that does not seem to include Utitia'q at all. (He is not explicitly excluded by name, but in the immediate context of the description of his song's basis in a similar event, it would be rhetorically bizarre not to mention that the guide was present on this second floe, if that were the case.) Moreover, the journal reports that it was Boas's own boat used for the rescue, whereas this version reports that it was "their little boats"—that is, boats belonging to kinspeople of the group in danger—that were taken out to the floe (Boas, *Eskimo Story*, 40). Stocking has speculated that perhaps Boas began this writing project during a period of convalescence a couple years after the turn of the century ("Another View," 252).

94. On borrowing within an Inuit framework of property norms, see Martin, *Stories*, 68, 86.

95. In the 1922 story, the latter difference (luck, not help) fits the fact that No-tongue is an outsider in the winter village, but Boas had already introduced this change in the earliest nonfictional publications about the song.

96. Boas, "Eskimo Winter," 368.

97. On Boas's sense, in the 1880s, of the potential disappearance of the Inuit—and on the probable influence on this expectation of an 1880 study by Rudolf

Virchow—see Baehre, "Early Anthropological Discourse," 19. Boas discusses the population reduction in *Baffin-Land*, 70.

98. See Vizenor on "the potentiality of native irony" (*Native Provenance*, 3).

99. The commonality of geographic experience that Boas hints at here is fraught in ways that Wilderson, in an Afro-pessimist critique of settler colonialism, describes; he writes that a "capacity for cartographic coherence . . . secures subjectivity for both the Settler and the 'Savage,'" and only by disclaiming this capacity, and instead "embrac[ing] its structural nonpresence," will Native theory be able to coarticulate its ontologies with those of the "Slave" in Black studies (*Red, White, and Black*, 181, 182). The cartographic capacity of Inuit people was a direct topic of settler scientists' debate in the early twentieth century (with Boas's *Central Eskimo* often cited in these discussions) and even featured in the daily press in articles with such titles as "The Eskimo as a Map-Maker" (*Boston Evening Transcript*, October 20, 1909).

100. Boas, *Eskimo Story*, 26, 51–52.

101. This version appears in Boas, "Year among the Eskimo," 385; and Boas, *Eskimo Story*, 41; and, with slightly different formatting, Boas, "Poetry and Music" (*Science*), 384.

102. On the racial politics of "geography's discursive attachment to stasis and physicality, the idea that space 'just is,'" see McKittrick, *Demonic Grounds*, xi.

103. Boas, "Study of Geography," 139, 139, 140.

104. Boas, "Study of Geography," 141.

105. Boas, "Study of Geography," 140, 141.

106. "By 1888," Harper writes, Boas's "metamorphosis from geographer to ethnographer was complete" ("Collaboration," 57).

107. Boas, *Baffin-Land*, 62. (Much of the material in this section of *Baffin-Land* will be reprised, lightly edited in English translation, in a section of *The Central Eskimo* titled "Distribution of the Tribes.") "The Study of Geography" uses the same term in a slightly different definition: "anthropo-geography—the life of man as far as it depends on the country he lives in" (137). One contemporaneous synonym for "anthropogeography" (in the sense meaning the study of population distribution) was "anthropography" (Jefferson, "Anthropography"). "Anthropography" was itself also used, in distinction from "ethnographic" studies of custom, to refer to the comparative study of human anatomy and physiology (Garson, introduction to *Notes and Queries*, 5). And it appears in a third sense in the British anthropologist R. R. Marett's 1923 review of *American Indian Life* for *American Anthropologist*. As Marett writes, the book's inclusion of a number of full-page illustrations was a telling reflection of, but incidental to, a more metaphorically pictorial narrative principle: "strictly germane to the scientific purpose is the resolve to be not only anthropological but, so to say, anthropographic" ("*American Indian Life*," 267).

108. Boas, *Baffin-Land*, 62 (my translations).

109. Boas's fieldnotes include two rough drawings of the circular space of the *qaggiq* (spelled by Boas *Kaggi*), with indications of conventional placements for participants ("Eskimo ethnographic notes from Baffinland").

110. See, for instance, "Donald B. MacMillan to Sail Again into the Arctic," *New York Tribune*, January 13, 1921.

111. H. R. Holmden, quoted in G. Smith, "Transfer of Arctic Territories," 69.

112. Mariano Aupilarjuk, quoted in Bennett and Rowley, introduction to *Uqalurait*, xxv.

113. Igloolik elder Abraham Ullijuruluk describes these shifts of snowdrift orientation as effects of the earth tilting (Mauro, "Uqalurait.")

114. Hollander, *American Poetry*, 725. This anthology is part of the Library of America series.

Postscript

1. hifi nub, "Do you guys get sound blindness?," Head Fi, January 10, 2015, 4:49 p.m., https://www.head-fi.org/threads/do-you-guys-get-sound-blindness.750223/.

2. BrownBear, comment on hifi nub, "Do you guys get sound blindness?," January 18, 2015, 3:11 p.m.

3. ProtegeManiac, comment on hifi nub, "Do you guys get sound blindness?," January 18, 2015, 6:04 a.m.

4. billybob_jcv, comment on hifi nub, "Do you guys get sound blindness?," January 10, 2015, 6:26 p.m.

5. rasur, comment on WheelsAtLarge, "Deep Learning enables hearing aid wearers to pick out a voice in a crowded room," Hacker News, March 10, 2017, https://news.ycombinator.com/item?id=13836167#13890701. On the controversies of cochlear implants, see Mills, "Do Signals Have Politics?" Depictions of "the history of cochlear implants as a binary conflict between Deaf culture and normative biomedicine," Mills argues, "obscure the radical aspirations of a minority of deaf implant users" who articulate a program of "deaf futurism" (336).

6. I wasn't able to contact rasur and ask about this, but I did reach hifi nub, a few years after the original post, through Head-Fi's private message function. Explaining that I was interested in the history of the term, I wondered whether anything in particular had brought that phrase to mind. "I definitely didn't look it up," hifi nub replied. The term simply seemed to suggest the way that people "adapt to their surroundings." hifi nub, personal communication to author on head-fi.org, April 11, 2018.

7. On the historiography of the diffusion-invention debate—and for a polemical argument about the imperialist logic of diffusio*nism*, as an ideological stance rather than a historiographical method—see Blaut, "Diffusionism."

8. "Sound Leads Elsewhere," per Kahn. Sonic "diffusion" may connote differently for different readers; those familiar with acoustic design may think of "diffusers" as modular architectural elements designed to evenly distribute reverberations, but what I mean to emphasize here is instead the more general sense of diffusion as scattering.

Bibliography

Archives Consulted

American Council of Learned Societies Committee on Native American Languages Collection. Mss.497.3.B63c. American Philosophical Library. Philadelphia, PA.

Anne Ross Piburn Collection. Western History Collections. University of Oklahoma Libraries. Norman, OK.

David Efron Gesture Research. MS2004-07. National Anthropological Archives, Smithsonian Institution. Suitland, MD.

Elsie Clews Parsons Papers. Mss.Ms.Coll.29. American Philosophical Library. Philadelphia, PA.

Franz Boas Papers. Mss.B.B61. American Philosophical Library. Philadelphia, PA.

Helen Keller Archive. American Foundation for the Blind. The American Printing House for the Blind. Louisville, KY.

John Ross Papers. Thomas Gilcrease Library and Archive. Tulsa, OK.

W. E. B. Du Bois Papers. MS 312. Special Collections and University Archives, University of Massachusetts Amherst Libraries. Amherst, MA.

Newspapers and Magazines Cited

American Magazine of Useful and Entertaining Knowledge

Arizona Daily Star (Tucson)

Atlantic Monthly

Binghamton (NY) Press

Birmingham (AL) News

Book News

Boston Evening Transcript

Boston Globe

Branding Iron (Atoka, Indian Territory)

Brooklyn Daily Eagle

Buffalo Commercial

Buffalo Evening News

Buffalo Evening Times

Buffalo Express

Burlington (VT) Daily News

Butte (MT) Miner

The Century

Cherokee Phoenix, and the Indians' Advocate (New Echota, GA)

Chicago Tribune

Columbia (SC) Spectator

Corpus Christi (TX) Times

The Crisis

Daily Chieftain (Vinita, Indian Territory)

Daily Oklahoman (Oklahoma City, OK)

Daily Palo Alto (CA)

Daily Press (Newport News, VA)

Democrat and Chronicle (Rochester, NY)

Fortune

The Forum

Fort Gibson (OK) New Era

Fort Gibson (Indian Territory) Post

Indian Chieftain (Vinita, Indian Territory)

Indian Leader (Lawrence, KS)
(Topeka) Kansas Democrat
LaCrosse (WI) Tribune and Leader-Press
Ladies' Home Journal
The Liberator
Longman's Magazine
Los Angeles Evening Express
Magazine for the Scottish Deaf
McAlester (Indian Territory) Capital
Minneapolis Journal
Minneapolis Star
Minneapolis Tribune
Montgomery (AL) Advertiser
Munsey's Magazine
Muskogee (Indian Territory) Times-Democrat
New-England Magazine
New York Herald
New York Times
Oakland Tribune
Oklahoma Daily (Norman, OK)
Oklahoma State Capital (Guthrie, OK)
The Oldhallian
Outing
Overland Monthly
Popular Science Monthly
Progressive Woman

Readers' Digest
Salt Lake (UT) Tribune
San Francisco Examiner
Saturday Evening Post
Science News Letter
Scientific American
The Sequoia
Selma (AL) Times
Sooner State Press (Norman, OK)
Southern Workman
South McAlester (Indian Territory) Capital
South McAlester (Indian Territory) News
Star-Gazette (Elmira, NY)
The State (Columbia, SC)
Stillwater (OK) Daily Press
St. Louis Globe-Democrat
St. Louis Post-Dispatch
St. Nicholas
Swiss Cross
Themis of Zeta Tau Alpha
Waco (TX) Morning News
Weekly Chieftain (Vinita, Indian Territory)
Youth's Companion

Other Sources

Abbate, Carolyn. "Music—Drastic or Gnostic?" *Critical Inquiry* 30, no. 3 (Spring 2004): 505–36.

Abel, Elizabeth. "Shadows." *Representations* 84 (Fall 2003): 166–99.

———. *Signs of the Times: The Visual Politics of Jim Crow.* Berkeley: University of California Press, 2010.

Abu-Lughod, Lila. "Writing against Culture." In *Recapturing Anthropology: Working in the Present,* edited by Richard Fox, 137–62. Santa Fe, NM: School of American Research Press, 1991.

Accinno, Michael. "Extraordinary Voices: Helen Keller, Music, and the Limits of Oralism." *Journal of Interdisciplinary Voice Studies* 4, no. 2 (October 2019): 139–56.

Adams, Andy. *Cattle Brands.* 1934. Freeport, NY: Books for Libraries Press, 1971.

———. *Wells Brothers: The Young Cattle Kings.* Boston: Houghton Mifflin, 1911.

Agamben, Giorgio. "Notes on Gesture." In *Infancy and History: Essays on the Destruction of Experience,* translated by Liz Heron, 133–40. London: Verso, 1993.

Allen, Paula Gunn, ed. *Voice of the Turtle: American Indian Literature, 1900–1970.* New York: Ballantine Books, 1994.

Andrews, Steve. "Toward a Synaesthetics of Soul: W. E. B. Du Bois and the Teleology of Race." In *Re-cognizing W. E. B. Du Bois in the Twenty-First Century: Essays on W. E. B. Du Bois,* edited by Mary Keller and Chester J. Fontenot Jr., 142–85. Macon, GA: Mercer University Press, 2007.

Appadurai, Arjun. *Modernity at Large: Cultural Dimensions of Globalization.* Minneapolis: University of Minnesota Press, 1996.

Aptheker, Herbert, ed. *Writings by W. E. B. Du Bois in Non-Periodical Literature Edited by Others.* Millwood, NY: Kraus-Thomson, 1982.

Arnold, Matthew. *Culture and Anarchy: An Essay in Political and Social Criticism.* London: Smith, Elder, 1869.

Asad, Talal. "Comments on Conversion." In *Conversion to Modernities: The Globalization of Christianity,* edited by Peter Van der Veer, 263–73. New York: Routledge, 1996.

Auerbach, Erich. *Mimesis: The Representation of Reality in Western Literature.* Translated by Willard R. Trask. Princeton, NJ: Princeton University Press, 1953.

Baehre, Rainer. "Early Anthropological Discourse on the Inuit and the Influence of Virchow on Boas." *Études/Inuit/Studies* 32, no. 2 (2008): 13–34.

Bailey, Flora L. "Navaho Motor Habits," *American Anthropologist* 44, no. 2 (April–June 1942): 210–34.

Bank, Rosemarie K. "Representing History: Performing the Columbian Exposition." *Theatre Journal* 54, no. 4 (December 2002): 589–606.

Barthes, Roland. "The Reality Effect." In *The Rustle of Language,* translated by Richard Howard, 141–48. New York: Hill and Wang, 1986.

Bauman, Richard, and Charles L. Briggs. *Voices of Modernity: Language Ideologies and the Politics of Ideology.* Cambridge: Cambridge University Press, 2003.

Beard, George M. *American Nervousness: Its Causes and Consequences.* New York: Putnam, 1881.

Bell, Chris. "Introducing White Disability Studies: A Modest Proposal." In *The Disability Studies Reader,* 2nd ed., edited by Lennard J. Davis, 275–82. New York: Routledge, 2006.

Benadon, Fernando. "Gridless Beats." *Perspectives of New Music* 47, no. 1 (Winter 2009): 135–64.

Bender, Margaret. *Signs of Cherokee Culture: Sequoyah's Syllabary in Eastern Cherokee Life.* Chapel Hill: University of North Carolina Press, 2002.

Benedict, Ruth. "Anthropology and the Abnormal." *Journal of General Psychology* 10, no. 1 (1934): 59–82.

Benjamin, Walter. *Illuminations: Essays and Reflections.* Translated by Harry Zohn. Edited and with an introduction by Hannah Arendt. Preface by Leon Wieseltier. New York: Schocken Books, 2007.

Bennett, John, and Susan Rowley. Introduction to *Uqalurait: An Oral History of Nunavut,* xxv–xxix. Montreal: McGill-Queen's University Press, 2004.

——, eds. *Uqalurait: An Oral History of Nunavut.* Foreword by Suzanne Evaloardjuk, Peter Irniq, Uriash Puqiqnak, and David Serkoak. Montreal: McGill-Queen's University Press, 2004.

Berman, Roger. "Fitzgerald and the Idea of Society." *F. Scott Fitzgerald Review* 12, no. 1 (2014): 32–43.

Bérubé, Michael. "Autobiography as Performative Utterance." *American Quarterly* 52, no. 2 (June 2000): 339–43.

Bird, Traveller. *Tell Them They Lie: The Sequoyah Myth.* Los Angeles: Westernlore, 1971.

Blakney, Sherrie Lee. "Connections to the Land: The Politics of Health and Wellbeing in Arviat Nunavut." PhD diss., University of Manitoba, 2009.

Blaut, J. M. "Diffusionism: A Uniformitarian Critique." *Annals of the Association of American Geographers* 77, no. 1 (1987): 30–47.

Boas, Franz. *Anthropology and Modern Life.* 1928. Introduction by Ruth Bunzel. New York: Courier Dover, 1986.

——. *Baffin-Land: Geographische Ergebnisse einer in den Jahren 1883 und 1884 ausgeführten Forschungsreise.* Gotha, Germany: Justus Perthes, 1885.

——. *The Central Eskimo.* In *Sixth Annual Report of the Bureau of Ethnology to the Secretary of the Smithsonian Institution, 1884–85,* by J. W. Powell, 409–669. Washington, DC: US Government Printing Office, 1888.

——. "Changes in the Bodily Form of the Descendants of Immigrants." *American Anthropologist,* n.s., 14, no. 3 (July–September 1912): 530–62.

——. "Dance and Music in the Life of the Northwest Coast Indians of North America." In *The Function of Dance in Human Society: A Seminar Directed by Franziska Boas,* edited by Franziska Boas, 5–19. 1944. Reprint, Brooklyn: Dance Horizons, 1972.

——. *Eskimo Story (Written for My Children): My Arctic Expedition, 1883–1884.* Edited by Norman F. Boas. Mystic, CT: Seaport Autographs, 2007.

——. "Eskimo Tales and Songs." *Journal of American Folklore* 7, no. 24 (January–March 1894): 45–50.

——. "An Eskimo Winter." In *American Indian Life: By Several of Its Students,* edited by Elsie Clews Parsons, 363–80. New York: G. W. Huebsch, 1922.

——. Foreword to *Coming of Age in Samoa: A Psychological Study of Primitive Youth for Western Civilization,* by Margaret Mead, xiv–xv. New York: William Morrow, 1928.

——. Foreword to *Gesture and Environment: A Tentative Study of the Spatio-temporal and "Linguistic" Aspects of the Gestural Behavior of Eastern Jews and Southern Italians in New York City, Living under Similar as well as Different Environmental Conditions,* by David Efron, i–ii. New York: King's Crown, 1941.

——. *Franz Boas among the Inuit of Baffin Island 1883–1884: Journals and Letters.* Translated by William Barr. Edited by Ludger Müller-Wille. Toronto: University of Toronto Press, 1998.

——. *The Handbook of American Indian Languages.* Washington, DC: US Government Printing Office, 1911.

——. "Journey in Cumberland Sound and on the West Shore of Davis Strait in 1883 and 1884." *Journal of the American Geographical Society of New York* 16 (1884): 242–72.

——. *The Mind of Primitive Man*. Rev. ed. New York: Macmillan, 1938.

——. "On Alternating Sounds." *American Anthropologist* 2, no. 1 (January 1889): 47–54.

——. "Poetry and Music of Some North American Tribes." *Science* 9, no. 220 (April 22, 1887): 383–85.

——. *Primitive Art*. 1927. Reprint, New York: Dover, 1955.

——. "The Study of Geography." *Science* 9, no. 210 (February 11, 1887): 137–41.

——. "A Year among the Eskimo." *Journal of the American Geographical Society of New York* 19 (1887): 383–402.

Boone, Elizabeth Hill, and Walter D. Mignolo, eds. *Writing without Words: Alternative Literacies in Mesoamerica and the Andes*. Durham, NC: Duke University Press, 1994.

Boudinot, Elias. "Invention of a New Alphabet." *American Annals of Education* 2 (April 1, 1832): 174–80.

Braddock, Alan C. *Thomas Eakins and the Cultures of Modernity*. Berkeley: University of California Press, 2009.

Brady, Erika. *A Spiral Way: How the Phonograph Changed Ethnography*. Jackson: University Press of Mississippi, 1999.

Breitwieser, Mitchell. "False Sympathy in Melville's *Typee*." *American Quarterly* 34, no. 4 (Autumn 1982): 396–417.

——. *National Melancholy: Mourning and Opportunity in Classic American Literature*. Stanford, CA: Stanford University Press, 2007.

Brinton, Daniel G. "The Language of Palaeolithic Man." Philadelphia: Press of MacCalla, 1888.

Brodhead, Richard H. *Cultures of Letters: Scenes of Reading and Writing in Nineteenth-Century America*. Chicago: University of Chicago Press, 1993.

Brooks, Peter. *Reading for the Plot: Design and Intention in Narrative*. Cambridge, MA: Harvard University Press, 1984.

Brooks, Van Wyck. *Helen Keller: Sketch for a Portrait*. New York: E. P. Dutton, 1956.

Brown, Kirby. *Stoking the Fire: Nationhood in Cherokee Writing, 1907–1970*. Norman: University of Oklahoma Press, 2018.

Bruccoli, Matthew. *Some Sort of Epic Grandeur: The Life of F. Scott Fitzgerald*. Columbia: University of South Carolina Press, 2002.

Brudvig, Jon L. "Hampton Normal & Agricultural Institute American Indian Students (1878–1923) Tribal Affiliations." twofrog, 1996. http://twofrog.com/hampton2.txt.

Brueggemann, Brenda Jo. *Lend Me Your Ear: Rhetorical Constructions of Deafness*. Washington, DC: Gallaudet University Press, 1999.

Bucholtz, Mary. "The Politics of Transcription." *Journal of Pragmatics* 32 (2000): 1439–65.

Bunker, M. N. *What Handwriting Tells You about Yourself, Your Friends, and Famous People: A Key to Grapho-analysis*. Cleveland: World, 1951.

Carmody, Todd. "Rehabilitating Analogy." *J19* 1, no. 2 (Fall 2013): 431–39.

Chambaud, Lewis. *A Grammar of the French Tongue: With a Preface, Containing an Essay on the Proper Method of Teaching and Learning That Language*. Revised by M. Des Carrieres. London: Longman, Brown, 1846.

Chang, David A. *The Color of the Land: Race, Nation, and the Politics of Landownership in Oklahoma, 1832–1929*. Chapel Hill: University of North Carolina Press, 2012.

Chapman, John W. *Ten'a Texts and Tales from Anvik, Alaska*. With vocabulary by Pliny Earle Goddard. Publications of the American Ethnological Society 6. Leyden: Brill, 1914.

Cheng, Anne Anlin. "Skins, Tattoos, and Susceptibility." *Representations* 108 (Fall 2009): 98–119.

Chow, Juliana. *Nineteenth-Century American Literature and the Discourse of Natural History*. Cambridge: Cambridge University Press, 2021.

Chow, Rey. "Where Have All the Natives Gone?" In *Displacements: Cultural Identities in Question*, edited by Angelika Bammer, 125–51. Bloomington: Indiana University Press, 1994.

Clifford, James. *The Predicament of Culture: Twentieth-Century Ethnography, Literature, and Art*. Cambridge, MA: Harvard University Press, 1988.

Cohen, Rachel. *A Chance Meeting: Intertwined Lives of American Writers and Artists, 1854–1967*. New York: Random House, 2004.

Comeau, Raymond F. "The Friendship of Helen Keller and John Greenleaf Whittier." *Wavelengths*, September 7, 2021. http://whav.net/2021/09/07/the -friendship-of-helen-keller-and-john-greenleaf-whittier/.

Conlon, Paula Thistle. "Drum-Dance Songs of the Iglulik Inuit in the Northern Baffin Island Area: A Study of Their Structures." PhD diss., Université de Montréal, 1992.

Connor, Steven. "Two-Step, Nerve-Tap, Tanglefoot: Tapdance Typologies in Cinema." In *Sounding Modernism: Rhythm and Sonic Mediation in Modern Literature and Film*, edited by Julian Murphet, Helen Groth, and Penelope Hone, 211–27. Edinburgh: Edinburgh University Press, 2017.

Cook, Simon John. "The Making of the English: English History, British Identity, Aryan Villages, 1870–1914." *Journal of the History of Ideas* 75, no. 4 (October 2014): 629–49.

Coward, John M. *The Newspaper Indian: Native American Identity in the Press, 1820–90*. Urbana: University of Illinois Press, 1999.

Cox, James H. "'Learn to Talk Yaqui': Mexico and the Cherokee Politics of John Milton Oskison and Will Rogers." *Western American Literature* 48, no. 4 (Winter 2014): 400–421.

Crain, Patricia. *The Story of A: The Alphabetization of America from "The New England Primer" to "The Scarlet Letter."* Stanford, CA: Stanford University Press, 2000.

Crary, Jonathan. *Techniques of the Observer: On Vision and Modernity in the Nineteenth Century.* Cambridge, MA: MIT Press, 1990.

Cressman, Jodi. "Helen Keller and the Mind's Eyewitness." *Western Humanities Review* 54, no. 2 (Fall 2000): 108–23.

Crutchfield, Susan. "'Play[ing] Her Part Correctly': Helen Keller as Vaudevillian Freak." *Disability Studies Quarterly* 25, no. 3 (Summer 2005). http://dsq-sds.org /article/view/577/754.

Darnell, Regna. *Invisible Genealogies: A History of Americanist Anthropology.* Lincoln: University of Nebraska Press, 2001.

Daston, Lorraine. "On Scientific Observation." *Isis* 99, no. 1 (March 2008): 91–110.

Dauchy and Company's Newspaper Catalogue. New York: Dauchy, 1904.

Davidson, Michael. "Disability Poetics." In *The Oxford Handbook of Modern and Contemporary American Poetry,* edited by Cary Nelson, 581–601. Oxford: Oxford University Press, 2012.

Davis, Adam, ed. *Hearing the Call across Traditions: Readings on Faith and Service.* Foreword by Eboo Patel. Woodstock, VT: SkyLight Paths, 2009.

Davis, Lennard J. *Enforcing Normalcy: Disability, Deafness, and the Body.* London: Verso, 1995.

Davy, Charles. *Conjectural Observations on the Origin and Progress of Alphabetic Writing.* London, 1772.

Deacon, Desley. *Elsie Clews Parsons: Inventing Modern Life.* Chicago: University of Chicago Press, 1997.

Decker, Jeffrey Louis. "Gatsby's Pristine Dream: The Diminishment of the Self-Made Man in the Tribal Twenties." *NOVEL: A Forum on Fiction* 28, no. 1 (Autumn 1994): 52–71.

de Laguna, Frederica. *Travels among the Dena: Exploring Alaska's Yukon Valley.* Seattle: University of Washington Press, 2000.

Deleuze, Gilles, and Félix Guattari. *Anti-Oedipus: Capitalism and Schizophrenia.* Translated by Robert Hurley, Mark Seem, and Helen R. Lane. Preface by Michel Foucault. Minneapolis: University of Minnesota Press, 1983.

Derrida, Jacques. *Limited Inc.* Evanston, IL: Northwestern University Press, 1988.

——. *Of Grammatology.* Translated by Gayatri Chakravorty Spivak. Baltimore: Johns Hopkins University Press, 1997.

Dewalt, Robert. "Tom's Investigation: The Development of the Surveillance Theme in the Composition of *The Great Gatsby.*" *F. Scott Fitzgerald Review* 14, no. 1 (2016): 110–35.

Dickens, Charles. *American Notes for General Circulation.* Paris: Baudry's European Library, 1842.

——. *Bleak House.* London: Bradbury and Evans, 1853.

Dimock, Wai Chee. *Through Other Continents: American Literature across Deep Time.* Princeton, NJ: Princeton University Press, 2006.

——. *Weak Planet: Literature and Assisted Survival.* Chicago: University of Chicago Press, 2020.

Dinius, Marcy. "'Look!! Look!!! at This!!!!': The Radical Typography of David Walker's Appeal." *PMLA* 126, no. 1 (2011): 55–72.

Doane, Mary Anne. "The Voice in the Cinema: The Articulation of Body and Space." *Yale French Studies* 60 (1980): 33–50.

Donald, James. "Jazz Modernism and Film Art: Dudley Murphy and *Ballet mécanique*." *Modernism/modernity* 16, no. 1 (January 2009): 25–49.

Dorais, Louis-Jacques. "*Tusaaji Tusilaartuq*: When the Translator Must Be Hard of Hearing." *Tusaaji: A Translation Review* 4, no. 4 (2015): 30–42.

Du Bois, W. E. B. *The Souls of Black Folk: Essays and Sketches*. Chicago: A. C. McClurg, 1903.

Edwards, Brent Hayes. *Epistrophies: Jazz and the Literary Imagination*. Cambridge, MA: Harvard University Press, 2017.

Efron, David. *Gesture and Environment: A Tentative Study of the Spatio-temporal and "Linguistic" Aspects of the Gestural Behavior of Eastern Jews and Southern Italians in New York City, Living under Similar as well as Different Environmental Conditions*. Sketches by Stuyvesant Van Veen. New York: King's Crown, 1941.

Elliott, Michael A. *The Culture Concept: Writing and Difference in the Age of Realism*. Minneapolis: University of Minnesota Press, 2002.

"English Orthography." *American Annals of Education* 2 (April 1, 1832): 167–73.

Evans, Brad. *Before Cultures: The Ethnographic Imagination in American Literature, 1865–1920*. Chicago: University of Chicago Press, 2005.

———. "Introduction: Rethinking the Disciplinary Confluence of Anthropology and Literary Studies." *Criticism* 49, no. 4 (2007): 429–45.

Evans, Nicholas. *Writing Jazz: Race, Nationalism, and Modern Culture in the 1920s*. New York: Garland, 2000.

Fabian, Johannes. *Time and the Other: How Anthropology Makes Its Object*. Foreword by Matti Bunzl. New York: Columbia University Press, 2014.

Fanon, Frantz. *Black Skin, White Masks*. Translated by Charles Lam Markmann. London: Pluto, 1986.

Fechner, Gustav. *Elements of Psychophysics*. Vol. 1. Translated by Helmut E. Adler. Edited by David H. Dowes and Edwin G. Boring. New York: Holt, Rinehart and Winston, 1966.

Felski, Rita. "'Context Stinks!'" *New Literary History* 42 (2011): 573–91.

Fewkes, Jesse Walter. *Preliminary Report on a Visit to the Navaho National Monument, Arizona*. Washington, DC: US Government Printing Office, 1911.

"Field Meeting at Manchester, Thursday, August 10, 1876." *Bulletin of the Essex Institute* 8, no. 7 (August 1876): 61–76.

Firth, Raymond. "Postures and Gestures of Respect." In *The Body Reader: Social Aspects of the Human Body*, edited by Ted Polhemus. 88–108. New York: Pantheon, 1978.

Fitzgerald, F. Scott. "Bernice Bobs Her Hair." In *The Short Stories of F. Scott Fitzgerald: A New Collection*, edited by Matthew J. Bruccoli, 25–47. New York: Charles Scribner's Sons, 1989.

———. "The Captured Shadow." In *The Short Stories of F. Scott Fitzgerald: A New Collection*, edited by Matthew J. Bruccoli, 412–30. New York: Charles Scribner's Sons, 1989.

———. *Correspondence of F. Scott Fitzgerald*. Edited by Matthew J. Bruccoli and Margaret M. Dungan, with the assistance of Susan Walker. New York: Random House, 1980.

———. *The Crack-Up*. Edited by Edmund Wilson. New York: New Directions, 1956.

———. "Dice, Brassknuckles & Guitar." In *The Short Stories of F. Scott Fitzgerald: A New Collection*, edited by Matthew J. Bruccoli, 237–58. New York: Charles Scribner's Sons, 1989.

———. *The Great Gatsby*. New York: Charles Scribner's Sons, 1953.

———. *The Great Gatsby*. Preface and notes by Matthew J. Bruccoli. New York: Collier Books, 1992.

———. *The Great Gatsby: A Facsimile of the Manuscript*. Edited by Matthew J. Bruccoli. Washington, DC: Microcard Editions Books, 1973.

———. *"The Great Gatsby": The Revised and Rewritten Galleys*. Edited by Matthew J. Bruccoli. F. Scott Fitzgerald Manuscripts 3. New York: Garland, 1990.

———. *The Last Tycoon: Manuscript and Revised Typescript for the First 17 Episodes, with the Author's Notes and Plans*. Vol. 3. New York: Garland, 1990.

———. *The Love of the Last Tycoon: A Western*. Edited by Matthew J. Bruccoli. Cambridge: Cambridge University Press, 1993.

———. *The Short Stories of F. Scott Fitzgerald: A New Collection*. Edited and with a preface by Matthew J. Bruccoli. New York: Charles Scribner's Sons, 1989.

———. *Tender Is the Night: A Romance*. Preface by Malcolm Cowley. New York: Charles Scribner's Sons, 1951.

———. *The Vegetable; or, From President to Postman*. New York: Charles Scribner's Sons, 1923.

Fletcher, Karen, and John Davis. Introduction to *Helen Keller (Rebel Lives)*, edited by John Davis, 1–12. Melbourne: Ocean, 2003.

Fogelson, Raymond. "On the Varieties of Indian History: Sequoyah and Traveller Bird." *Journal of Ethnic Studies*, 2, no. 1 (1974): 105–12.

Forster, George. *A Voyage round the World in His Brittanic Majesty's Sloop, Resolution, Commanded by Capt. James Cook, during the Years 1772, 3, 4, and 5*. Vol. 1. London: B. White, 1777.

Fragos, Emily, ed. *Poems of Gratitude*. New York: Knopf, 2017.

Frankenberg, Ruth. "The Mirage of an Unmarked Whiteness." In *The Making and Unmaking of Whiteness*, edited by Birgit Brander Rasmussen, Eric Klinenberg, Irene J. Nexica, and Matt Wray, 72–96. Durham, NC: Duke University Press, 2001.

Fretwell, Erica. *Sensory Experiments: Psychophysics, Race, and the Aesthetics of Feeling*. Durham, NC: Duke University Press, 2020.

Friedner, Michele, and Stefan Helmreich. "Sound Studies Meets Deaf Studies." *Senses and Society* 7, no. 1 (2012): 72–86.

Fuller, Sarah. "How Helen Keller Learned to Speak." *American Annals of the Deaf* 37, no. 1 (January 1892): 23–30.

Gallagher, Catherine. "Raymond Williams and Cultural Studies." *Social Text* 30 (1992): 79–99.

Garcia, Edgar. *Signs of the Americas: A Poetics of Pictography, Hieroglyphs, and Khipu*. Chicago: University of Chicago Press, 2020.

Garland, Hamlin. *Crumbling Idols: Twelve Essays on Art Dealing Chiefly with Literature, Painting and the Drama*. Chicago: Stone and Kimball, 1894.

Garland-Thomson, Rosemarie. *Extraordinary Bodies: Figuring Physical Disability in American Culture and Literature*. New York: Columbia University Press, 1997.

Garson, John George. Introduction to *Notes and Queries on Anthropology*, 2nd ed., edited by John George Garson and Charles Hercules Read, 5-6. London: Anthropological Institute, 1892.

Gaskill, Nicholas. *Chromographia: American Literature and the Modernization of Color*. Minneapolis: University of Minnesota Press, 2018.

Geertz, Clifford. "Thick Description." In *The Interpretation of Cultures*, 3-30. New York: Basic Books, 2000.

Gibson, William. *The Miracle Worker: A Play in Three Acts*. London: Samuel French, 1960.

Giemza, Bryan. "The Strange Case of Sequoyah *Redivivus*: Achievement, Personage, and Perplexity." *Mississippi Quarterly* 60, no. 1 (Winter 2006-07): 129-50.

Gilles de la Tourette, Georges. *Études cliniques et physiologiques sur la marche: La marche dans les maladies du système nerveux: Étudiée par la méthode des empreintes (avec 31 figures)*. Paris: Delahaye et Lecrosnier, 1886.

———. "Étude sur une affection nerveuse caractérisée par de l'incoordination motrice accompagné d'écholalie et de coprolalie (Jumping Latah Myriachit)." *Archives de Neurologie* 9 (1885): 19-42.

Gitelman, Lisa. *Paper Knowledge: Toward a Media History of Documents*. Durham, NC: Duke University Press, 2014.

Glenn, Susan A. "'Funny, You Don't Look Jewish': Visual Stereotypes and the Making of Modern Jewish Identity." In *Boundaries of Jewish Identity*, edited by Susan A. Glenn and Naomi B. Sokoloff, 64-90. Seattle: University of Washington Press, 2010.

Goldsmith, Meredith. "White Skin, White Mask: Passing, Posing, and Performing in *The Great Gatsby*." *Modern Fiction Studies* 49, no. 3 (Fall 2003): 443-68.

Golston, Michael. *Rhythm and Race in Modernist Poetry and Science*. New York: Columbia University Press, 2007.

Graham, Laura A. "From 'Ugh' to Babble (or Babel): Linguistic Primitivism, Sound-Blindness, and the Cinematic Representation of Native Amazonians." *Current Anthropology* 61, no. 6 (December 2020): 732-62.

Gramsci, Antonio. *Selections from the Prison Notebooks of Antonio Gramsci*. Edited and translated by Quintin Hoare and Geoffrey Nowell Smith. New York: International, 1971.

Greenblatt, Stephen. "The Touch of the Real." *Representations* 59 (Summer 1997): 14-29.

Greg, W. W. "The Rationale of Copy-Text." *Studies in Bibliography* 3 (1950-51): 19-36.

Grover, Gwin E. "The Society of American Indians: Too Many Chiefs and not Enough Indians." Master's thesis, University of Nebraska at Omaha, 1989.

Hale, Dorothy J. *Social Formalism: The Novel in Theory from Henry James to the Present*. Stanford, CA: Stanford University Press, 1998.

Hale, Horatio. "On Some Doubtful or Intermediate Articulations: An Experiment in Phonetics." *Journal of the Anthropological Institute of Great Britain and Ireland* 14 (January 1, 1885): 233–43.

Hamilton, Walter. *The Aesthetic Movement in England*. London: Reeves and Turner, 1882.

Handler, Richard. "Raymond Williams, George Stocking, and Fin-de-Siècle U.S. Anthropology." *Cultural Anthropology* 13, no. 4 (November 1998): 447–63.

Haraway, Donna. *The Companion Species Manifesto: Dogs, People, and Significant Otherness*. Chicago: Prickly Paradigm, 2003.

Harjo, Joy. *Crazy Brave: A Memoir*. New York: Norton, 2012.

Harper, Kenn. "The Collaboration of James Mutch and Franz Boas, 1883–1922." *Études/Inuit/Studies* 32, no. 2 (2008): 53–71.

Hartman, Saidiya V. *Scenes of Subjection: Terror, Slavery, and Self-Making in Nineteenth-Century American*. New York: Oxford University Press, 1997.

Harvey, Sean. *Native Tongues: Colonialism and Race from Encounter to the Reservation*. Cambridge, MA: Harvard University Press, 2015.

Hawthorne, Nathaniel. *Grandfather's Chair: True Stories from History*. London: Standard, 1931.

——. *The Scarlet Letter and Other Writings*. Edited by Leland S. Person. New York: Norton, 2005.

——. *Tanglewood Tales: A Wonder-Book for Girls and Boys*. New York: Fred DeFau, 1896.

Hay, Louis. "Genetic Criticism: Another Approach to Writing?" In *Research on Writing: Multiple Perspectives*, edited by Sylvia Plane et al., 531–47. Fort Collins, CO, and Metz, France: WAC Clearinghouse and CREM, 2017.

Hayles, N. Katherine. "Print Is Flat, Code Is Deep: The Importance of Media-Specific Analysis." *Poetics Today* 25, no. 1 (Spring 2004): 67–90.

"Helen Keller." *Science* 11, no. 270 (April 6, 1888): 160–61.

Heller-Roazen, Daniel. *Echolalias: On the Forgetting of Language*. Princeton, NJ: Princeton University Press, 2005.

Hemingway, Ernest. *A Moveable Feast*. New York: Charles Scribner's Sons, 1964.

——. *Selected Letters, 1917–1961*. Edited by Carlos Baker. New York: Scribner Classics, 1981.

Herrmann, Dorothy. *Helen Keller: A Life*. Chicago: University of Chicago Press, 1998.

Herskovits, Melville J. *Franz Boas: The Science of Man in the Making*. New York: Charles Scribner's Sons, 1953.

Hitz, John. "Helen Keller." *American Anthropologist*, n.s., 8, no. 2 (April–June 1906): 308–24.

Hochman, Brian. *Savage Preservation: The Ethnographic Origins of Modern Media Technology*. Minneapolis: University of Minnesota Press, 2014.

Hollander, John, ed. *American Poetry: The Nineteenth Century*. London: Routledge, 2016.

Horvarth, Ricardo. *Memorias y recuerdos de Blackie*. Buenos Aires: Todo es Historia S.R.L., 1979.

Hudson, Brian K. "Domesticated Species in D'Arcy McNickle's *The Surrounded* and John M. Oskison's *Brothers Three*." *SAIL* 28, no. 2 (Summer 2016): 80–108.

Hurston, Zora Neale. "The Characteristics of Negro Expression." In *Negro: An Anthology*, edited by Nancy Cunard, 24–31. New York: Frederick Ungar, 1970.

Ingold, Tim. "Four Objections to the Concept of the Soundscape." In *Being Alive: Essays on Movement, Knowledge, and Description*, 136–39. New York: Routledge, 2011.

——. *Lines: A Brief History*. New York: Routledge, 2007.

Iyer, Vijay. "Exploding the Narrative in Jazz Improvisation." In *Uptown Conversation: The New Jazz Studies*, edited by Robert G. O'Meally, Brent Hayes Edwards, and Farah Jasmine Griffin. 393–403. New York: Columbia University Press, 2004.

Jackson, Zakiyyah Iman. *Becoming Human: Matter and Meaning in an Antiblack World*. New York: New York University Press, 2020.

Jakobson, Roman. "Franz Boas' Approach to Language." *International Journal of American Linguistics* 10, no. 4 (October 1944): 188–95.

——. "Two Aspects of Language and Two Types of Aphasic Disturbances." In *Selected Writings*, vol. 2, *Word and Language*, 239–59. The Hague: Mouton, 1971.

James, William. "The Laws of Habit." In *Talks to Teachers on Psychology: And to Students on Some of Life's Ideals*, 64–78. New York: Henry Holt, 1907.

Jastrow, Joseph. "Psychological Notes on Helen Kellar [*sic*]." *Psychological Review* 1, no. 4 (1894): 356–62.

Jefferson, Mark. "The Anthropography of North America." *Bulletin of the American Geographical Society* 45, no. 3 (1913): 161–80.

Jemisin, N. K. *The Broken Earth Trilogy*. 3 vols. New York: Hachette, 2015–17.

Johnson, Russell L. "'Disease Is Unrhythmical': Jazz, Health, and Disability in 1920s America." *Health History* 13, no. 2 (2011): 13–42.

Jones, Gavin. *Strange Talk: The Politics of Dialect Literature in Gilded Age America*. Berkeley: University of California Press, 1999.

Justice, Daniel Heath. *Our Fire Survives the Storm: A Cherokee Literary History*. Minneapolis: University of Minnesota Press, 2006.

Kahn, Douglas. "Sound Leads Elsewhere." In *The Routledge Companion to Sounding Art*, edited by Marcel Cobussen, Vincent Meelberg, and Barry Truax, 41–50. New York: Routledge, 2016.

Kalter, Susan. "'America's Histories' Revisited: The Case of 'Tell Them They Lie.'" *American Indian Quarterly* 25, no. 3 (Summer 2001): 329–51.

Kane, Brian. *Sound Unseen: Acousmatic Theory in Theory and Practice*. Oxford: Oxford University Press, 2014.

Kaplan, Amy. "Nation, Region, Empire." In *The Columbia History of the American Novel*, edited by Emory Elliott, 240–66. New York: Columbia University Press, 1991.

Keller, Helen. *Midstream: My Later Life*. Garden City, NY: Doubleday, Doran, 1929.

———. "My Recollections of Boston: The City of Kind Hearts." In *Fifty Years of Boston: A Memorial Volume*, xv–xx. Boston: Subcommittee on Memorial History of the Boston Tercentenary Committee, 1932.

———. *My Religion*. Garden City, NY: Doubleday, Page, 1927.

———. *The Story of My Life; With Her Letters (1887–1901), and a Supplementary Account of Her Education, Including Passages from the Reports and Letters of Her Teacher, Anne Mansfield Sullivan, by John Albert Macy*. New York: Doubleday, 1903.

———. *The World I Live In*. New York: Century, 1908.

Kesserling, Marion L. *Hawthorne's Reading, 1828–1850: A Transcription and Identification of Titles Recorded in the Charge-Books of the Salem Athenaeum*. New York: Haskell House, 1975.

Kingsford, Jane. *The Soprano: A Musical Story*. Boston: Loring, 1869.

Kinsey, A. A. *Report of the Proceedings of the International Congress of the Deaf, Held at Milan, September 6th–11th, 1880*. London: W. H. Allen, 1880.

Kittler, Friedrich A. *Discourse Networks 1800/1900*. Translated by Michael Metteer, with Chris Cullens. Foreword by David W. Wellbery. Stanford, CA: Stanford University Press, 1990.

Klages, Mary. *Woeful Afflictions: Disability and Sentimentality in Victorian America*. Philadelphia: University of Pennsylvania Press, 1999.

Kleege, Georgina. *Blind Rage: Letters to Helen Keller*. Washington, DC: Gallaudet University Press, 2006.

Knapp, Samuel L. *Lectures on American Literature: With Remarks on Some Passages of American History*. New York: Elam Bliss, 1829.

Kohn, Eduardo. *How Forests Think: Toward an Anthropology Beyond the Human*. Berkeley: University of California Press, 2013.

Korenman, Joan S. "'Only Her Hairdresser . . .': Another Look at Daisy Buchanan." *American Literature* 46, no. 4 (January 1975): 574–78.

Kroeber, A. L. Introduction to *American Indian Life: By Several of Its Students*, edited by Elsie Clews Parsons, 5–16. New York: G. W. Huebsch, 1922.

———. "The Place of Boas in Anthropology." *American Anthropologist*, n.s., 58, no. 1 (February 1956): 151–59.

———. "The Superorganic." *American Anthropologist*, n.s., 19, no. 2 (April–June 1917): 163–213.

Kroeber, Theodora. *Ishi in Two Worlds: A Biography of the Last Wild Indian in North America*. Foreword by Karl Kroeber. 1961. Reprint, Berkeley: University of California Press, 2002.

Krupat, Arnold. "On the Translation of Native American Song and Story: A Theorized History." In *On the Translation of Native American Literatures*, edited by Brian Swann, 3–32. Washington, DC: Smithsonian Institution Press, 1992.

Kuehl, John. "Scott Fitzgerald's Reading." *Princeton University Library Chronicle* 22, no. 2 (Winter 1961): 58–89.

Kushner, Howard I. *A Cursing Brain? The Histories of Tourette's Syndrome*. Cambridge, MA: Harvard University Press, 1999.

Lamson, Mary Swift. *The Life and Education of Laura Bridgman, the Deaf, Dumb and Blind Girl*. Boston: New England Publishing, 1878.

Lane, Harlan. *The Mask of Benevolence: Disabling the Deaf Community*. New York: Knopf, 1992.

Larré, Lionel. Introduction to *Tales of the Old Indian Territory and Essays on the Indian Condition*, by John M. Oskison, 1–61. Lincoln: University of Nebraska Press, 2012.

——. Introduction to *Unconquerable: The Story of John Ross, Chief of the Cherokees, 1928–1866*, xi–xl. Lincoln: University of Nebraska Press, 2022.

Latour, Bruno. *We Have Never Been Modern*. Translated by Catherine Porter. Cambridge, MA: Harvard University Press, 1993.

Lauter, Paul, ed. *The Heath Anthology of American Literature*. 2nd ed. Vol. 2. Lexington, MA: D. C. Heath, 1994.

LeConte, Joseph. "Sound-Blindness." Letter to the editor. *Science* 10, no. 255 (December 23, 1887): 312.

Lepore, Jill. *A Is for American: Letters and Other Characters in the Newly United States*. New York: Vintage, 2002.

Levin, Thomas Y. "Tones from out of Nowhere: Rudolph Pfenninger and the Archaeology of Synthetic Sound." *Grey Room* 12 (Summer 2003): 33–79.

Lewis, George E. "Improvised Music after 1950: Afrological and Eurological Perspectives." *Black Music Research Journal* 16, no. 1 (Spring 1996): 91–122.

Lewis, Richard, ed. *I Breathe a New Song: Poems of the Eskimo*. Illustrated by Jessie Oonark. Introduction by Edmund Carpenter. New York: Simon and Schuster, 1971.

Lindsey, Donal F. *Indians at Hampton Institute, 1877–1923*. Urbana: University of Illinois Press, 1995.

Lippit, Akira Mizuta. *Electric Animal: Toward a Rhetoric of Wildlife*. Minneapolis: University of Minnesota Press, 2000.

"List of Members." *Journal of Hellenic Studies* 4 (1883): xxi–xxxiv.

Littlefield, Daniel F., Jr. *Alex Posey: Creek Poet, Journalist, and Humorist*. Lincoln: University of Nebraska Press, 1992.

Littlefield, Daniel F., Jr., and James W. Parins. "Short Fiction Writers of the Indian Territory." *American Studies* 23, no. 1 (Spring 1982): 23–38.

Livermore, Mary. *My Story of the War*. Hartford, CT: A. D. Worthington, 1889.

Lockwood, Samuel. *Animal Memoirs. Part I: Mammals*. New York: Ivison, Blakeman, 1888.

Longmore, Paul K. *Why I Burned My Book: And Other Essays on Disability*. Philadelphia: Temple University Press, 2003.

Lopenzina, Drew. "'Good Indian': Charles Eastman and the Warrior as Civil Servant." *American Indian Quarterly* 27, nos. 3–4 (Summer–Autumn 2003): 727–75.

Lott, Eric. *Black Mirror: The Cultural Contradictions of American Racism*. Cambridge, MA: Harvard University Press, 2017.

Love, Heather. "Close but Not Deep: Literary Ethics and the Descriptive Turn." *New Literary History* 41, no. 2 (Spring 2010): 371–91.

Lowie, Robert H. *The History of Ethnological Theory*. New York: Holt, Rinehart and Winston, 1937.

Lutz, Tom. *American Nervousness, 1903: An Anecdotal History*. Ithaca, NY: Cornell University Press, 1991.

Mackert, Michael. "Franz Boas' Theory of Phonetics." *Historiographia Linguistica* 21, no. 3 (1994): 351–84.

Malcomson, Scott L. *One Drop of Blood: The American Misadventure of Race*. New York: Farrar, Straus and Giroux, 2000.

Manzanas, Ana M^a. "Ethnicity, *Mestizaje*, and Writing." In *Narratives of Resistance: Literature and Ethnicity in the United States and the Caribbean*, edited by Ana Mª Manzanas and Jesús Benito. 27–42. Cuenca, Spain: Ediciones de la Universidad de Castilla–La Mancha, 1999.

Marett, R. R. "*American Indian Life. By Several of Its Students* by Elsie Clews Parsons" (review). *American Anthropologist*, n.s., 25, no. 2 (April–June 1923): 266–69.

Margolies, Alan. "The Maturing of F. Scott Fitzgerald." *Twentieth-Century Literature* 43, no. 1 (April 1997): 75–93.

Martin, Keavy. *Stories in a New Skin: Approaches to Inuit Literature*. Winnipeg: University of Manitoba Press, 2012.

Mauro, Ian. "Uqalurait: The Snow Is Speaking." Isuma TV, November 23, 2009. http://www.isuma.tv/inuit-knowledge-and-climate-change/uqalurait-snow -speaking.

Mauss, Marcel. "The Techniques of the Body." Translated by Ben Brewster. *Economy and Society* 2, no. 1 (February 1973): 70–88.

Mayfield, Sara. *Exiles from Paradise: Zelda and Scott Fitzgerald*. New York: Delacorte, 1971.

McGill, Meredith. *American Literature and the Culture of Reprinting*. Philadelphia: University of Pennsylvania Press, 2003.

McKittrick, Katherine. *Demonic Grounds: Black Women and the Cartographies of Struggle*. Minneapolis: University of Minnesota Press, 2006.

Mead, George Herbert. "Social Consciousness and the Consciousness of Meaning." *Psychological Bulletin* 7 (1910): 397–404.

Mead, Margaret. *Coming of Age in Samoa: A Psychological Study of Primitive Youth for Western Civilization*. Foreword by Franz Boas. New York: William Morrow, 1928.

Melville, Herman. *Moby-Dick; or, the Whale*. Evanston, IL: Northwestern- Newberry, 1988.

Mencken, H. L. *The American Language: An Inquiry into the Development of English in the United States*. New York: Knopf, 1945.

——. *A Book of Prefaces*. New York: Knopf, 1917.

——. *Prejudices: Fifth Series*. New York: Knopf, 1926.

"Mental Science." *Science* 12, no. 301 (November 9, 1888): 222–23.

Michaels, Walter Benn. *Our America: Nativism, Modernism, and Pluralism*. Durham, NC: Duke University Press, 1995.

——. *The Shape of the Signifier: 1967 to the End of History*. Princeton, NJ: Princeton University Press, 2004.

Mieszkowski, Sylvia. *Resonant Alterities: Sound, Desire and Anxiety in Non-realist Fiction*. Bielefeld, Germany: transcript Verlag, 2014.

Miller, Ray E. "A Strobophotographic Analysis of a Tlingit Indian's Speech."
    International Journal of American Linguistics 6, no. 1 (March 1930): 47–68.
Mills, Mara. "Deaf Jam: From Inscription to Reproduction to Information." *Social
    Text* 28, no. 1 (2010): 35–58.
———. "Do Signals Have Politics? Inscribing Abilities in Cochlear Implants."
    In *The Oxford Handbook of Sound Studies*, edited by Trevor Pinch and Karin
    Bijsterveld, 320–46. Oxford: Oxford University Press, 2012.
Mitchell, David T., and Sharon L. Snyder. *Narrative Prosthesis: Disability and the
    Dependencies of Discourse.* Ann Arbor: University of Michigan Press, 2000.
Monroe, Lewis B. *The Fourth Reader.* Philadelphia: Cowperthwait, 1872.
Mooney, James. *History, Myths, and Sacred Formulas of the Cherokees.* Asheville,
    NC: Historical Images (Bright Mountain Books), 1992.
Moores, Donald F. "*The Mask of Benevolence: Disabling the Deaf Community*"
    (book review). *American Annals of the Deaf* 138, no. 1 (March 1993): 4–9.
Morell, Thomas. *Sacred Annals, or The Life of Christ, as Recorded by the Four
    Evangelists.* 2nd ed. London: T. Longman, 1784.
Morson, Gary Saul. *Narrative and Freedom: The Shadows of Time.* New Haven, CT:
    Yale University Press, 1994.
Moten, Fred. *Black and Blur.* Durham, NC: Duke University Press, 2017.
———. *In the Break: The Aesthetics of the Black Radical Tradition.* Minneapolis:
    University of Minnesota Press, 2003.
Mowitt, John. *Percussion: Drumming, Beating, Striking.* Durham, NC: Duke
    University Press, 2002.
Murphy, James Emmett, and Sharon Murphy. *Let My People Know: American
    Indian Journalism, 1828–1978.* Norman: University of Oklahoma Press,
    1981.
Murray, Stephen O. "The Creation of Linguistic Structure." *American
    Anthropologist*, n.s., 85 no. 2 (June 1983): 356–62.
Nagel, James, ed. *Anthology of the American Short Story.* Boston: Houghton
    Mifflin, 2007.
Nagel, James, and Tom Quirk, eds. *The Portable American Realism Reader.*
    New York: Penguin, 1997.
Napolin, Julie Beth. "Elliptical Sound: Audibility and the Space of Reading." In
    *Sounding Modernism: Rhythm and Sonic Mediation in Modern Literature and
    Film*, edited by Julian Murphet, Helen Groth, and Penelope Hone, 109–30.
    Edinburgh: Edinburgh University Press, 2017.
———. *The Fact of Resonance: Modernist Acoustics and Narrative Form.* New York:
    Fordham University Press, 2020.
Native American Cultural Center, Stanford University. "History Timelines: Native
    American History at Stanford." Accessed September 5, 2021. http://nacc
    .stanford.edu/about-nacc/history-timelines.
Ngai, Mae M. *Impossible Subjects: Illegal Aliens and the Making of Modern America.*
    Princeton, NJ: Princeton University Press, 2004.
Nielsen, Kim E. *The Radical Lives of Helen Keller.* New York: New York University
    Press, 2004.

Noland, Carrie. *Agency and Embodiment: Performing Gestures/Producing Culture.* Cambridge, MA: Harvard University Press, 2009.

———. *Voices of Negritude in Modernist Print: Aesthetics, Subjectivity, Diaspora, and the Lyric Regime.* New York: Columbia University Press, 2015.

"Notes and News." *Science* 8, no. 204 (December 31, 1886): 628–31.

Nowlin, Michael. *F. Scott Fitzgerald's Racial Angles and the Business of Literary Greatness.* New York: Palgrave Macmillan, 2007.

Nurhussein, Nadia. *Rhetorics of Literacy: The Cultivation of American Dialect Poetry.* Columbus: Ohio State University Press, 2013.

Obasogie, Osagie K. *Blinded by Sight: Seeing Race through the Eyes of the Blind.* Stanford, CA: Stanford University Press, 2013.

Ochoa Gautier, Ana María. *Aurality: Listening and Knowledge in Nineteenth-Century Colombia.* Durham, NC: Duke University Press, 2014.

Ochs, Elinor. "Transcription as Theory." In *Developmental Pragmatics*, edited by Elinor Ochs and Bambi B. Schieffelin, 43–72. New York: Academic, 1979.

Oliveros, Pauline. "Some Sound Observations." In *Audio Culture: Readings in Modern Music*, edited by Christoph Cox and Daniel Warner, 102–6. New York: Continuum, 2004.

Ong, Walter J. *Orality and Literacy.* New York: Routledge, 2002.

Oskison, John M. *Black Jack Davy.* New York: Appleton, 1926.

———. *The Brothers Three.* New York: Macmillan, 1935.

———. "A Laboratory Fancy." Introduction by Alex Benson. *PMLA* 137, no. 1 (January 2022): 107–11.

———. *The Singing Bird: A Cherokee Novel.* Edited by Timothy B. Powell and Melinda Smith Mullikin. Foreword by Jace Weaver. Norman: University of Oklahoma Press, 2007.

———. "Tale of the Old I.T." In *Tales of the Old Indian Territory and Essays on the Indian Condition*, edited by Lionel Larré, 65–132. Lincoln: University of Nebraska Press, 2012.

———. *Tales of the Old Indian Territory and Essays on the Indian Condition.* Edited by Lionel Larré. Lincoln: University of Nebraska Press, 2012.

———. *Unconquerable: The Story of John Ross, Chief of the Cherokees, 1928–1866.* Edited by Lionel Larré. Lincoln: University of Nebraska Press, 2022.

Oskison, John M., and Angie Debo, eds. *Oklahoma: A Guide to the Sooner State.* Norman: University of Oklahoma Press, 1941.

Padden, Carol A., and Darline Clark Gunsauls. "How the Alphabet Came to Be Used in a Sign Language." *Sign Language Studies* 4, no. 1 (Fall 2003): 10–33.

Parry, Albert. *Tattoo: Secrets of a Strange Art as Practiced among the Natives of the United States.* New York: Simon and Schuster, 1933.

Parsons, Elsie Clews, ed. *American Indian Life: By Several of Its Students.* New York: G. W. Huebsch, 1922.

———. "A Narrative of the Ten'a of Anvik, Alaska." *Anthropos* 16 (January–June 1921): 51–71.

———. Preface to *American Indian Life: By Several of Its Students*, 1–4. New York: G. W. Huebsch, 1922.

———. "Waiyautitsa of Zuñi, New Mexico." In *American Indian Life: By Several of Its Students*, 157–73. New York: G. W. Huebsch, 1922.

Paterson, Mark. *Seeing with the Hands: Blindness, Vision, and Touch after Descartes*. Edinburgh: Edinburgh University Press, 2016.

Peirce, Charles Sanders. *Collected Papers of Charles Sanders Peirce*. Vols. 2–4. Edited by Charles Hartshorne and Paul Weiss. Cambridge, MA: Harvard University Press, 1932–33.

Peirce, Charles Sanders, and J. Jastrow. "On Small Differences of Sensation." *Memoirs of the National Academic of Sciences* 3 (1884): 73–83.

Penn, Arthur, dir. *The Miracle Worker*. Screenplay by William Gibson. United Artists, 1962.

Pestalozzi, Johann Heinrich. *Leonard and Gertrude*. Translated and abridged by Eva Channing. Boston: D. C. Heath, 1892.

Peters, Cynthia L. *Deaf American Literature: From Carnival to the Canon*. Washington, DC: Gallaudet University Press, 2002.

Piatote, Beth. *Domestic Subjects: Gender, Citizenship, and Law in Native American Literature*. New Haven, CT: Yale University Press, 2013.

Platt, George, dir. *Deliverance*. Written by Francis Trevelyan Miller. Helen Keller Film Corporation, 1919. http://loc.gov/item/mbrs00093858/.

Portelli, Alessandro. *The Death of Luigi Trastulli and Other Stories: Form and Meaning in Oral History*. Albany: State University of New York Press, 1991.

Porter, Edna, ed. *Double Blossoms: Helen Keller Anthology*. 2nd ed. New York: Lewis Copeland, 1931.

Porter, Joy. *To Be Indian: The Life of Iroquois-Seneca Arthur Caswell Parker*. Norman: University of Oklahoma Press, 2001.

Posey, Alexander. *Lost Creeks: Collected Journals*. Edited by Matthew Wynn Sivils. Lincoln: University of Nebraska Press, 2009.

———. *The Poems of Alexander Lawrence Posey*. Edited by Minnie H. Posey. Memoir by William Elsey Connelley. Topeka, KS: Crane, 1910.

Pound, Louise. "Popular Variants of 'Yes.'" *American Speech* 2, no. 3 (December 1926): 132.

Powell, J. W. *Introduction to the Study of Indian Languages with Words Phrases and Sentences to Be Collected*. 2nd ed. Washington, DC: US Government Printing Office, 1880.

Powell, Timothy B. Introduction to *The Singing Bird: A Cherokee Novel*, by John M. Oskison, xix–xlvii. Norman: University of Oklahoma Press, 2007.

Powers, William K. "Translating the Untranslatable: The Place of the Vocable in Lakota Song." In *On the Translation of Native American Literatures*, edited by Brian Swann, 293–310. Washington, DC: Smithsonian Institution Press, 1992.

Pratt, Lloyd. *Archives of American Time: Literature and Modernity in the Nineteenth Century*. Philadelphia: University of Pennsylvania Press, 2010.

Puckett, Kent. *Bad Form: Social Mistakes and the Nineteenth-Century Novel*. New York: Oxford University Press, 2008.

Qaggiavuut. "The Pisiq Song Book." Qaggig School of Performing Arts. Accessed September 5, 2021. http://pisiqsongbook.com.

Raboteau, Albert J. *Slave Religion: The "Invisible Institution" of the Antebellum South*. Oxford: Oxford University Press, 1978.

Radick, Gregory. *Simian Tongue: The Long Debate about Animal Language*. Chicago: University of Chicago Press, 2007.

Rancière, Jacques. *The Politics of Aesthetics: The Distribution of the Sensible*. Translated and with an introduction by Gabriel Rockhill. London: Continuum, 2004.

Rankin, Jean Sherwood. "Helen Keller and the Language-Teaching Problem." *Elementary School Teacher* 9, no. 2 (October 1908): 84–93.

Rasmussen, Birgit. *Queequeg's Coffin: Indigenous Literacies and Early American Literature*. Durham, NC: Duke University Press, 2012.

"Reader's Notes, A." *Wisconsin Journal of Education* 18, no. 2 (February 1888): 79–90.

Reckson, Lindsay V. *Realist Ecstasy: Religion, Race, and Performance in American Literature*. New York: New York University Press, 2020.

Reed, Anthony. *Soundworks: Race, Sound, and Poetry in Production*. Durham, NC: Duke University Press, 2021.

Reed, Thomas B., and Elsie Clews Parsons. "Cries-for-salmon, a Ten'a Woman." In *American Indian Life: By Several of Its Students*, edited by Elsie Clews Parsons, 337–62. New York: G. W. Huebsch, 1922.

Reichel, A. Elizabeth. *Writing Anthropologists, Sounding Primitives: The Poetry and Scholarship of Edward Sapir, Margaret Mead, and Ruth Benedict*. Lincoln: University of Nebraska Press, 2021.

Rhea, John M. *A Field of Their Own: Women and American Indian History, 1830–1941*. Norman: University of Oklahoma Press, 2016.

Richardson, Robert D. *William James: In the Maelstrom of American Modernism: A Biography*. Boston: Houghton Mifflin, 2006.

Rifkin, Mark. *Temporal Sovereignty and Indigenous Self-Determination*. Durham, NC: Duke University Press, 2017.

Robinson, Dylan. *Hungry Listening: Resonant Theory for Indigenous Sound Studies*. Minneapolis: University of Minnesota Press, 2020.

Rogers, Will. *The Papers of Will Rogers: The Early Years, November 1879–April 1904*. Edited by Wertheim, Arthur Frank, and Barbara Bair. Norman: University of Oklahoma Press, 1996.

Rogoff, Leonard. "Is the Jew White? The Racial Place of the Southern Jew." *American Jewish History* 85, no. 3 (September 1997): 195–230.

———. "Types Distinct from Our Own: Franz Boas on Jewish Identity and Assimilation." *American Anthropologist*, n.s., 84, no. 3 (September 1982): 545–65.

Rose, Deborah Bird. *Hidden Histories: Black Stories from Victoria River Downs, Humbert River, and Wave Hill Stations*. Canberra, Australia: Aboriginal Studies Press, 1991.

Ross, Dorothy. *G. Stanley Hall: The Psychologist as Prophet*. Chicago: University of Chicago Press, 1972.

Rossi, Michael. *The Republic of Color: Science, Perception, and the Making of Modern America*. Chicago: University of Chicago Press, 2019.

Round, Phillip H. *Removable Type: Histories of the Book in Indian Country, 1663–1880*. Chapel Hill: University of North Carolina Press, 2010.

Ruby, Jay. *Picturing Culture: Explorations of Film and Anthropology*. Chicago: University of Chicago Press, 2000.

Ryle, Gilbert. "The Thinking of Thoughts: What Is 'Le Penseur' Doing?" In *Collected Essays, 1929–1968*, 480–96. New York: Barnes and Noble, 1971.

Saint-Amour, Paul. "Weak Theory, Weak Modernism." *Modernism/Modernity* 25, no. 3 (September 2018): 437–59.

Salerno, Abigail. "Helen Keller, Hollywood and Political Celebrity." In *In the Limelight and under the Microscope: Forms and Functions of Female Celebrity*, edited by Su Holmes and Diane Negra, 37–60. London: Continuum, 2011.

Samuels, Ellen. *Fantasies of Identification: Disability, Gender, Race*. New York: New York University Press, 2014.

Sandler, Wendy. "The Phonological Organization of Sign Languages." *Language and Linguistics Compass* 6, no. 3 (March 2012): 162–82.

Sapir, Edward. *Language: An Introduction to the Study of Speech*. New York: Harcourt, Brace, 1921.

———. "Sayach'apis, a Nootka Trader." In *American Indian Life: By Several of Its Students*, edited by Elsie Clews Parsons, 297–324. New York: G. W. Huebsch, 1922.

Sargent, Porter. *A Handbook of Private Schools for American Boys and Girls*. 7th ed. Cambridge, MA: Cosmos, 1922.

Sayce, A. H. "Address to the Anthropological Section of the British Association at Manchester." *Journal of the Anthropological Institute of Great Britain and Ireland* 17 (1888): 166–81.

———. *Introduction to the Science of Language*. Vol. 1. London: C. Kegan Paul, 1880.

Schafer, R. Murray. *The Tuning of the World*. New York: Knopf, 1977.

Schalk, Sami. "Reevaluating the Supercrip." *Journal of Literary and Cultural Disability Studies* 10, no. 1 (2016): 71–86.

Schneider, Lucien. *Ulirnaisigutiit: An Inuktitut-English Dictionary of Northern Quebec, Labrador and Easter Arctic Dialects (with an English-Inuktitut Index)*. Quebec City: Les Presses de l'Université Laval, 1985.

Schor, Naomi. "Blindness as Metaphor." *differences: A Journal of Feminist Cultural Studies* 11, no. 2 (Summer 1999): 76–105.

———. *Reading in Detail: Aesthetics and the Feminine*. New York: Routledge, 1997.

Schreier, Benjamin. "Desire's Second Act: 'Race' and *The Great Gatsby*'s Cynical Americanism." *Twentieth-Century Literature* 53, no. 2 (2007): 153–81.

Schweik, Susan. "Disability Politics and American Literary History: Some Suggestions." *American Literary History* 20, nos. 1–2 (Spring–Summer 2008): 217–37.

Scott, James C. *The Art of Not Being Governed: An Anarchist History of Upland Southeast Asia*. New Haven, CT: Yale University Press, 2009.

———. *Domination and the Arts of Resistance: Hidden Transcripts*. New Haven, CT: Yale University Press, 1990.

Sedgwick, Eve Kosofsky. "Paranoid Reading and Reparative Reading, or, You're so Paranoid, You Probably Think This Essay Is about You." In *Touching Feeling: Affect, Pedagogy, Performativity*, edited by Michèle Aina Barele, Jonathan Goldberg, Michael Moon, and Eve Kosofsky Sedgwick, 123–51. Durham, NC: Duke University Press, 2003.

"Self-Taught Men." *American Annals of Education* 2 (April 1, 1832): 161–67.

Shakespeare, William. *A Midsummer Night's Dream*. Edited by Sukanta Chaudhuri. London: Bloomsbury Arden Shakespeare, 2017.

Shipley, Lori. "Musical Education of American Indians at Hampton Institute (1878–1923) and the Work of Natalie Curtis (1904–1921)." *Journal of Historical Research in Music Education* 34, no. 1 (October 2012): 3–22.

Shklovksy, Viktor. "Art as Technique." In *Russian Formalist Criticism: Four Essays*, translated by Lee T. Lemon and Marion J. Reis, 3–24. Lincoln: University of Nebraska Press, 1965.

Sider, Gerald M. *Skin for Skin: Death and Life for Inuit and Innu*. Durham, NC: Duke University Press, 2014.

Silko, Leslie Marmon. *Storyteller*. New York: Penguin, 2012.

Silverstein, Michael. "'Cultural' Concepts and the Language-Culture Nexus." *Current Anthropology* 45, no. 5 (December 2004): 621–52.

———. "From Inductivism to Structuralism: The 'Method of Residues' Goes to the Field." *History and Philosophy of the Language Sciences*, September 11, 2013. http://hiphilangsci.net/2013/09/11/from-inductivism-to-structuralism-the -method-of-residues-goes-to-the-field/.

———. "Indexical Order and the Dialectics of Sociolinguistic Life." *Language & Communication* 23 (2003): 193–229.

Silverstein, Michael, and Greg Urban. "The Natural History of Discourse." In *Natural Histories of Discourse*, edited by Michael Silverstein and Greg Urban, 1–17. Chicago: University of Chicago Press, 1996.

Simpson, Audra. *Mohawk Interruptus: Political Life across the Borders of Settler States*. Durham, NC: Duke University Press, 2014.

———. "Why White People Love Franz Boas; or, The Grammar of Indigenous Dispossession." In *Indigenous Visions: Rediscovering the World of Franz Boas*, edited by Ned Blackhawk and Isaiah Lorado Wilner, 166–81. New Haven, CT: Yale University Press, 2018.

Skinner, Hubert M. *The Story of the Letters and Figures*. Chicago: O. Brewer, 1905.

Sklar, Deidre. "Remembering Kinesthesia: An Inquiry into Embodied Cultural Knowledge." In *Migrations of Gesture*, edited by Carry Noland and Sally Ann Ness, 85–111. Minneapolis: University of Minnesota Press, 2008.

Slater, Peter Gregg. "Ethnicity in *The Great Gatsby*." *Twentieth-Century Literature* 19, no. 1 (January 1973): 53–62.

Smith, Gordon W. "The Transfer of Arctic Territories from Great Britain to Canada in 1880, and Some Related Matters, as Seen in Official Correspondence." *Arctic* 14, no. 1 (March 1961): 53–73.

Smith, Mark M. *Listening to Nineteenth-Century America*. Chapel Hill: University of North Carolina Press, 2001.

Society of American Indians. *Report of the Executive Council on the Proceedings of the First Annual Conference of the Society of American Indians.* Washington, DC: Society of American Indians, 1912.

"Sound Blindness." *Phrenological Journal and Science of Health* 86, no. 2 (February 1888): 113–14.

"Sound-Blindness." *Science* 10, no. 250 (November 18, 1887): 244–45.

Spaar, Lisa Russ, ed. *Acquainted with the Night: Insomnia Poems.* New York: Columbia University Press, 1999.

Spillers, Hortense J. "Mama's Baby, Papa's Maybe: An American Grammar Book." *Diacritics* 17, no. 2 (Summer 1987): 64–81.

Spinden, Herbert. "The Understudy of Tezcatlipoca." In *American Indian Life: By Several of Its Students,* edited by Elsie Clews Parsons, 237–50. New York: G. W. Huebsch, 1922.

Spivak, Gayatri. "Three Women's Texts and a Critique of Imperialism." *Critical Inquiry* 12, no. 1 (Autumn 1985): 243–61.

Stallybrass, Peter. "Printing and the Manuscript Revolution." In *Explorations in Communication and History,* edited by Barbie Zelizer, 111–18. London: Routledge, 2008.

Statue of Sequoyah: Proceedings in Statuary Hall of the United States Capitol upon the Unveiling and Presentation of the Statue of Sequoyah by the State of Oklahoma. Sixty-Fifth Congress, June 6, 1917. Washington, DC: US Government Printing Office, 1924.

Sterne, Jonathan. *The Audible Past: Cultural Origins of Sound Reproduction.* Durham, NC: Duke University Press, 2003.

Stewart, Garrett. *Reading Voices: Literature and the Phonotext.* Berkeley: University of California Press, 1990.

Stewart, Susan. *On Longing: Narratives of the Miniature, the Gigantic, the Souvenir, the Collection.* Durham, NC: Duke University Press, 1993.

Stocking, George W., Jr. "Another View of 'Papa Franz.'" Review of *Eskimo Story (Written for My Children): My Arctic Expedition, 1883–1884,* by Franz Boas. *American Anthropologist,* n.s., 110, no. 2 (June 2008): 251–53.

——. *The Ethnographer's Magic and Other Essays in the History of Anthropology.* Madison: University of Wisconsin Press, 1992.

——. "From Physics to Ethnology." In *Race, Culture, and Evolution: Essays in the History of Anthropology,* 133–60. Chicago: University of Chicago Press, 1968.

——. "Polarity and Plurality: Franz Boas as a Psychological Anthropologist." In *Delimiting Anthropology: Occasional Essays and Reflections,* 49–62. Madison: University of Wisconsin Press, 2001.

——. *Race, Culture, and Evolution: Essays in the History of Anthropology.* Chicago: University of Chicago Press, 1968.

Stoddard, Lothrop. *The Rising Tide of Color against White World-Supremacy.* Introduction by Madison Grant. New York: Charles Scribner's Sons, 1920.

Stoever, Jennifer Lynn. *The Sonic Color Line: Race and the Cultural Politics of Listening.* New York: New York University Press, 2016.

Sundquist, Eric J. *To Wake the Nations: Race in the Making of American Literature.* Cambridge, MA: Harvard University Press, 1993.

Swann, Brian, ed. *Native American Songs and Poems: An Anthology.* New York: Dover, 2012.

———. *On the Translation of Native American Literatures.* Washington, DC: Smithsonian Institution Press, 1992.

Swyers, Holly. "Rediscovering Papa Franz: Teaching *Anthropology and Modern Life.*" *HAU: Journal of Ethnographic Theory* 6, no. 2 (2016): 213–31.

Talalay, Kathryn. *Composition in Black and White: The Life of Philippa Schuyler.* New York: Oxford University Press, 1995.

Tarde, Gabriel. *The Laws of Imitation.* Translated by Elsie Clews Parsons. New York: Holt, 1903.

———. *Les Lois de l'imitation.* Paris: Félix Alcan, 1890.

Tarver, J. C. "Sound-Blindness." *Journal of Education* (London), November 1, 1887, 475–76.

Thompson, Carlyle Van. *The Tragic Black Buck: Racial Masquerading in the American Literary Imagination.* New York: P. Lang, 2004.

Tuck, Eve, and K. Wayne Yang. "Decolonization Is Not a Metaphor." *Decolonization: Indigeneity, Education & Society* 1, no. 1 (2012): 1–40.

Tylor, Edward B. *Primitive Culture: Researches into the Development of Mythology, Philosophy, Religion, Language, Art, and Custom.* 2 vols. London: John Murray, 1871.

Ustinov, Peter, dir. *Billy Budd.* Allied Artists, 1962.

US World's Columbian Commission, Committee on Awards. *Report of the Committee on Awards of the World's Columbian Exposition.* Vol. 1. Washington, DC: US Government Printing Office, 1901.

VanStone, James W. *Ingalik Contact Ecology: An Ethnohistory of the Lower-Middle Yukon, 1790–1935.* Chicago: Field Museum of Natural History, 1979.

Vaught, L. A. *Vaught's Practical Character Reader.* Chicago: L. A. Vaught, 1902.

Vazquez, Alexandra. *Listening in Detail: Performances of Cuban Music.* Durham, NC: Duke University Press, 2013.

Vizenor, Gerald. *Native Provenance: The Betrayal of Cultural Creativity.* Lincoln: University of Nebraska Press, 2019.

Vogel, Shane. *Stolen Time: Black Fad Performance and the Calypso Craze.* Chicago: University of Chicago, 2018.

Wagner, Bryan. *Disturbing the Peace: Black Culture and the Police Power after Slavery.* Cambridge, MA: Harvard University Press, 2009.

Wang, Orrin N. C. "Against Theory beside Romanticism: The Sensation of the Signifier." *diacritics* 35, no. 2 (Summer 2005): 3–29.

Wead, Charles K. "The Study of Primitive Music." *American Anthropologist*, n.s., 2, no. 1 (January 1900): 75–79.

Weaver, Jace. Foreword to *The Singing Bird: A Cherokee Novel*, by John M. Oskison, ix–xv. Norman: University of Oklahoma Press, 2007.

Weheliye, Alexander G. *Habeas Viscus: Racializing Assemblages, Biopolitics, and Black Feminist Theories of the Human*. Durham, NC: Duke University Press, 2014.

———. *Phonographies: Grooves in Sonic Afro-Modernity*. Durham, NC: Duke University Press, 2005.

Weinstein, Cindy. *Time, Tense, and American Literature: When Is Now?* New York: Cambridge University Press, 2015.

Werkmeister, Sven. "Postcolonial Media History: Historical Arguments for a Future Field of Research." In *Postcolonial Studies Meets Media Studies: A Critical Encounter*, edited by Kai Merten and Lucia Krämer, 235–56. Bielefeld, Germany: transcript Verlag, 2016.

Werner, Marta L. "Helen Keller and Anne Sullivan: Writing Otherwise." *Textual Cultures* 5, no. 1 (Spring 2010): 1–45.

West, James L. W., III. Introduction to *Trimalchio: An Early Version of "The Great Gatsby,"* by F. Scott Fitzgerald, xiii–xxii. Cambridge: Cambridge University Press, 2000.

———. "Mencken's Review of Tales of the Jazz Age." *Menckeniana* 50 (Summer 1974): 2–4.

Whitney, W. D. "On Inconsistency in Views of Language." *Transactions of the American Philological Association* 11 (1880): 92–112.

Whittier, John Greenleaf. *Anti-Slavery Poems: Songs of Labor and Reform*. Boston: Houghton Mifflin, 1893.

Whyte, Kyle. "Sciences of Consent: Indigenous Knowledge, Governance Value, and Responsibility." In *Routledge Handbook of Feminist Philosophy of Sciences*, edited by Sharon Crasnow and Kristen Intemann, 117–30. New York: Routledge, 2020.

Wiegman, Robyn. *Object Lessons*. Durham, NC: Duke University Press, 2012.

Wilderson, Frank B., III. *Red, White, and Black: Cinema and the Structure of U.S. Antagonisms*. Durham, NC: Duke University Press, 2010.

Will, George F. "No-Tongue, a Mandan Tale." *Journal of American Folklore* 26, no. 102 (October–December 1913): 331–37.

———. "The Story of No-Tongue." *Journal of American Folklore* 29, no. 133 (July–September 1916): 402–6.

Williams, Raymond. *Keywords: A Vocabulary of Culture and Society*. New York: Oxford University Press, 1976.

Williamson, Gordon. "Two Inuit Folk Songs (for Mixed Chorus)." November 30, 2006. SSRN. http://ssrn.com/abstract=1928881.

Wiltse, Sara E. "Experimental." *American Journal of Psychology* 1, no. 4 (August 1888): 702–5.

———. "Sound-Blindness." In *The Place of the Story in Early Education and Other Essays*, 99–106. Boston: Ginn, 1902.

Winefield, Richard. *Never the Twain Shall Meet: Bell, Gallaudet, and the Communications Debate*. Washington, DC: Gallaudet University Press, 1987.

Winkler, Peter. "Writing Ghost Notes: The Poetics and Politics of Transcription." In *Keeping Score: Music, Disciplinarity, Culture*, edited by David Schwartz,

Anahid Kassabian, and Lawrence Siegel, 169–203. Charlottesville: University Press of Virginia, 2007.

Wolfe, Patrick. "Settler Colonialism and the Elimination of the Native." *Journal of Genocide Research* 8, no. 4 (December 2006): 387–409.

Womack, Craig. *Red on Red: Native American Literary Separatism*. Minneapolis: University of Minnesota Press, 1999.

Woolf, Virginia. *Mr. Bennett and Mrs. Brown*. London: Hogarth, 1924.

Wordsworth, William. *The Prelude; or, Growth of a Poet's Mind: An Autobiographical Poem*. New York: D. Appleton, 1850.

Wynter, Sylvia. *On Being Human as Praxis*. Durham, NC: Duke University Press, 2015.

Yusoff, Kathryn. *A Billion Black Anthropocenes or None*. Minneapolis: University of Minnesota Press, 2018.

Zumwalt, Rosemary Lévy. *Wealth and Rebellion: Elsie Clews Parsons, Anthropologist and Folklorist*. Urbana: University of Illinois Press, 1992.

Index

Note: Page numbers in italics refer to figures.

Efron, Paloma, 107, *108*, 195n62
Eliot, John, 34, 36, 37
Ellingson, Dorothy, 125
Emancipation Group (Ball), 89
embodiment of writing, 65–66, 94, 105,
   129, 188n73, 193n13, 202n121
empiricism, 3, 93, 94, 105, 107
English language: boarding schools
   and, 143, 208n76; Cherokee syllabary
   and, 21, 34, 37–38, 43; dialectal forms
   of, 18, 65, 79, 81, 106, 118; imperialism and, 37, 43; plural form of
   "cultures" in, 3; pronunciation of, 17,
   38, 106; spelling of, 38, 40, 43,
   178–79n88; translation and, 21, 52,
   67, 138, 151
enrollment, Native American, 47, 48,
   54. *See also* land allotment in Indian
   Territory
environment, social, 93–94, 102, 105,
   106, 112, 113–14, 195n56
ethnographic authority, 145–47, 171n46,
   207n57
ethnographic present, 148
etiquette manuals, 100, 102, 194n36
Evans, Brad, 5, 166n15
expansionism, settler. *See* settler
   colonialism

fancy, 23–24, 27, 53, 135
Fechner, Gustav, 165n4, 171n44
fences, 17, 18, 21, 22, 53, 55, 173n13
Fewkes, Jesse Walter, 26, 30–31, 174n27,
   176n48
fidelity, 7, 55, 67, 123, 174n30, 183n137,
   208n81, 208n83
fieldnotes, 131, 134, 135, 154, 157,
   210n109
fieldwork, 3, 7, 106, 108, 131, 132, 135,
   202n3
film, 74–82, 93, 108–9, 100, 116, 121,
   196n65, 200n105
film criticism, 76–77
film title cards, 74–78, 79–81, 189n89
fingerspelling. *See* manual alphabet

Fitzgerald, F. Scott: "Bernice Bobs Her
   Hair," 100–103, 194n41; "Captured
   Shadow," 126; "Dice, Brassknuckles &
   Guitar," 117–18, 198n85, 198n87;
   "Echoes of the Jazz Age," 118; *Great
   Gatsby*, 15, 91–95, 100–101, 115–30;
   letter to Annabel from, 100, 101–2,
   104–5; *Love of the Last Tycoon*, 116,
   129; *Tales of the Jazz Age*, 126–27,
   201n116; *Tender is the Night*, 125,
   194n34, 198n82, 200n110; *Vegetable*,
   198n82
fonts, 19
foot tapping, 91–93, 116–18, 122–30,
   192n8, 198n87
forms, blank, 61, 185n21
Franklin, Benjamin, 101
free indirect discourse, 51
frequency, 122, 148–49, 159. *See also*
   temporality; tone
fugues, 126, 129, 201n113
Fuller, Sarah, 68–69, 76, 186–87n50

Gallaudet College, 68
Garland, Hamlin, 28, 31, 203n14
geographies, 10, 13, 30, 31, 153, 156, 158,
   160, 199n100, 210n102
gestures: aesthetics and, 104; culture
   and, 95, 104, 105, 193n15; dance and,
   111–12; filmed, 108–9, 110; Fitzgerald
   and, 94–95, 100, 116–18, 120–23, 125,
   126, 129, 198n87; gendered, 93, 99,
   103, 124; *Gesture and Environment*
   and, 106–11, 112, 113, 195n56,
   196nn64–66, 197n75; Keller and,
   73–74; self-reflexivity of, 99; Ryle
   and, 198n90, 201n119; speech and, 106,
   109–10, 195n55; study of, 93–94,
   104–5; as syllogisms, 110–11; writing
   and, 94–95, 120, 129, 199n93,
   202n120. *See also* rhythmic tattoos
Gibson, William, 70, 72, 73–74, 188n73
Gilles de la Tourette, Georges, 96, 99,
   105, 193n17, 193n20
Goddard, Pliny, 150

Johnston, Frances Benjamin, 20
Jones, Wilson, 46–48, 49, 53

Keller, Helen: "Chat about the Hand,"
  183n1; *Deliverance* and, 74–82,
  189n89; *Double Blossoms* and, 83–88,
  190n11, 191n116; *My Religion*, 56–57,
  59, 83, 183n1; *Out of the Dark*, 71;
  photographs of, 56–57, 59, 183n1;
  Story of My Life, 61–63, 71, 73–74, 79,
  90, 106–7, 188n88, 189n94; "What
  the Blind Can Do," 71
Kenningnang, 138, 139
King, Charles Bird, 43
Knapp, Samuel, 37–38, 39, 178n76
Kraitsir, Charles, 36
Kroeber, Alfred L., 29–30, 60, 132
Kroeber, Theodora, 59–60

laboratories, 23–24, 26–27, 58, 171n46,
  173n16
Lamson, Mary Swift, 63
land allotment in Indian Territory, 14,
  21, 46–48, 50, 53–55, 143, 173n10,
  181n112. *See also* enrollment, Native
  American
Lane, Harlan, 6, 184n16
Latin alphabet: cattle brands and, 17,
  18–19, 20–21, 53; Inuktitut in, 131,
  140; Keller and, 69, 75–76, 78, 80, 83;
  syllabaries and, 35, 38, 40–41, 131.
  See also alphabetic writing
LeConte, Joseph, 6
letter *H*, 22, 53, 183n133, 204n30
Lind, Jenny, 79
lines: blank, 61; drawn, 96, 110–11, 112,
  114, 202n120; of Harjo's brand, 17,
  53, 54–55; Ingold on, 202n120; of
  handwriting, 62–64, 66, 91, 128;
  shore-, 153, 157; temporal, 11, 36, 78,
  111, 160; color, 81, 84, 87, 172n55; of
  musical notation, 140–41, 151, 160;
  species, 23, 27, 73, 139; of gait
  analysis, 96, 202n120; tattoos and,
  124; of type, 13, 18, 55; of verse, 12,

45–46, 86–87, 136, 140; waveform, 7,
  67, 75, 158, 167n25
linguistic assimilation, 9, 14, 60
literacy: Cherokee, 39–40, 41, 176n96;
  Keller's education and, 61, 64, 66, 67,
  75, 78, 79, 81–82, 185n25; sign-
  language, 160, 161
listening. *See* aurality. *See also* deep
  listening; hungry listening
literary history, 3, 5, 7, 24, 31
literature: "American," 16, 38, 133, 158,
  161; medial plurality of, 15–16, 202n21;
  social-scientific methods and, 4,
  10–11, 93, 119, 132, 137, 168n28
Livermore, Mary A., 8–9, 169n33
local color writing, 18, 22, 24, 31–32,
  203n14
Love, James Kerr, 83
lyrics, song, 135–36, 137–40, 141–42,
  151, 157, 205n34

MacMillan, Donald B., 157
Macy, John Albert, 185n18, 189n94
manual alphabet: Keller's use of, 71–72,
  74–76, 78, 80, 187n70, 187n73,
  184n54, 188n86, 188n88; versus sign
  language, 187n54. *See also* alphabetic
  writing
mapping, 31, 155–57, 210n99
Marett, R. R., 210n107
masks: ceremonial, 144, 157; metaphorical, 100, 104–5, 115, 197n78
Mauss, Marcel, 99, 106
McGirt v. Oklahoma, 182n127
McKeown, Tom D., 41
McMahon, Henry, 77
McRonald, Dorothy, 62–63
Mead, Margaret, 195n47
measurement, psychophysical, 2,
  58–59
Melville, Herman, 19, 73, 183n133,
  200n107
Mencken, H. L., 125–26, 128, 199n98,
  201n113, 201n116
microscopy, 17, 23, 25, 26, 42, 174n26

pain sensitivity, 58, 184n12
painting the town, 29, 32
pantomime, 77, 110
parentheses, 19, 146, 148, 207n54
Parker, Arthur C., 29, 31, 175n43
Parry, Albert, 124
Parsons, Elsie Clews: *American Indian Life*, 15, 131–39, 142, 145–53, 157; career of, 132, 149, 186n46, 203n7; "Cries-for-salmon," 142, 144–49, 207n54, 207n57, 207n59; at Hampton Institute, 144–45, 206nn48–49; "Narrative of the Ten'a of Alaska," 145–46, 147; Tarde translation by, 67–68, 186n46; "Value of Folk Tales" lecture, 206n48; "Waiyautitsa of Zuñi, New Mexico," 131–33, 202n4
Peck, Edmund, 137
Peirce, Charles Sanders, 10–11, 56, 58, 183n4, 184n8
Penn, Arthur, 73
perceptual labor, 77
perceptual measurement, 58–59
periodization, historical, 9–10
periods, typographic, 75, 88, 136, 142
Perkins, Max, 115–16
Perkins School for the Blind, 63, 68–69, 84
Perry, Adeline G., 64, 65, 66–67
phonautographs, 67
phonetics: culture concept and, 129; Keller and, 72, 186–87n50; sound-blindness and, 2, 161, 167n22; speech and, 13, 69, 81, 136, 138; spelling and, 12, 40–41, 43; syllabaries and, 14, 21–22, 40–41, 43. *See also* alternating sounds
phonographs, 26, 41–42, 144, 174nn26–27
photography, 9, 56, 59, 65–66, 93, 132, 144, 149, 183–84n4
phrenology, 103
physiognomy, 103, 156, 195n56

Piburn, Anna Ross, 43–44, 179nn98–100
pisiit, 135–37, 138–42, 151, 157, 203n20, 205nn32–33
Platt, George Foster, 74
poetry, 2, 43–46, 86–87, 89–90, 132, 158, 203n20
polygamy, 48–52, 182n130
population distribution, 156–57, 210n107
Porter, Edna, 83–88, 189n101, 190n111, 196n71
Posey, Alex, 43–44, 46–48, 181n113, 181n115, 181n118
posture, 101, 114, 194n34, 196n70
Powell, J. W., 11, 171n42, 178–79n88
print culture, 12, 17, 32, 34, 57, 137, 142
printing: blank forms and, 185n21; Cherokee syllabary and, 34–35, 39, 173n14; deaf education and, 183n3; Oskison and, 19, 28, 31, 35, 54–55
protozoa, 22–24
psychophysics, 2, 58–59
public transcript, 8
punctuation: errors of, 130, 135–36, 142; film titles and, 75; sound-blindness and, 6, 161; tattooing as, 92, 192n5; voice and, 121, 134. *See also* commas; parentheses; periods, typographic; quotation marks
Putnam, Frederic Ward, 58, 59

qaggiq, 137, 157
quotation marks, 4, 47, 51, 52–54, 75, 161

Raboteau, Albert J., 8, 169n33
race: Boas and, 3, 197n76; *Deliverance* and, 79–80, 81–82; Du Bois and, 86–89, 191n116, 191–92n132, 196n71; Fanon and, 197n78; Fitzgerald and, 94–95, 103, 114–16, 118–20, 124, 129–30, 193n14, 199n95; gestural habit and, 93–95, 104, 106, 107–8,

200n106; imaginaries of, 92, 115–16, 198nn80–81; Jewishness and, 114, 197nn74–75, 197n78; Jim Crow signs and, 197n76; Keller and, 86, 87–90, 189n96, 191n116, 200n111; Sequoyah and, 37–38; social evolutionism and, 3, 160

Radcliffe College, 60, 185n18

recognition, 53, 87, 91

Reed, Claudia, 149

Reed, Lucinda, 149

Reed, Thomas B.: biography of, 133, 143–44, 149, 208n72; "Cries-for-salmon," 142, 144–49, 207n54, 207n57, 207n59; "Fishing on the Yukon," 144; presentations at Hampton by, 144, 147, 148, 206nn42–43, 208n81; Sapir and, 149–50

refusal, 5, 14, 22, 53–54, 55, 86, 112, 134, 160

regionalist literature, 18. *See also* local color writing

relativism, 3, 13, 132, 165n6, 175n43

reproduction: autographic, 56, 57, 59–60, 61, 62; biological, 49–51, 182n129, 182n131; ethnographic, 131, 139–40, 144, 208n93; mechanical, 54, 55; social, 22, 189n96; of study methods, 96; writing as, 16, 160

revision: of *Deliverance* screenplay, 78; by Du Bois, 86–88; by Fitzgerald, 92, 95, 101, 122–23, 125, 127–28; historical, 4, 71, 154–55, 169–70n33; by Holden, 45–46; by Parsons, 145–47; of "Utitia'q's Song," 151–52, 154–55; by Wiltse, 6

rhythmic tattoos, 91–94, 116–18, 122–25, 127–30, 192n8

Robinson, Dylan, 10, 170n36

Rogers, Emma Savage, *19*

Rogers, Will, 30, 40, 175n45

Ross, Anna, 43–44, 179nn98–100

Ross, Etna, 74, *80*

Ross, John, 35, 43, 176–77n63

Roulston, Jane A., 83

Ruskin, John, 24, 32–33

salvage anthropology, 3, 26, 59, 155. *See also* anthropology; vanishing race myth

Sapir, Edward, 99–100, 149–50, 208n80

Sayce, A. H., 13, 171n49

scientific authority, 93, 99

Scott, James C., 8, 169–70n33

seismography, 122, 199–200n100

self-presentation, 100–101

sentimentalist framing of disability, 73, 85, 188n76

sequoias, 34

Sequoyah: Cadmus analogy with, 36–37, 38–39, 43; fictional representation of, 21, 42, 51–52; historiography of, 22, 34, 39–40, 178n83; poetic odes to, 43–46; 180n104, 180nn108–10; state naming for, 33–34, 46, 180n110; statue of, 40–45, 179n99, 180n104; syllabary of (*See* Cherokee syllabary)

Sequoyah Club, 33

settler colonialism: Oskison and, 14, 26–27, 48, 50, 53, 175–76n79; Sequoyah and, 34, 39, 40; "settler indigeneity" and, 38, 176n58, 178n75; social evolutionism and, 5, 37–38; territory and, 21, 133, 157

shades of sound, 2, 13

shadows, 114–16, 198n83

sightedness, 59, 62, 64, 66, 82

sign languages, 9, 44, 68, 69, 77, 78, 92, 159, 161, 186n48. *See also* American Sign Language (ASL)

signals, 117–21, 198n90

signatures, 59–60. *See also* autograph of Helen Keller

silent film, 74, 77

Simpson, Audra, 5

Skaggs, Drennen C., 47, 48, 181n115

snowdrifts, 157–58

Printed in the USA
CPSIA information can be obtained
at www.ICGtesting.com
LVHW012311191023
761576LV00004B/392